FRONT YARD
& BACKYARD
IDEA BOOK

FRONT YARD
& BACKYARD
IDEA BOOK

Jeni Webber and Lee Anne White

The Taunton Press

The Taunton Press, Inc., 63 South Main Street, PO Box 5506,
Newtown, CT 06470-5506
e-mail: tp@taunton.com

EDITORS: Marilyn Zelinsky-Syarto and Lee Anne White
JACKET/COVER DESIGN: Sandra Mahlstedt
INTERIOR DESIGN: Lori Wendin
LAYOUT: Laura Lind Design and Suzie Yannes
ILLUSTRATORS: Christine Erickson and Jeni Webber
COVER PHOTOGRAPHERS: Front cover (top row, left to right): © Lee Anne White;
(bottom row, left to right): © Tim Street-Porter; © Karen Poussolini/Positive Images;
© Brian Vanden Brink, photographer 2004; © Robert Stein; Back cover: all photos
© Lee Anne White, except bottom right photo © Allan Mandell

Library of Congress Cataloging-in-Publication Data

Webber, Jeni.
  Front yard and backyard idea book / Jeni Webber & Lee Anne White.
    p. cm.
  ISBN 1-56158-795-8
  1. Landscape gardening. 2. Garden structures. 3. Garden ornaments and furniture. I.
White, Lee Anne. II. Title.
  SB473.W396 2005
  712'.6--dc22
                          2004021959

Printed in Singapore
10 9 8 7 6 5 4 3 2

Contents

Introduction—Front Yard Idea Book ▪ 2

Introduction—Backyard Idea Book ▪ 4

Chapter 1
Getting Started ▪ 6

Take Stock of Your Situation ▪ 12

Make the Most of Your Space ▪ 15

Take Cues from Your Architecture ▪ 17

Designing a Master Plan ▪ 21

Budgets, Schedules, and Priorities ▪ 22

Chapter 2
Entries ▪ 28

Stoops and Landings ▪ 31

Porches ▪ 37

Courtyards ▪ 39

Chapter 3
Paths and Steps ▪ 46

Main Paths ▪ 49

Secondary Paths ▪ 56

Sidewalks ▪ 59

Steps and Handicap Ramps ▪ 63

Chapter 4
Driveways and Parking ▪ 66

Driveways ▪ 72

Parking Bays, Pull-Offs, and Parking Courts ▪ 77

Street Entries ▪ 84

Chapter 5
Property Boundaries ▪ 86

Fences ▪ 91

Walls ▪ 95

Hedges · 100

Periphery Plantings · 104

Chapter 6

Foundation Plantings · 108

Architectural Cues · 112

Bed Layout · 120

Three-Dimensional Plantings · 123

Plant Selection · 129

Chapter 7

Ground Covers · 132

Lawns · 139

Alternative Ground Covers · 143

Nonliving Ground Covers · 149

Chapter 8

Plantings · 152

Beds and Borders · 158

Container Gardens · 164

Cottage Gardens · 166

Woodland Groves · 170

Chapter 9

Lighting · 174

Lighting Paths, Steps, and Driveways · 179

Lighting Entries and Activity Areas · 182

Accent Lighting · 185

Contents *(continued)*

Chapter 10

The Inviting Backyard · 188

Expand Your Living Space · 190

Create Your Own Domain · 192

Start by Dividing Spaces · 194

Collaborate with Nature · 198

Chapter 11

Dining and Relaxing · 200

Under the Shelter of a Porch or Portico · 202

A Dream Deck · 212

A Patio and Terrace Link to the Landscape · 222

A Peaceful Courtyard · 248

Cooking Out · 252

Keeping Warm · 260

Adding a Garden Structure · 266

Creating a Casual Seating Area · 276

Lighting the Outdoors · 282

Fortunately, times are changing. Individual homeowners, entire neighborhoods, and even many developers have begun to realize the personal and environmental benefits, as well as cost-effectiveness, of designing more suitable front-yard landscapes. Lawns are getting smaller and, in many cases, have been replaced by alternative ground covers and native plants. Homeowners are also beginning to use their front yards again and are finding creative and socially acceptable ways to distinguish their homes from those of their neighbors while still fitting them into the surrounding landscape. In many cities, front-yard gardens are now almost commonplace.

There are also new types of residential communities being developed. Narrow, tree-lined streets keep these neighborhoods cooler, and natural drainage swales reduce the amount of water carried away in storm drains and make that water more readily available to plants. A network of pathways and shared green spaces support neighborhood activities—everything from potluck dinners to baseball games. Front porches and courtyards serve as outdoor rooms for reading, dining, and visiting with neighbors. It is a pleasure to wander through these neighborhoods—to see the diversity of plantings, discover homes with personality, and see children playing games and people sitting on their porches.

It only takes one person to make a difference. I've seen it in the landscaping projects I've been involved with, and in the dozens of neighborhoods across the country that we visited while creating this book. As soon as one homeowner updates a front yard, others follow suit.

In this book, I hope you'll find some new ways to think about front yards, as well as practical, hands-on advice for dealing with everything from foundation plantings and parking spaces to designing spaces for family activities. May it spark your imagination so that you can start a new revolution to reclaim the front yards in your neighborhood.

—Jeni Webber

BACKYARD IDEA BOOK

It may not be obvious as you drive down the street, but there's a minor revolution taking place in America's backyards. Behind those picket fences, we are retreating to the backyard after long work weeks and relaxing on our decks, porches, and patios. We're fleeing the comfort of air-conditioned interiors to cook, dine, and entertain alfresco. We're escaping to backyard playgrounds, courts, and pools for hours of family fun and games. Now that we've rediscovered the joys of staying at home, we're finding new ways to spend that time outdoors.

This shift toward outdoor living is changing the way we design backyards. Large expanses of green grass are surren-

dering to smaller patches of more easily managed lawn. Long, regimented rows of vegetables are being replaced by small yet efficient kitchen gardens planted just outside the back door. Folding chairs on concrete surfaces are being deserted for cushioned sofas on flagstone patios and redwood decks, often flanked by cozy fireplaces, outdoor kitchens, and soothing water features. The lines between indoors and out are forever blurred.

Our concept of backyard activities is expanding, too. Swings may never lose their attraction, but they are just one element in a backyard playground that also includes slides, forts, bridges, and climbing structures. Badminton nets and cro-

quet hoops are still common, but so are bike paths, bocce courts, and putting greens. And swimming pools—once little more than rectangular holes in the ground—now run the gamut from pint-sized plunge pools and long, narrow lap pools to naturalistic pools with boulders, beaches, and waterfalls.

Here you'll get a look at the latest trends in outdoor design to help you sort through the many new products and innovative ideas designed for outdoor living. And you'll find inspiration for enhancing your own backyard with inviting spaces in which you'll want to spend many sunny afternoons and starry evenings while relaxing among family and friends.

—Lee Anne White

Getting Started

For too many years, front yards have been the misfits of the landscape. What started off as utilitarian spaces in the founding days of our country were transformed into something quite ornamental by the mid-1800s. But after World War II, when the housing boom hit the suburbs, front yards became, well, boring. Now, in the early years of a new century, front yards are finally getting the attention they deserve. After all, the front yard is the first thing you see when you pull up in front of your house—whether you own many acres or a tiny plot of land. It can cloak your home with warmth and personality.

With the rising cost of real estate, it makes perfect sense to make the most of this space. In fact, any real estate agent will tell you about the importance of curb appeal when it's time to sell your home. But you should landscape for your own enjoyment, not for potential buyers. When you keep this in mind, the front yard should do three things:

- Visually tie your house to the surrounding landscape, giving your home personality and a sense of place
- Create a welcoming environment
- Serve your family's needs—whether for outdoor activities, parking, or entertaining guests

▲ A CAREFULLY CRAFTED STONE WALL softened by lush plantings marks a driveway entry.

◄ A LANDSCAPE THAT MATURES GRACEFULLY requires planning. Shrubs should be sited so that they can grow naturally to their full stature. Pathways should enhance logical circulation patterns. Views should be envisioned before trees are cut or planted.

▲ SEMIPUBLIC SPACES ARE UNIQUE. Because they are yours, they should reflect your personality and be places you can enjoy. Because they are constantly on view to others, they should be designed with more restraint than a back yard might be. The goal is not to make your yard look like your neighbors'; it's to make it look cared for and in keeping with the surrounding landscape and architecture.

In many ways, landscaping a front yard is much like decorating a room in your house. You want to convey a sense of style; make good use of shape, texture, and your favorite colors; and arrange all the elements so they are both functional and inviting. But outdoors, you have a few new elements to add to the equation. First of all, front yards are semipublic spaces. You may own the land, but your yard is part of a neighborhood and a broader regional landscape. While it's important to distinguish your landscape from others, it also has to blend in. In addition, you'll be working with plants, which add a living element to the design palette. Not only do plants grow over time but they change throughout the seasons. Though working with plants is a little more complex than working with fabrics and paints, I believe it's what makes landscaping exciting.

Some of you will be starting with a blank slate—a bare patch of land in front of a new home. Others will be updating existing landscapes. In either case, you'll start at the same place. Before you go shopping for plants or supplies, you need to consider the following:

- **Site**—the physical terrain, your neighborhood, and the regional landscape in which you live
- **Space**—how you desire to use your front yard, what you want it to look like, and how you want to feel when you are in it
- **Budget**—how much time and money you have to invest, and whether you will do the work yourself or hire professionals to help with the job
- **Schedule**—the time frame you have for realizing your goals (whether immediate or long term) and what you consider your priorities
- **Maintenance**—how much time and money you want to spend maintaining your landscape

We'll look at all of these issues in a broad sense in this chapter, and in more detail throughout the book. But by taking time to address them up front, you will come up with some basic principles to guide you through the landscape design process.

▼ IT CAN BE DIFFICULT TO CREATE both a place to garden and a lawn where growing children can play, especially on a busy street. Here, the picket fence makes the yard safe for play while serving as the backdrop for a perennial border. The fancifully detailed arbor echoes architectural elements of the home.

A Color-Coordinated Landscape

If the soul is in the details, there's plenty of soul in this front yard. It's not a very big yard, but it's certainly worth exploring. At first glance, you'll notice a rhapsody of earthy colors—from the aubergine-colored house with silky brown curtains to the terra-cotta pots, soft-toned stonework, and wine-foliaged foundation plants. Then the lush plantings, which create a frame within which to view the house, will pique your interest. And finally, upon closer inspection, you'll find the intricate details of the stonework will capture your fancy—from the artfully crafted retaining walls, paths, and steps to a curbside landing strip and a pebble-mosaic water feature where homeowner Tim O'Hearn sits with his son to feed the fish.

Landscape designer and artist Jeffrey Bale is the mastermind behind this creation. He started by terracing what was once a small, sloped lawn to create flat planting beds filled with flowering shrubs, perennials, ornamental grasses, and bulbs. He color-coordinated the house, hardscaping, and plantings and created a focal point with the water feature—which doubles as front-yard seating. Because the area is loosely enclosed by flowering shrubs, it makes a wonderful gathering place at the end of a busy day.

▲PLANTINGS NEATLY FRAME the view of this home's entry, while creating comfortable surroundings that enable the homeowners to enjoy their front yard.

◀ A LOW RETAINING WALL can transform A sloped yard into a flat one—whether it's used for lawn or plantings. This one is as artful as it is practical.

▲ THE GENTLE SPLASH OF a water feature can help drown out distracting neighborhood noise to create a soothing setting. This pebble-mosaic water feature was designed with built-in seating walls where friends and family can gather in the evening.

House

Pool

Stepping-stone path

Main path

Driveway

Sidewalk   Wall

Street

► YOU CAN EASILY ENHANCE your view from inside by adding a focal point. Here, a large container planting draws the eye.

Take Stock of Your Situation

Whenever I take on a new landscaping job for a client, I first have to take stock of the situation; as a homeowner, you should do the same. Allow some time for this. Get out a notepad and pencil, and involve your entire family in the process. Even though you may be anxious to start digging, it's important not to rush this first crucial step.

Start by sizing up your site. You may love your house and property—and hopefully, you do—but you still need to take a good, close look at it with a critical eye. There are 10 steps to this process that involve different ways of looking at your yard. To help you through this process, I've included a list of questions to ask as you evaluate your front yard from different points of view (see the sidebar on the facing page). Jot down any observations and ideas on your notepad as you do this.

It's a good idea to make a scale drawing of your site while you're at it. You don't have to be an artist—just handy with a tape measure and ruler (see the sidebar on p. 12). With several photocopies of a site plan, you can make notes about light patterns, aspect (which way your house faces), existing plants, problem areas, and other observations on this "map" of your property. A site plan will also serve as the basis for your landscape plan.

A landscape plan allows you to play around with ideas and change your mind without pulling out the garden tools—to go from wildly impractical dreams to workable solutions before you dig the first hole or lay the first brick. A plan also helps when there are two or more interested parties—perhaps you and a spouse or other family members—as you can more amicably work out solutions to your differing needs and desires. And a plan lets you place plants thoughtfully, keeping in mind how large they'll grow over time.

How to Evaluate Your Site

To evaluate your site, follow these steps:

1. Look out your windows and doors. Are there views to screen? Can others see into your house? Would you like to create views of gardens or children's play areas?

2. Look at your house from the street. What's your general impression? Is there a clear path to the door? Are plants overgrown or growing against the house? What architectural elements do you wish to accent or screen?

3. Walk around your front yard. How is the space shaped? Where do you need paths? Are steps loose and wobbly? Is there a place for a comfortable chair?

4. Notice how you feel in your yard. Is it too open or exposed, or do you feel claustrophobic? Do you want more or less privacy?

5. Look at the land. Is it flat, sloped, or rolling? Damp or dry? What kind of soil do you have? Does it drain well after a heavy rain?

6. Inspect existing plantings. Are they healthy and attractive, or do certain plants need to be pruned, moved, or removed? Do they offer seasonal interest? Do you have enough variety in plantings? Or perhaps too much variety?

7. Look at how the light falls on your property. Do you have full sun, heavy shade, something in between, or a mix? Do you need to create more shade or open up the site to create more sunlight? Which direction does your house face?

8. Think about your local weather patterns. Does your house need to be screened from strong winter winds? Should your paths be easy to shovel in snow? Would a breezeway between the house and garage keep you dry in the rainy season?

9. Stop and listen. Do you hear the pleasant sounds of chirping birds or children's laughter? Do you need to buffer sounds from passing cars?

10. Drive around your neighborhood and the surrounding countryside. What plants, construction materials, and landscaping styles distinguish your region from other parts of the country? What landscaping ideas do you like that would be right for your site?

11. Evaluate your property at night. Do paths and steps need to be better illuminated? Can you see to back up your car? Is there a glare that needs to be screened?

▲ THIS CORNER LOT had little back yard, so a play space was created out front. It features screening for safety, a lawn for activities, and a kid-sized fort for quiet moments.

Sketching a Site Plan

Site plans aren't difficult to draw, but you do need accurate measurements. Start by roughly sketching your property boundaries, your house, and any significant structures on a large sheet of paper. You can write the measurements on this plan as you go. Keep in mind that you're only working with the front yard, so that's all you need to show. Stake the corners of your property and measure the distance between them with a long tape measure. Next, measure your house. To place the house in relation to the property boundaries, measure from each corner of the house perpendicularly (two directions) to the property boundary. Next, add any driveways, paths, or other structures. It's also a good idea to show existing planting beds, paths, and trees.

Once you have your measurements, make a scale drawing on paper with a ruler, T-square, and drafting triangle. A three-sided architect's ruler will easily convert your measurements to scale. To determine your working scale, divide the length of your property by the working length of the paper. For instance, to draw a 100-foot property line in a 25-inch space, you'll work in ¼-inch scale (¼- and ⅛-inch scale are the most commonly used).

Start by drawing the house to scale, then systematically place the other elements of the page—starting

with the property lines and moving on to other structures, hardscaping, and, finally, any plantings. If something looks out of place, you can always go outside and check your measurements. Once you've finished, make several photocopies for playing around with different design ideas. Tracing paper also works well for experimenting with ideas.

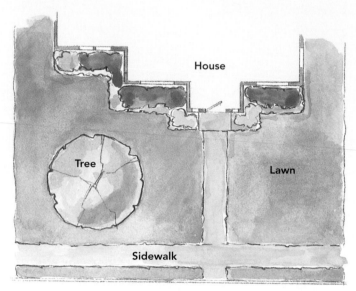

Landscape design is a practical, intuitive, and creative process. An effective design weaves together family needs and interests, architectural elements, plantings, and landforms into a synergistic whole. No single solution suits any one site or family, and certainly, no single solution suits all the homes in a neighborhood. I once thought that landscape design was the fine art of compromise—identifying and including only things that everyone could agree upon. Over the years, however, I've realized that's just designing to the lowest common denominator, and the results are rarely good. Unless you're the only person living in your house, talk it over with the others. You can almost always include something for everyone.

Make the Most of Your Space

A front yard should be designed for those who live there. It must be functional as well as attractive. You need a place to park your car and a convenient route for hauling arm-loads of groceries to the kitchen. If someone in your home is handicapped, he or she must be able to get around easily. If you have young children or pets and live on a busy street, an enclosed space will help ensure their safety.

The front yard is often an excellent place for activities. When doing things in your front yard, you'll begin to feel more in touch with your community. It's nice to see other people in a neighborhood, even if you don't know them well. This is especially true for

people with reduced mobility. Some of the activities you might consider include gar-dening, relaxing, entertaining, dining, recre-ation and games, washing the car, and more.

◀ TROUBLE SPOTS CAN become treasured spaces. With a separate garage built into the front hillside, the owners transformed the rooftop into a terrace for gardening. In nice weather, they can also bring out patio furniture.

▼ THINK BEYOND THE BOX. Instead of straight courtyard walls, this homeowner added an interesting curve to create an outdoor dining area.

Consider practical needs too. Some households get by with one small car; others need space for an assortment of cars, trucks, sport utility vehicles, boats, and campers. Parking, in fact, is a major element in many front landscapes. Vehicles are wider and families have more cars per household than ever before. For this reason, most new homes have wider driveways, multiple-bay garages, turnaround slots, and expanded parking areas. Older landscapes are often renovated to widen driveways and add extra parking slots.

Every house has its own unique set of circumstances that must be addressed in the landscape planning process. If you live on a hill, you may need to improve access or solve erosion and runoff problems. Perhaps you live in a neighborhood where safety or security is an issue, or maybe you just prefer your privacy. Do you live on an exposed mountainside where the wind rattles your windows in winter, or in the middle of a

field where the sun bakes your house in summer? Along busy urban and suburban streets, you may need to design walls and hedges to help lessen the impact of traffic noise. On small lots, you may need a fence or other screening for privacy. And if you

▲ STUDY YOUR ARCHITECTURE. The formal, symmetric design of this colonial home dictated balanced, clipped shrubs; a period-style fence painted to match the house trim; and a central path of brick to complement the house façade.

have a steep lot, you'll need easy access to your home as well as hillside landscaping that requires very little upkeep.

Take Cues from Your Architecture

One of the best places to look for inspiration is your house. The style of your house will, to a large degree, dictate the style of your landscape, whether formal, informal, or contemporary. The shape of your house, whether tall, boxy, or horizontal, should be echoed in many of the plants you choose. Architectural features—such as doors, bay windows, or porches—are elements to be

either emphasized or downplayed with landscaping. The relationship between entries and parking areas will signal where paths should be laid.

Often, there are architectural elements or building materials that can be used throughout the landscape—split-rail fencing with a natural wood home; a brick path leading to a home with a brick foundation; a matching stucco courtyard wall surrounding the entry of a stucco house; Victorian wood trim details echoed in arbors or fence posts. Colors can also be repeated or contrasted in a complementary way—both with construction materials and plantings.

Landscape Elements Common to Architectural Styles

For a unified look, it helps to include landscape elements that suit the style of your home. Here are some common planting, hardscaping, and decorative elements to consider for different types of architecture.

COTTAGE

- Picket fences—all styles and colors
- Geometric beds with a profusion of plants
- Little or no lawn
- Mix of flowers, herbs, and vegetables
- Often eclectic or personalized style
- Painted-wood or wrought-iron garden furniture

COLONIAL

- Picket fences and clipped hedges (especially boxwood)
- Brick paths
- Symmetric plantings
- Geometric beds
- Classic teak garden furniture

VICTORIAN

- Usually symmetric plantings
- Colorful bedding schemes and window boxes
- Elaborate details in house, fences, arbors, and gazebos
- Wrought-iron garden furniture

CAPE COD

- Usually symmetric plantings
- Small lawn
- Simple plantings and window boxes
- Naturally weathered or painted wooden garden furniture
- Stone walls and paths

CRAFTSMAN BUNGALOW

- Symmetric or asymmetric plantings, depending on house design
- Layered, naturalistic plantings
- Small lawn
- Detailed hardscaping, often with a mix of brick, wood, and stone
- Wooden garden furniture with simple lines
- Front porches and terraces

MEDITERRANEAN

- Symmetric or asymmetric plantings, depending on house design
- Little or no lawn
- Mediterranean herbs and plants with silver foliage
- Stucco walls, often draped in brightly colored vines

▲ **ARCHITECTURAL LINES** of the house are picked up in the lamppost.

- Tile and cut-stone pavers
- Often with terracing and water features

SOUTHWESTERN
- Often asymmetric plantings
- Succulents and other drought-tolerant plants
- Little or no lawn
- Gravel ground covers; tile and sandstone pavers
- Stucco or adobe walls
- Heavy, carved wooden garden furniture

ENGLISH/COUNTRY
- Usually symmetric plantings
- Large expanses of lawn (may be mown or natural)
- Extensive use of mixed beds and borders
- Flagstone and brick used for walls, paths, and terraces
- Prominent but simply designed garden features (arbors, pergolas)
- Teak or heavy wrought-iron garden furniture

RUSTIC
- Symmetric or asymmetric plantings, depending on house style
- Naturalistic plantings—often with natives or in a woodland setting
- Split-rail fences
- Adirondack, primitive, or weathered garden furniture
- Stone, gravel, and mulched paths

FARMHOUSE
- Often symmetric plantings
- Large shade trees close to house
- Larger lawns, meadows, or naturalistic ground covers
- Loose foundation plantings, usually with some perennials or bulbs mixed in
- Picket, split-rail, or cattle fencing
- Brick and stepping-stone paths
- Simple painted garden furniture

▲ **DISTINCTIVE PLANTINGS** and decorative items carry out an Asian theme.

CONTEMPORARY
- Usually asymmetric plantings
- Extensive use of lawns and evergreens
- Stained or weathered garden furniture
- Flagstone paths and low walls

POSTMODERN
- Usually asymmetric plantings—simple, yet bold
- Little or no lawn; highly manicured where the lawn exists
- Geometric planting beds and hardscaped areas
- Often without foundation plantings
- Courtyard entries with sculptures
- Metal, glass, and concrete materials
- Metal, contemporary, or artistic garden furniture

JAPANESE
- Usually asymmetric but regularly pruned plantings
- Mix of geometric and naturalistic paths
- Extensive use of evergreens and flowering trees—emphasis on plant form
- Color used subtly
- Symbolic use of stone, water, and earth
- Stone or wooden garden benches
- Boulders used for accent

◀THIS CORNER BENCH was built into a retaining wall. It serves as an invitation to neighbors to stop and visit with one another and to enjoy the homeowner's garden.

▼THIS VICTORIAN FARMHOUSE has an inviting front porch and is surrounded by lush plantings. Though most of the plantings—boxwood, hydrangeas, heavenly bamboo, and Lenten rose—are common in temperate climates, the hardy palm gives this setting a tropical feel.

Keeping in mind that front yards are semipublic spaces, it's a good idea to review any subdivision covenants before getting too far into the planning process to make sure you are aware of any restrictions. And though your yard doesn't have to look just like all the others on your street—in fact, it shouldn't—you do want to make sure that in a traditional neighborhood, you don't make changes too quickly or radically. For instance, it's usually easier to begin by expanding foundation plantings, resurfacing paths, and adding mailbox plantings than by constructing tall walls or converting manicured lawns to meadows.

The oft-quoted English poet and literary critic Alexander Pope wrote as long ago as the 1700s about "consulting the genius of a place" as you landscape. That just means designing a landscape that looks and feels at home—created in response to the specific terrain, environmental conditions, history, architecture, and inhabitants of a place. When you drive around your neighborhood and the countryside, look at things with a fresh eye. What gives your region a sense of

◀ A CASUAL SETTING suits this informal house. Large stone slabs serve as steps to the front door. The lawn, which would have been difficult to mow on this slope, was replaced with a mix of evergreen and deciduous plants. Teak chairs offer a place to sit and enjoy the garden.

uniqueness? Is it certain plants, a particular building style, or common landscaping materials? By incorporating some of those elements in your front yard, you gain the ability to vary the other elements while your landscape continues to fit in.

Designing a Master Plan

Armed with your site evaluation, list of ideas, and several copies of your site plan, it's time to begin thinking about the space and how it will be used. Details—such as

what kind of stone you want for the retaining wall or which shrubs to use in foundation plantings—come later. For now, just focus on the big picture.

I like to start with what landscape designers call a "bubble diagram." It's where you draw loose circles on your site plan around areas based on how you plan to use them. For example, you might draw a circle in a shady area for sitting, in a flat area for a patch of lawn, next to the side door for parking, or in a sunny spot for a garden. Include practical things too—like a place for the trash cans on pickup day or im-

► THIS COURTYARD is intimate, not private. The low wall doubles as seating so the owners can visit with their neighbors. Notice how the wall height varies at the corner, and how the tiles are laid at an angle to the wall for a subtle visual effect.

BUBBLE DIAGRAM

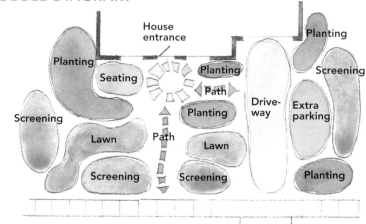

proved access from the garage to the kitchen door. Look back over your notes, and draw some more circles to mark areas where you need screening or more sun or that are too steep to mow. Think about how these spaces relate to each other and how you would get from one area to another. Did you just place the trash cans next to a seat-

ing area? Or do you need a series of paths to get around easily?

Next, try your hand at sketching what you think the design might look like—the lawn, the paths, parking, sitting areas, and such. Draw up several different approaches, and get some feedback from other family members. Don't worry about your drawing skills. The point is to think through the changes on paper before you begin making them in the yard. It's much easier to redraw something that doesn't work than it is to move a path, dig up a plant, or reseed the lawn.

Budgets, Schedules, and Priorities

Budgets and schedules go hand in hand. Few of us are blessed with unlimited financial resources. As a result, we tend to scale back our plans to what our current budget allows, rather than thinking about what's ideal for our property. I'd like to encourage you to think in a long-term way about your landscape. Just because you're thinking about the finished landscape doesn't mean that you have to install it all at once. By installing a landscape in phases, you can better manage your expenses and, if you like, do much of the hands-on work yourself. In the end, you'll be much more satisfied with the results.

Lawns, trees, and certain hardscaping features like patios or retaining walls are usually installed first. Lawns give children a place to play and provide a ground cover to prevent erosion. Trees need the longest time to get established. And for logistical reasons, many hardscaping features must be installed before gardens can be planted. It's also important to take care of grading projects early in the process, and to install any utilities—

▲ YOU CAN SAVE MONEY while you help save the environment. This retaining wall is built from broken concrete.

Native Flora for a Southwest Landscape

When landscape designer Carrie Nimmer starting digging up struggling front lawns in one of Phoenix's historic districts, she raised more than a few eyebrows. Pristine lawns were the pride of the neighborhood, but they weren't an appropriate ground cover in a region that receives fewer than 8 inches of rainfall a year. She replaced her lawn and that of two neighbors with drought-tolerant succulents and native wildflowers that flourish in the surrounding Saguaro desert.

Yet there's more to Carrie's approach to designing landscapes than replacing lawns with native plants. She also believes in creating inviting spaces. That's why she ripped out her concrete driveway, replaced it with ochre-toned chipped gravel, and

▲ SUCCULENTS, CACTI, AND DESERT WILDFLOWERS now thrive where lawn once languished. The seductively curving path issues an invitation to explore the garden.

◄ONCE A GARAGE, now a cozy courtyard. Concrete paving was replaced with dry-laid flagstone and pea gravel—which is both more permeable and better looking.

▲A LARGE OUTDOOR TABLE is tucked into a terraced alcove not far from the front door, creating a place to dine, work, and gather with friends.

allowed plantings to soften the edges. In the evening, she can roll out the barbecue grill and transform the area into an outdoor patio where she sips wine with neighbors and watches children skate, bike, and play ball nearby.

With the help of her husband, Peter, an architect, she transformed the garage into a dramatic courtyard with a water feature and seating for two. And for larger gatherings, mesquite trees and other plantings provide screening for a dining area on a patio not far from the front door.

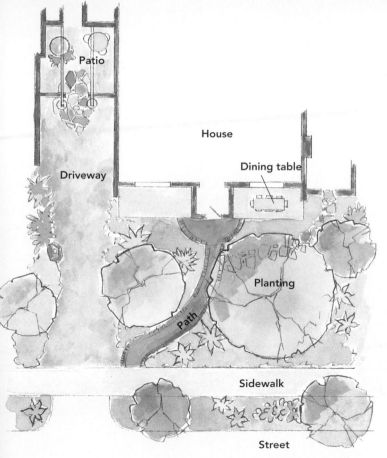

Patio

House

Driveway

Dining table

Planting

Path

Sidewalk

Street

Hiring a Design Professional

Landscape design is both an art and a science, drawing on the fields of design, horticulture, and construction. That's why it often makes sense to hire a professional—either for an overall concept plan, construction details, planting plans, installation, or all of the above. Whether you hire a landscape architect, landscape designer, or garden designer depends on your individual needs.

If you are situating a new home on a lot, installing a driveway, or rebuilding your front stoop, a landscape architect may be your best choice. Make sure you find one who specializes in residential design, as many landscape architects handle only commercial or municipal projects. Most states license landscape architects, who have generally attained advanced degrees in their field. Many are members of the American Society of Landscape Architects (ASLA).

Most landscape designers are not licensed, although they may have studied design or horticulture and be certified by the Association of Professional Landscape Designers (APLD). As a group, they tend to specialize in residential design and can help you create a master plan, address specific problems in your landscape, and install plantings.

Garden designers, who tend to focus more on creating gardens and working with plants than on overall landscape plans, don't have a governing body or membership organization. However, a garden designer may be just what you need for a small-scale project.

Ask to see examples of their work and check their references. Find out whether their specialty is space planning, hardscaping, or working with plants. Ask about the services they provide and how they bill for them. Most, but not all, will draw up concept plans, especially if there are hardscaping details. Some have their own crews and supervise the installation; others work with contractors; a few provide only design services and let you handle the installation. You can find design professionals in the Yellow Pages, by asking at local nurseries, by calling the ASLA or APLD, or by asking for referrals from homeowners with landscapes you admire.

such as outdoor lighting or irrigation systems. I also like to get a head start on amending the soil for any beds and borders.

One trick I've learned is to figure out where you'll get the most bang for your buck. In a front yard, that's often a new path to the front door, courtyard walls, updated foundation plantings, or a spruced-up entry. Driveway improvements, secondary paths, garden areas, and ornamental accents can be dealt with in subsequent years. Until you can invest in other plantings, vines will quickly and inexpensively give your place a lived-in look as they cover fences, walls,

◀ INSTEAD OF TRADITIONAL foundation plantings, this house sports raised beds filled with rich garden soil. A garden designer lives here, and he enjoys changing the bulbs and annuals for spectacular seasonal displays.

◀ IF YOU'RE ON A LIMITED budget and want to spread your landscaping out over several years, focus on your main path first. This one zigzags its way to the front door and is wide enough for a couple of chairs where the owners can enjoy watching the sunset.

and arbors, or are trained up and around windows and doorways.

Depending on your time, interests, and abilities, and the complexity of your site, you can either do the design work yourself or hire a professional to help. If you have a small yard and fairly simple plans and are reasonably handy, you may be able to tackle the entire project yourself. But for challeng-

ing sites or plans that call for lots of hard-scaping elements such as terraces, retaining walls, parking courts, or steps, it's often a good idea to hire a landscape architect or landscape designer to draw up detailed plans, even if you want to serve as your own contractor or do much of the installation yourself.

2

Entries

▶ DETAILS like these eye-catching house numbers make a difference.

T he front entry—whether a porch, stoop, landing, or courtyard—is the gateway to your home. It's here that you meet and greet visitors and see them off after a good visit. It's where you want them to pause and feel welcomed or to linger just a bit longer before leaving.

What does your front entry look like? Is it warm and inviting for those who wait at the door, or is it a cramped, stark environment with little to please the eye? Small details count for much here—a freshly painted door, a shiny brass knob, a colorful gathering of container plantings. Is there a roof to provide cover from rain and a convenient place to leave packages? Do the steps and paving complement your home? Are your house numbers visible from the street, and can guests find their way to the door safely and easily after dark?

At a minimum, entries offer a place to wait after someone knocks on your door. Yet they have the potential to be so much more—gathering places just waiting to be transformed into outdoor rooms. Expand a stoop or landing, and it becomes a terrace that can also be used for dining or entertaining. Hang some planted baskets and a swing on your porch, and it beckons you to relax with a glass of lemonade and a good book. Enclose your entry and you have an intimate courtyard setting perfect for dining, relaxing, or gardening.

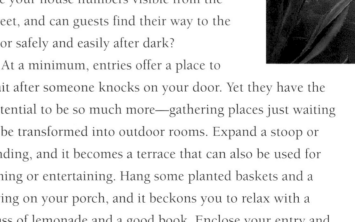

◀ PLANTS SOFTEN HARD SURFACES, whether they are grown in pots, trained along eaves, or allowed to spill over onto pathways. Here, manicured boxwood topiaries mix with a gently draping evergreen clematis to create a semiformal entry. The combination of architecture, plantings, and teal paint leads easily to the door.

► EXPRESS YOURSELF at the door. Paint, hardware, plantings, and ornamental accents can all be used to convey personality. Here, it's clear that an artist and gardener lives within.

When you compose your landscape, make your front door the primary focal point. Most traditional homes are designed with the front door as the dominant feature. On many other houses, however, the garage may be more prominent or the entry may be obscured. When the front door is not the dominant focal point, strong visual cues such as lighted pathways or eye-catching containers placed at bends in the path are often needed to guide the way.

The architectural symmetry of your house is a good starting point. A symmetrically designed house calls for a symmetrical arrangement of objects or plantings on either side of the front door. For instance, you may have matching sconces, identical plantings, the same number of rocking chairs or matching box planters on either side of the door. Asymmetrical designs—those in which the front door is not centered on the house façade—need a different approach. What you place on either side of the door may be balanced, but it doesn't necessarily match. You may have a small deciduous tree, small evergreen shrub, and perennials on one side, balanced by a cluster of medium-sized evergreen shrubs on the other.

▲ THE TWO CONICAL EVERGREEN shrubs add a subtle sense of formality to this otherwise informal, asymmetric entry. Flowering rhododendrons and pieris offer year-round interest with evergreen foliage and spring blossoms.

Stoops and Landings

▲ COLOR-COORDINATED accents like this awning draw attention. Instead of growing a wisteria (which can get unruly) over her door, the owner had an artist paint one that flowers year-round and never needs pruning.

The most common entries are stoops and landings. The only real difference between the two is their height. Landings are paved surfaces at or just above ground level, while stoops are raised, with two or more steps. Because they are raised, most stoops also have some sort of railing for safety. Stoops and landings may be covered with an awning or portico; local weather conditions are usually the driving factor behind these coverings. Because they provide shelter from rain and snow, they are more common in areas that receive ample precipitation than in arid regions. But even where the weather isn't a factor, awnings and porticos can help define an entry.

Another alternative for shelter—and one that is easy to add—is an arbor. Though an arbor won't keep you dry in a rainstorm, it can offer shade and wind protection, as well as add dimension, to your entry. Baskets of flowering plants can be hung from arbors, and colorful vines can be allowed to scramble up their sides and spill over the top. By planting several vines that flower in different seasons, you can enjoy color from spring through fall, or all year long in mild climates. Fragrant vines are a bonus for those passing through an arbor. If you don't have an arbor but want to achieve a similar effect, simply train vines up and over your doorway on a trellis or wire.

With a little patience, you can also create an attractive overhead canopy with trees. Your choice of trees is important, as they will be planted close to the house and your front path. Choose varieties that will not grow taller than about 25 feet (to prevent large branches from falling on your roof), with a more upright rather than a spreading canopy and with a deep root system that won't cause your path or

Big Ideas Transform a Tiny Entry

You don't need a big entry to make a memorable impression. Anna and Verne Davis's entry is slightly recessed and located at the corner of their house. Despite its somewhat unlikely location, Atlanta garden designer Brooks Garcia has called attention to the area with attractive plantings and a cozy seating area.

To begin, he created an enclosed terrace surrounded by plantings on the front, a stone retaining wall on the side, and a green moon gate that leads to Anna's garden in the back yard. Vines soften the walls of the house and retaining wall, while loose plantings screen views and an unfortunately placed utility box, and an iron bench offers a place to sit. Small containers filled with succulents, geraniums, and other favorite flowers accent the area nicely, and a statuary dog stands sentinel, as if to offer fresh bouquets to arriving guests.

▲ THOUGH THE ENTRY is recessed, plantings and a pathway clearly point the way to this front door. The cluster of small ornamental trees also screens a utility box.

◄ PLACE INTERESTING DETAILS where they can be viewed up close. This succulent-filled container is right next to the front door.

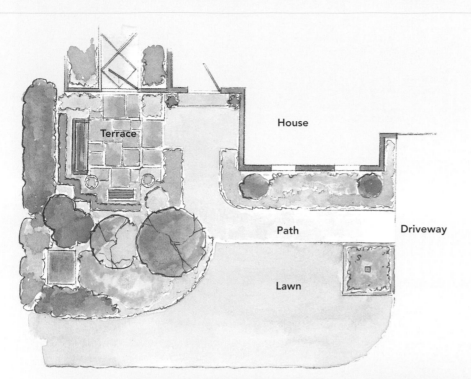

Terrace

House

Path

Driveway

Lawn

▼ A COMBINATION of plantings, structures, and the house itself enclose this cozy entry garden. A bench offers a quiet place to sit.

foundation to buckle. The smaller maples (*Acer* spp.), crape
myrtles (*Lagerstroemia* spp.), and shadblow (*Amelancier
canadensis*) are all good selections.

Though typically small, stoops and landings have long
been gathering spots. A couple of chairs or a bench are ideal
for sitting a spell. If your space is tight, a chair or bench isn't
even necessary as long as you have a few steps. Widened
into a terrace, a stoop or landing takes on the character of
an outdoor room, with seating space for a family or even a
table and chairs for outdoor dining.

Vines to Train around Doors

EVERGREEN VINES

Carolina jessamine (*Gelsemium sempervirens*)
Chilean jasmine (*Mandevilla laxa*)
Evergreen clematis (*Clematis armandii*)
Honeysuckle (*Lonicera* spp.)
Jasmine (*Jasminum polyanthum*)
Star jasmine (*Trachelospermum jasminoides*)
Wintercreeper (*Euonymous fortunei* var. *radicans*)

DECIDUOUS VINES

American bittersweet (*Celastrus scandens*)
Clematis (*Clematis* spp.)
Climbing hydrangea (*Hydrangea petiolaris*)
Climbing roses (*Rosa* spp.)
Fiveleaf akebia (*Akebia quintata*)
Porcelain berry (*Ampelopsis brevipedunculata*)

▲ CLEMATIS

ANNUALS AND TENDER PERENNIALS

Black-eyed Susan vine (*Thunbergia alata*)
Cup and saucer vine (*Cobaea scandens*)
Hyacinth bean (*Lablab purpureus*)
Morning glory (*Ipomoea* spp.)
Purple coral pea (*Hardenbergia violaceae*)
Sweet pea (*Lathyrus odoratus*)

▲ UPDATE AN OLD STOOP. This house, once a white cottage with a shingle roof and small concrete stoop, was transformed with a coat of paint, metal roof, lush plantings, and a new stoop. This stoop is wider, built from stone and accented with eye-catching container plantings.

▲ SMALL STOOPS can be artfully detailed. This one features an interesting combination of cut stone and random stone—all placed in an octagonal arrangement.

Update an Old Stoop

For a front-yard facelift, consider sprucing up your existing stoop or steps. You can enlarge them, resurface them, add new railings or posts, and even change the portico design above them. Widening a small stoop to 6 by 9 feet or larger will give you extra space for a couple of containers, a small bench, and a few last words to guests. Resurfacing your stoop with thin flagstone, tile, or concrete pavers in a diagonal pattern will make your stoop look bigger even if it's not. And attaching planks of wood between the treads of open wooden stairs to create risers is a simple way to dress up a staircase. You'll enjoy the changes, and they'll add to the resale value of your home.

▲ A BROAD STOOP can double as a terrace so there's enough room for the entire family to sit out front on a nice evening. Here, the chair colors reflect house, shutter, and window-box colors to tie the space together.

Even if your entry is tiny, attention to details can make a big impression. And because you're working in a small space, you can put your money toward quality materials and craftsmanship rather than quantity. Consider upgrading your door hardware, buying a unique container for plantings, adding an antique light fixture, or resurfacing your landing and steps with thin stone, tile, or brick pavers. A small entry is the ideal spot for a patterned floor—whether treated concrete, a tile mosaic, or brick laid in a ruglike pattern. You can also add life to confined spaces by accenting the upright—vine-covered trellises, window boxes overflowing with trailing and erect flowers, planted baskets hanging from your portico, or clusters of containers with conical evergreens or tall topiaries.

TINY ENTRY

Focus on details with a small entry.

Porches

The housing boom after World War II that resulted in oversimplified landscapes of little more than lawns and evergreen foundation plantings also contributed to the demise of front porches. Once common to architectural styles ranging from low-country cottages to grand Victorians to simple farmhouses, porches—like front-yard landscaping—are making a comeback. Not only do many new homes include a porch in the design, but homeowners are adding porches in record numbers to existing residences.

If you're adding on a porch, make sure it is at least 6 feet wide. Larger homes can easily support porches that are 8 or 10 feet wide. As with other outdoor structures, you'll need to check local building codes—especially those that apply to setbacks, the distance from the road that structures can be built.

▼ MATCHING RAIL PLANTERS help unite this home's two porches. The lower porch also features container plantings and a place to sit. Shrubs hide the foundation but not the porch railing.

Porches come in many shapes and sizes. There are small corner porches, porches that run the length of the house front, and wraparound porches that surround the entire house. Many are screened—especially in mosquito-prone areas—and others are open. Porch railings run the gamut from wood to wrought iron, from simple wooden palings to elaborately turned and painted palings. Porches are the perfect spot for a bench, wicker chairs, porch swing, or set of rockers. If you have a large porch, you can even create a series of small outdoor living rooms.

Low plantings are often the most pleasing beneath porch railings, with taller plants at the house corners and on either side of the front steps. Fragrant, flowering vines can be trained up and across a porch—as long as you realize that the eave is likely to reduce the amount of sun and natural rainfall a vine receives. Choose from vines with greater shade tolerance, and consider adding supplemental irrigation for any plantings (vines or otherwise) beneath an eave. Pots of ferns, impatiens, and other shade-loving plants will love a porch setting. Porches are also perfect for hanging baskets or box planters (including the kind that hang on rails). For variety, try including small vines and trailing plants along with the annual flowers in your baskets. And if your hanging baskets are exposed to drying winds, make sure you choose large baskets that are better able to hold moisture.

▲ PERENNIALS FRAME this low porch, with towering hollyhocks anchoring the corners in summer.

Courtyards originated in warm-climate regions like southern California, the Southwest, and parts of the South settled by the Spanish, but they are becoming increasingly common throughout the country. They can be used to create outdoor living rooms screened from public view as well as from the environment. Walls, arbors, and plantings provide relief from the hot sun, wind, and noise (though rarely from rain, snow, or cold). These walls don't have to be high to offer a sense of enclosure; even low walls can create a cozy atmosphere.

▼ A COVERED ENTRY and attractive gate make a dramatic entrance to this New Orleans–style courtyard. A large pot filled with fragrant gardenias serves as a focal point as you enter. Inside are a water feature and several benches.

The principal reason for building a courtyard is to provide a protected area for enjoying the outdoors. Most often, that means a place to sit and talk, drink a cup of tea, or read the morning paper. But there are other uses too—dining, cooking, napping, entertaining, and even gardening. So when designing your courtyard, it helps to first think about how you'll use the space, and then allow enough room for those activities. While a chair or bench can be tucked into almost any nook or cranny, you'll need a minimum of 12 by 12 feet for a 4-foot table and chairs. A café table with two chairs will occupy about half that space.

You'll also need to think about wall height and how that affects your activities. High walls will create the greatest amount of privacy but will limit the amount of sunlight for gardening and can make a small courtyard feel claustrophobic. An arbor overhead will add immensely to the sense of enclosure in the courtyard but is best if it only covers part of it. Then you won't feel completely cut off from the sky, and it won't darken interior rooms too much.

Mocking Up a Courtyard

Try mocking up the layout of a courtyard, including the height of the walls, before finishing your plans. You can easily do this with some tall stakes placed at the corners, with string tied between them at the anticipated wall height. Then sit in a chair in this area to see how you feel. Leave it for a few days; notice the sun patterns and think about how they'll affect your activities. Imagine the views both in and out of the courtyard that you will be hiding or preserving. Move your wall stakes and change your string height to make any necessary adjustments before beginning construction.

◄ THOUGH WALLS AND FENCES enclose most courtyards, hedges also work well. They just require frequent pruning to stay neat. This courtyard has a porous floor and doubles as a sunny garden spot. The owners enjoy sitting here in the evening, surrounded by fragrant roses and herbs.

► MASONRY WALLS can be softened with plants, both inside and out. Try espaliering a fruit tree, pyracantha, or pomegranate on a wide wall, and using climbing roses or other vines to scale tall walls or arbors.

▲ THIS FENCE-ENCLOSED courtyard features attractive flagstone paving and island beds for plantings. An arbor marks the entry and a pair of teak chairs offers a destination.

There are an infinite number of ways to define and enclose a courtyard. Your choice will be driven by your tastes, house style, budget, and time frame. The least expensive way to enclose an area is with a hedge, but even a fast-growing hedge can take several years to fill in. For more immediate results, you'll need to consider walls and fences. Those built from stone, brick, or wrought iron are the most expensive. Wooden fences and stuccoed concrete-block walls usually cost less and can be just as attractive in the right setting. Of course, not all your courtyard walls need to be the same. You might splurge on a stacked-stone wall near the front entry, with hedges or vine-covered fences along the sides.

To develop the gestalt of the various courtyard elements—the walls, ceiling (if any), flooring, and accents—the materials used need to complement rather than compete with each other. It's sort of a balancing act—providing contrast and interest without making the area too busy.

For flooring, a good rule of thumb is to make it interesting but not so busy that it calls attention to itself. An exception would be a courtyard where the flooring is the focal point—say, a pebble-mosaic "rug"—and the remainder of the courtyard is very simple. Most courtyards have masonry or gravel floors. Because courtyards are often shady areas and because they do not easily accommodate power equipment, a lawn is generally not a good choice—though there is no reason not to have a small patch of grass if you want.

▼ THE COURTYARD of this postmodern home is enclosed by the house and garage, as well as by a stucco fence, creating a private space for outdoor entertaining. An innovative water feature and plantings pay homage to the surrounding desert landscape. The principal colors of green, terracotta, and gray are echoed in the furniture, hardscape, containers, and plantings.

Buffering
Neighborhood Noise

We learn about and respond to our environment by listening, as sounds trigger activity in our brains. Sounds can relax us, awaken us, or carry us to other places and times. By their constancy and rhythm, sounds can be comforting. Many natural sounds—the sighing of pines, rustling of leaves, gentle lulling of waves, or purring of a cat—trigger a soothing emotional response. On the other hand, many sounds of urban life are distracting: Consider screeching tires, honking horns, lawn mowers, and leaf blowers. Even the voices of people at the wrong time, place, or pitch can put us on edge.

That's why screening some sounds, while adding or attracting others, is so important where we live. We can include elements to create, encourage, ricochet, and amplify sounds. Sounds that put us on edge can be buffered with dense screening and camouflaged by introducing soothing, rhythmic sounds like the trickling of water or gentle ringing of chimes. Other random but natural sounds can be encouraged through interplay with the environment—whether it's rain falling on a tin roof, birds splashing in a fountain, or wind rustling among leaves.

▲ A WATER FEATURE placed near a front entry will help lower the blood pressure of arriving guests who have been battling traffic jams. In a courtyard, water draws your attention from distracting neighborhood noise so you can enjoy visiting with friends or reading a book.

Plants are always pleasing in a courtyard, as they soften all the hard surfaces, provide a touch of color, and add another layer of texture to the walls, floor, and canopy. Vines are especially welcome, as they can cling to walls, twine up posts and trellises, and dangle from overhead structures.

Ever since the paradise gardens of Persia, water has been appreciated in courtyards for its sound, beauty, and cooling effect. The walls of a courtyard will magnify the sound of falling water, and dappled light will reflect off it, enlivening the walls. A water feature in a courtyard simply cannot have its praises sung too highly.

A Japanese-Inspired Courtyard

The moment you peer through Stephen and Meg Carruthers's courtyard gate, you're hooked. It's not possible to pass this view without being lured in to sit a spell on the simply but sturdily crafted bench, to meditate as the fish swim in the nearby pond, or to study the intricate patterns of the flagstone path laid in puzzlelike fashion. Even the fence is intriguing—simple board slats arranged randomly on alternating sides of horizontal supports.

Courtyards are among the most intimate of entries, and this one is no exception.

▲ THE HOMEOWNER designed this simply but sturdily built bench and placed it so one could sit and watch the fish in the pond.

◀ EVERGREENS ANCHOR this Japanese-style courtyard, though it's not devoid of flowers. Architectural elements are designed from simple materials but used in interesting ways. A fish pond adds to the calming atmosphere.

◀ THE ENTRY GATE is inviting. With its clean, simple lines, it allows the view within to dominate.

Stephen, a professional landscaper, drew inspiration from Japanese gardens for this courtyard. The hardscaping is deliberate and restrained, with strong use of lines and natural materials like wood, flagstone, and boulders. Plantings are lush and green, with an emphasis on foliage and texture rather than flowers. Small sculptures placed with care throughout the courtyard further personalize the space. The result is a peaceful, inviting atmosphere—a perfect transitional space for welcoming guests to their home on the outskirts of Portland, Oregon.

The house provides two of the courtyard walls; the other two are made from naturally weathered board fences. Both walls and fences are softened with plantings—from heavenly bamboo near the front door to Japanese maples, bamboo, and an assortment of evergreens along the fence and an espaliered pomegranate against the house.

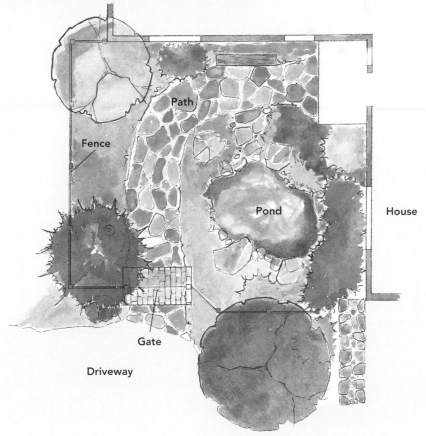

Path

Fence

Pond

House

Gate

Driveway

3

Paths and Steps

▶ THIS BRICK PATH is laid in a herringbone pattern.

Well-designed paths do more than get you from one place to another. A neatly laid brick walk to the front door welcomes guests to the place you call "home." A curved stepping-stone path that vanishes behind a hedge creates a sense of intrigue. A short, straight path from the garage clearly signals the quickest route to the house. And a meandering, mulched path through a front-yard garden says it's time to slow down and smell the roses.

Though basically utilitarian, well-designed paths can create a special setting or mood. The length, direction, materials, and points of interest along the way all contribute to the experience of walking down a path. Even the simplest—a short, straight, concrete path—can be enhanced by laying a row of cobbles or bricks on either side, by resurfacing with mortared flagstone, thin bricks, or pavers, or by bordering it with plants that spill out onto its surface.

The relative formality or informality of a path is expressed in the way the path is laid out, the materials chosen, and how those materials are used. A straight brick path surrounded by a manicured lawn is decidedly more formal than a curving, dry-laid flagstone path softened with creeping plants, which is still not as informal as a mulched path edged in railroad timbers. Whether you

◀ THIS GENTLY CURVED PATH is dry-laid in a running-bond pattern. It leads through an inviting arbor from the driveway to the front door and doubles as edging between a perennial border and lawn.

◀ AN INFORMAL PATH simply doesn't get any more charming than this. Stepping-stones are softened and surrounded by blue star creeper, geraniums, and epimediums, causing you to slow down and watch your footfalls.

▼ THE FLAGSTONE used for this informal path closely matches the color of the painted brick. Tile, brick, and other materials used for paths can be color-coordinated with a house.

design a formal or informal path is often guided by the architecture of your home. Generally, the larger and more traditional the home, the more formal the paths.

When possible, match the colors and materials of paths to your house. This is one of the best ways to tie your landscape and architecture together. Most of the time, the choice of materials is obvious. For instance, a concrete path edged in brick would complement a brick home, and a flagstone path would look nice leading to a house with a stone foundation. If you have a new wood-frame house and are pouring a concrete path, consider seeding it with colored pebbles or adding stain to complement the color of your house paint. One of the best-looking designs I've seen was a quarry-tile and granite-cobble path leading to a light terra-cotta-colored house with clay roof tiles. The variable color of the roof tiles, which ran from deep terra-cotta to gray-purple, beautifully matched the tiles and granite.

▲ A MAIN PATH to a front door should be the widest path in the front landscape. Four feet is a good starting point, but don't be afraid to go wider. This path climbs a hill, so it includes steps with railings, landings, and even a bench along the way. Note how the paving patterns change to differentiate the steps from the landings.

A well-laid front path clearly leads visitors to the main entrance of your home. It's like a red carpet rolled out to greet friends and family. As such, it should be your most formal path in the landscape, with the smoothest surface.

The main path to your front door should also be the widest path in your yard. A wide path, by its very nature, commands attention. You should follow it without hesitation. It's nice to make this path generous enough for two people to walk side by side. Four feet is a good width for most yards; wider paths may be best for a larger house or where plants spill onto the path. Occasionally, the front door is hidden or may not be the preferred entrance to a home. A wide path will lead visitors to your entry, no matter where the door.

One of the first issues you'll need to address is how visitors will reach your front entry. Will you speed them along, or give them reason to pause? The most basic path is a straight one that leads directly to the door. In fact, a straight path will

An Enchanting Entry

▲ ORIGINALLY A 14-STEP CLIMB, this front entry is now approached along a zigzagging path with short intermediate risers.

When Mahan Rykiel Associates was hired to renovate this residential landscape just outside the Baltimore city limits, among their first challenges was a front entry with a 14-riser stairway and a 7-foot drop in elevation between the front door and the driveway. Their solution was to spread the steps out by creating a series of garden terraces with paths running their length.

Near the driveway, matching stacked-stone piers and an allée of cherry trees—a sight to behold in early spring and inviting any time of year—mark the path's entrance. As you make your way along the bluestone path to the next terrace, you are greeted by three charming bronze piglets and you discover a tiny rectangular lawn surrounded by attractive plantings. And finally, as you approach the front entry, you are invited to relax on a generous flagstone terrace that offers seating for four and a lovely view of rolling hills and flowering dogwoods.

This path winds through rather than alongside plantings, and at each grade change, it jogs in a different direction through different scenery. As a result, it makes you want to slow down, breathe more deeply, and inhale the fragrance of freshly mown grass wafting from a nearby field.

◀ THE PATH TAKES several distinct jogs that change the scenery en route to the front door.

▼ THE LOWEST SECTION of the path travels through an allée of cherry trees that flower in early spring and form a graceful canopy in any season.

House

Driveway

Entry terrace

Lawn

Path

cause your eyes to immediately rest on the door, making you feel as if you have arrived even before you walk a few feet down that path. A straight path marks the shortest distance between two points, so it's the easiest and least expensive path to build. If you live in a snowy climate, that means less snow to shovel. A curving path, however, is enchanting. It is pleasing to look at and encourages one to slow down and enjoy the experience of walking down that path. Zigzagging paths have a similar effect and add interest to your landscape.

It's helpful to lay a garden hose (warmed by the sun so it bends easily) or planks of wood along the proposed route of a path. See how it looks up close and from a distance. Walk along the path to see how it feels. You'll know immediately if you've placed it too close to a prickly holly, headed it in the direction of an undesirable view, or sited it on uneven ground. You will also be able to tell whether the width is comfortable or feels a little crowded. Play with the layout: Change the width, flare the path at one or both ends, make the curves gentler or deeper, shift it either direction by a foot or two, or try an altogether different layout.

As you contemplate the layout of your path, think about its point of origination. Though that may seem obvious, paths are often misplaced. The guiding question is: Where do guests park? Or if you come and go regularly from the front door as well, where do you park? If there is ample parking in the driveway, there may be no need to run a path to the street. If you have little or no driveway parking, a path from the street may be sufficient. Often, two paths make the most sense—one from the sidewalk and a second from the driveway. Another option is to run a small path alongside the driveway to the street. This is a nice option if your driveway handles most of your parking needs but leaves little room for walking once it is filled with cars.

▲ CURVING PATHS are often more interesting than straight ones. They force you to slow down and enjoy the journey. This one originates in the driveway where visitors park.

Materials for Main Paths

Bricks are very durable. They range in color from sandy yellow to brown to deep red. The glazing process can render the finish either dull or slightly glossy, and bricks are sold in many textures, including smooth, stippled, and matte. They also vary in thickness: Common bricks used for paths are about twice the thickness of facing bricks for a wall or fireplace. You can also buy old or used bricks; just keep in mind that they are often porous and subject to spalling in cold, wet climates. They can also be odd sized.

Stone is also durable and immediately gives an established look to the landscape. One of the best choices for walkways is flagstone—a flat, hard, and irregularly shaped but evenly layered stone that is split into slabs. Bluestone, slate, sandstone, and water-washed sandstone are all flagstones. Because of its irregular shape, laying flagstone is like piecing together a puzzle. It's not difficult but can be time consuming.

▲ RANDOM FLAGSTONE Is usually mortared for front paths to keep it from shifting underfoot.

Many of these stones are also sold as cut pavers—which come as square or rectangular pieces of even thickness that can be fit together quickly. They are commonly used in formal settings. Flagstones, whether irregular or cut, can be either dry-laid or mortared.

Concrete pavers are versatile, attractive, and durable and can be laid in a multitude of patterns. Less expensive than stone or brick, they come in an assortment of shapes, sizes, and colors. Concrete pavers do not require mortar, are three times stronger than poured concrete, and shift without breaking as soil conditions change—making them ideal for cold climates.

Poured concrete has a new look. It can be pigmented, stained, texturized, scored, or combined with aggregate to create an attractive, durable surface. It's much easier to treat concrete at installation than it is to refinish existing concrete—though there are companies that have developed techniques for that too. To update an existing concrete path, it may be easier to widen it with a band of bricks or cobbles, or to mortar thin pavers or flagstone over the concrete base.

▲ CONCRETE IS THE MOST affordable paving material. It can be dressed up with bands of brick or cobbles as well as pigmented, stained, texturized, or seeded with aggregate.

▲ IN WET CLIMATES, you need paths with good traction. This Pacific Northwest garden features a coarse concrete path edged and banded with brick. It is both attractive and safe.

As well as being obvious in direction, a main path should provide secure footing in any weather. Loose materials, such as stepping-stones, chipped gravel, or mulch, are best reserved for secondary paths. Instead, select materials that provide a consistent surface and lay them so that they cannot shift underfoot. That's why poured-concrete and mortared-stone, -brick, and -tile paths are such good choices when they lead to a front door.

How the weather affects the surface of the materials should also be considered. Slate can be slippery in rainy weather, brick can become mossy in damp shade, and non-mortared surfaces are tough to shovel after a snowstorm. Flagstone with a slightly textured surface will be less slippery; concrete simply edged with brick may be a better choice for damp shade; and smooth, mortared surfaces make more sense in snow country.

Create Pattern with Brick

One of the greatest benefits of using brick is its ability to create a pattern in your walk. There are many classic brick patterns: Running bond, herringbone, stack bond, and basket-weave are just a few. Bricks can be laid as straight or gently curving paths, or even in a concentric circle as the focal point of a path. As a rule of thumb, a pattern that runs with the path (such as running bond) will move your eye quickly down a path. A pattern that crosses the width of the path (such as basketweave) will slow down eye movement. On long paths, try breaking up patterns into sections or panels with periodic header courses (bands of brick across a path) or com-

BRICK PATTERNS

Basketweave

Herringbone

Running bond

Stack bond

bining patterns for a more interesting pathway. You can also combine brick with stone or concrete for added visual texture, vary the hue in bricks, or replace some bricks with 8-inch-square tiles for an artistic touch.

Most bricks are 4 inches wide and 8 inches long, but they do come in different sizes. An odd-sized brick will throw off a pattern, so be sure to lay out a few sections of your pattern at the brickyard before placing your order.

◀ EXISTING CONCRETE PATHS and steps can often be overlaid with brick or other pavers. However, you need to be careful where the path meets the driveway. A slight grade change can easily cause someone to trip. Here, the owners solved that problem by cutting the transitional bricks at a slope.

Secondary Paths

Beyond the main path to the door, you may find it helpful to create one or more secondary paths that lead to the side yard, a seating area, the garage, a flower garden, or even the neighbor's yard. Such secondary paths should be less formal in style and slightly narrower—3 feet is ideal for frequently traveled paths, but as little as 1½ feet may do in other areas.

Another factor that influences a path's size and style is its relationship to the house and surrounding landscape. The farther from the house, the narrower and more informal paths tend to become. Of course, in all but the most casual of situations, it is still best to choose and place materials so people walking on the path don't have to pick their way carefully along.

▲ SECONDARY PATHS need not connect to a main path. In this case, a stepping-stone path runs from the front lawn through a narrow side yard. Though the stepping-stone path is much narrower, the materials complement those in the main path.

◄ DISTINGUISH BETWEEN primary and secondary paths. The widest, smoothest path should lead to the front door. Narrower, less formal paths can lead to other parts of the yard or garden. Here, the owner differentiated paths in both size and materials.

▶ A BREEZEWAY RUNS from the separate garage to the kitchen, offering protection in wet weather. A short path also connects the driveway to the breezeway—creating an attractive secondary entry for family and close friends.

▼ RECYCLE MATERIALS. This homeowner took out a concrete path that once led to the front door but recycled the broken concrete by mixing it creatively with bricks and a few river cobbles for a side-yard path.

I often match the materials to the main path but use them in a more casual way. For instance, if a main path is laid in mortared brick, a narrower secondary path in dry-laid brick would lend continuity to the landscape without drawing attention from the main path. Stepping-stone paths complement wider, mortared-stone paths in a similar way. If using stepping-stones, choose those with the smoothest surface possible and anchor them securely. The top of the stones should be flush with the ground.

Another option is to use different materials for secondary paths. Chipped gravel and granite fines are excellent choices, and mulched paths are ideal winding through a front-yard garden.

Materials for Secondary Paths

Chipped gravel is small, irregular stone that comes in an assortment of colors and crunches softly beneath your feet. It kicks up easily and is difficult to shovel after a snowstorm, but it drains quickly after a rain and is an excellent choice for informal paths. You'll need something to keep it in bounds; cobbles or some sort of wood or metal edging will do the trick.

Quarry fines have a finely crushed, irregular texture and come in both gray and a pleasant ochre-brown. A quarry-fine path is attractive, affordable, and easily maintained. Edging will keep it neat, or you can allow it to blend in more naturally with plants as a garden path.

Stepping-stones are generally flagstones or flat fieldstones secured at ground level with grass, herbs, or other creeping plants between them. Decorative stepping-stones made from concrete are also available, or you can make your own—perhaps with an imbedded tile, glass, or pebble mosaic.

Cobbles come in two varieties: cut-granite cobbles and rounded river cobbles. Because they form an uneven surface when laid, cobbles should be kept to secondary paths except when used as edging. Cut-granite cobbles may be dry-laid or mortared and are easier to walk on than river cobbles, which must be mortared for stability and are generally reserved for creative applications.

Mulch is the most casual and least expensive path material to install. It looks lovely winding through the woods or a garden. Edging can help keep it in place, though it's generally not a necessity. You must replenish a mulch path every year or so, but it nourishes the soil as it breaks down.

◄ SECONDARY PATHS ARE generally less structured than main paths. They can be narrower, less formal, and created from a broader range of materials. This quarry-fine path meanders through a naturalistic front-yard garden.

▲ STEPPING-STONES are an excellent choice for providing access to the water spigot or other utility area. Choose from flat stones, bricks, and concrete stepping-stones, or make your own. These feature pebble mosaics set in concrete rounds.

Sidewalks

Sidewalks come in two basic variations—those placed directly at the curb and those with a small strip of ground between the sidewalk and street. The first is more common in commercial districts, the second in residential areas—though it varies from one town or neighborhood to the next. My favorites are those with a strip of earth because they can be landscaped.

Most sidewalk strips are devoid of everything except grass, fire hydrants, and maybe a few street trees. But just think what a nicely planted sidewalk strip would do for your evening walks around the neighborhood, not to mention the setting for your house. By creating a small garden area on either side of the sidewalk (in the strip and in your yard), you actually make a small public garden that your neighbors can also enjoy. Use only the toughest plants—those that can handle the heat, dryness, piles of plowed snow, plants, and occasional footsteps— and avoid plants that will soon outgrow their allotted space or snag the cloth-

▼ THINK BEYOND the straight and narrow. This sidewalk landing flows like a river.

Paths Lead the Way

Not all house sites are flat, and not all front entries face the street. Take this contemporary home in the hills of northern California. Built on a steep curve, it can be accessed from the street in two locations—at house level by way of a short driveway, or from 15 feet below, near a detached garage. Both entries were designed for vehicular use, and neither approached the front door.

When Brad and Nancy Lewis hired the landscape firm of Four Dimensions, circulation was a top priority. The straight wooden staircase from the garage to the front door was beginning to decay, and the owners had to give detailed instructions on the phone to first-time visitors for

▲ FROM THE UPPER DRIVE, the wider, mortared path clearly leads to the front door, while the narrower, stepping-stone path leads to the kitchen door. A small cairn marks the diverging paths.

◀ THE MAIN ENTRY is actually from below. These meandering stone steps replaced a straight wooden staircase. Landings ease the climb, while plantings and a water feature make it more enjoyable.

▶ THESE CURVED STEPS make an attractive entry and match the stone paths. A bench serves as both a focal point and place to relax. The covered entry provides space for packages and cover in inclement weather.

how to reach the house. Four Dimensions started by replacing the staircase with a meandering curve of stone steps. The curve allowed the designers to break up the climb into a series of shorter flights with landings. This lessened the apparent steepness and made the passage more comfortable and inviting. Plantings, stacked-stone walls, and water features made it more interesting. Near the bottom of the steps, a new street entry was created and marked with a boulder and house numbers to encourage visitors to walk up the steps through the garden.

On the upper level, which is still used by the family and some guests, are two paths—the wider, mortared path is clearly the main path, and it leads to the front entry. A smaller stepping-stone path veers toward the kitchen door. A stone cairn marks the fork in the paths.

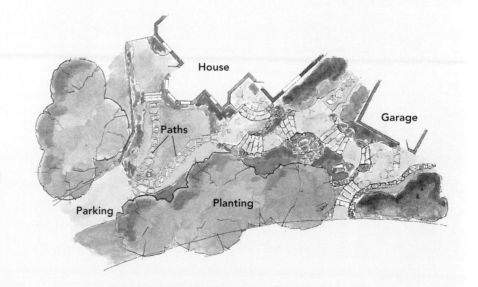

House

Garage

Paths

Parking

Planting

ing of those who park next to them. Plantings can run the gamut from evergreen ground covers to long-blooming perennials to mixed plantings with seasonal interest.

When you landscape your sidewalk strip, be sure to leave several landing areas for getting in and out of the car. Paving materials of some sort work best, as they'll keep your shoes dry in wet weather. Brick, flagstone, and pea gravel work equally well, so choose a surface that complements your other landscaping materials. If your main path runs from the house to the sidewalk, consider continuing it between the sidewalk and street by matching the width, materials, and any patterns. These landings should be at least 3 feet wide.

Though not all streets have sidewalks, just about any house can. If you have lawn that runs to the curb, consider adding a narrow sidewalk if your guests frequently park along the street. Then they won't step out of the car onto wet grass.

▲DON'T HAVE A SIDEWALK? Add one. Guests will appreciate stepping out onto a solid surface rather than into the grass or other plantings. This one also presents a trim appearance where the yard meets the street.

Steps and Handicap Ramps

▲ IF YOU NEED to add steps to your path for a grade change, try to avoid a single step. Two steps (counting the grade level, as shown here) are much easier to see. Changing the pattern at steps helps too. This cut-bluestone path features bull-nosed edges.

Unless your property is flat, you'll need to decide whether a gently sloped path or steps provide the safest passage. The guiding rule for deciding this is to consider the degree of the slope. If you have a 6 percent or less change in grade (which can be measured as a 3-inch drop over a 4-foot run), you're probably better off with a gentle slope, which is much easier to negotiate, easier to install, and less surprising than a single step. Just be sure to avoid paving materials that will dislodge easily or become slippery when wet, and make sure your slope tapers gradually and evenly. If the grade change is greater than 6 percent, you'll need to install steps.

Where there is a steep grade change, steps and surrounding retaining walls are major architectural features that should be carefully designed. The expertise of a landscape architect would be very helpful in this situation. As a general guideline, avoid long runs of steps. Try not to design more than eight steps without a landing, though in some cases this is difficult because the grade change is so great. At a landing, you can change the direction of the steps—veering slightly right or left—adding interest to the landscape and breaking up the climb. Provide a low wall or bench as a resting spot along the way.

If you're designing or installing your own steps, keep safety in mind. Your goal is to create a rise-to-run ratio in which most people would take a natural stride. Good combinations include a 5½-inch rise with a 15-inch tread, a 6½-inch rise with a 14-inch tread, and a 4½-inch rise with a 17-inch tread. Keep it consistent throughout and light the

◀ STEPS NEED NOT be straight. These broad steps are laid in an elegant curve, issuing an invitation to come see what lies beyond. The concrete is softened by plantings that gently spill over the edges without becoming a tripping hazard.

steps so they can be seen in the dark. With three or more steps, put in a handrail. If possible, highlight the beginning of a run of steps with a different paving material or pattern to call attention to the grade change. For instance, you might add a row of bricks to the edge of concrete steps. On brick steps, you might vary the brick color or turn the bricks a different direction along the edge. Boulders placed beside steps are also a good way to emphasize the grade change.

Concrete, flagstone, and brick are all excellent materials for steps. Aggregate can be added to concrete to create greater surface friction. And a slightly porous or textured flagstone, versus a solid, smooth-surfaced stone, will provide better traction in wet weather. In an informal setting, railroad ties can be used, but they will require ongoing maintenance to keep the fill behind them level for a safe climbing surface. As a general rule, railroad ties are best reserved for steps along secondary paths.

▲ A WROUGHT-IRON HANDRAIL was artfully crafted and attached to this wall for safety and support. Such unexpected details add a nice finishing touch to the landscape.

▶ MIXED MATERIALS create a pleasing contrast; here, that contrast calls attention to the steps, which improves safety. These poured-concrete steps are offset by boulders and patterned brick.

▼ THIS HANDICAP RAMP was designed both to be safe and to blend in with the house. It provides easy access to a charming cottage garden as well as the driveway.

Ease of accessibility to your home is a key consideration if a family member or frequent visitor uses a wheelchair or has difficulty negotiating steps. Most states have developed useful guidelines for providing access for disabled persons. These guidelines cover slope, length of run, ramp configuration, handrails, landings, and other features.

Wood is the most commonly used material for building ramps. It is affordable, versatile, and easy to build with. If you live in a brick or mortared home, a concrete ramp faced with brick or stone will blend more seamlessly with the architecture. Railings for ramps can be designed to match the house as well. Landscape a ramp much as you would a small porch or stoop, bringing plantings up to the edge without interfering with the use of the rails. A mix of evergreen and deciduous plants will screen the foundation and provide seasonal interest. And finally, a few fragrant plants placed at nose level will be much appreciated.

4

Driveways and Parking

▶ THIS SIMPLE, winding drive is laid in local crushed shells rather than gravel.

◀ THIS BRICK DRIVEWAY marks the beginning of a gracious entry. A low stone pillar topped with a planted urn creates a sort of gateway.

A s children, we view driveways as playgrounds— places for riding bikes, playing hopscotch, or shooting hoops. As adults, we view them a little differently. Driveways provide access to our house, give us a place to park our cars, and offer a smooth surface for rolling out the garbage and recyclables each week for pickup. Sometimes we hold yard sales there, wash the car, or even garden—either in containers or alongside the drive.

Though primarily utilitarian, new driveways and parking areas should be designed to complement your home and landscape. At a minimum, driveways shouldn't detract— though this can be a challenge considering the amount of space they often take up. Driveways can require a substantial outlay of cash, so it pays to think them through carefully before the bulldozer arrives. If you live in a house with a less than desirable driveway, there's no reason to lose hope. There are a number of ways to update a driveway without having to start from scratch.

The size and shape of a lot, its grade, the location of the house and garage entrances, additional parking needs, and the amount of street traffic all impact the design of a driveway. As you make plans to design a new driveway or update

▲ MEDIAN STRIPS in a driveway, whether the drive is paved or gravel, can be planted with low-growing herbs and wildflowers to create a colorful, low-maintenance carpet. In this case, the median strip complements the native desert wildflowers in the front-yard garden.

an existing one, you'll need to ask yourself the following questions:

- **Ingress and egress**—Is it safe to back out of your driveway or should you only drive forward onto the street? Can you see oncoming traffic?

- **Ease of access**—Do you have room to maneuver the car, open your doors, and get things in and out comfortably? Is the grade change too abrupt or a curve too tight? If your house is set back from the road, is there room for a fire truck in an emergency, or for delivery trucks to turn around without gouging your lawn?

- **Parking**—How many cars do you need to accommodate? Do you have adequate space for them or do you need more parking? Where might you place additional parking so that it can be somewhat screened from view?

- **Grade changes**—Does your driveway have a flat or gentle grade, or is it so steep that you can't see to back up and have difficulty getting in and out of the car? Would a longer, winding drive better suit your lot than a shorter, straight one? Does your car scrape anywhere along the drive, such as at the street or garage entry?

- **Drainage**—Where will the runoff from your driveway go? Do you have low points where you slosh through puddles after a rainstorm?

- **Function**—Will you use your driveway for activities besides parking, ingress, and egress? Does it currently double as a pathway for visitors parked on the road? Do children play there? Can it double as an area for entertainment? Would a smooth, natural, or decorative surface best suit these activities?

- **Aesthetics**—Would you like to de-emphasize your driveway or break it up visually? Are there certain areas such as the street entry, a parking court, or a half circle near your front door that you want to accent?

▼BECAUSE THE DRIVEWAY and parking area fall between the garage and front entry, this area was designed to double as a courtyard. It includes a bench and container plantings along the periphery, as well as an attractive stone wall surrounded by plantings.

Storm Spurs Landscape Makeover

When Hurricane Opal struck Atlanta in 1995, it toppled more than 5,000 of the city's largest oaks. One of those was in Arabelle and Grant Luckhardt's front yard. It knocked out the power and blocked traffic for a full week, and left their shady front-yard plantings exposed to full sun. But the Luckhardts turned this event into a good excuse for a complete landscape makeover and called in landscape designer Paula Refi for the job.

Arabelle loved gardens, and that's what she wanted to see when she looked out all

▲ AFTER THE STORM, an up-rooted tree and other plantings were removed. This shot was taken before the new, wider driveway had been paved, the additional parking space had been added, and the front-yard garden had been planted.

◄ THIS FRONT GARDEN looks as good from the street as it does from the living room window. Shrubs loosely enclose a small lawn and serve as a backdrop for perennials, annuals, and bulbs.

▶ DURING THE LANDSCAPE renovation, the driveway was widened and repaved. A parallel parking slot was created when a section of sloped lawn was cut out and replaced with an attractive stone wall.

her windows. As she says, "I wanted the front garden to be directed as much at me in the house as at the public." So Paula enclosed the front yard with a mix of small ornamental trees and shrubs and then planted both the inside and street side with perennials and bulbs. Window boxes were also added to bring flowers within even closer view. A small patch of lawn remains in the center of the yard.

Of course, this makeover entailed more than transforming the front yard into a garden. The slope next to the driveway was replaced with a stacked-stone retaining wall, and the old driveway was replaced with a new, wider one. In addition, a pull-in parking slot was added between the driveway and stone wall for the large van Arabelle was driving at the time. Says Arabelle, who has since retired the van to plantmobile status, "This was one of the best decisions we made. Having a dry-stacked wall gave a finished look to the front yard, and that parking space made it so much easier to load and unload the van." Originally, the stone wall was planted with sun-loving creeping perennials, but things continue to change in this garden—as the new trees are now creating shade of their own.

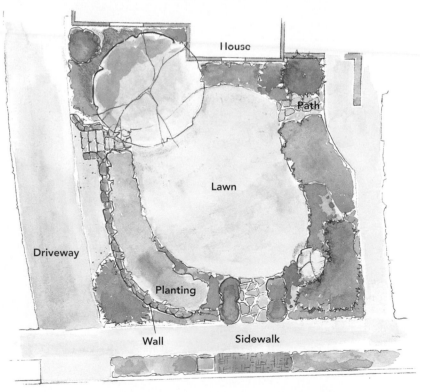

Driveways

Not only do we have more cars per household than ever before, but the average car is bigger than before. Just look at the number of luxury cars, trucks, and sport-utility vehicles on any highway. That's why most new driveways are 11 or 12 feet wide for a single-car garage and 20 feet wide for a two-car garage. Older driveways, which accommodated smaller cars, were often only 8 or 9 feet wide. Though cars can still be driven on them, they are more difficult to maneuver, and when you step out of these cars, you often find yourself standing on the lawn. As a result, some homeowners are ripping out and replacing old driveways, while others are widening existing drives by edging them with bricks, pavers, cut cobbles, and stone.

The simplest driveway, both to install and maneuver, is a straight one with plenty of clearance from walls, steep

▲ ATTRACTIVELY DETAILED valances placed over garage doors give vines a place to grow and soften the doors' visual impact.

shoulders, and plantings. Though it's easy to pull into a straight driveway, backing out can be difficult if you live on a busy road or have limited visibility. Flaring the drive at the street will give you more room to turn, and adding a turnaround slot will eliminate the need to back out into the street. In a pinch, the turnaround can also serve as an additional parking space.

Straight driveways, when they lead to a garage, pose a unique landscaping challenge: They lead your eyes (as well as your car) straight to the garage door. What you really want to call attention to is your home and the landscaping. There are several good ways to deal with this. First, create pattern in the driveway with bands of bricks, stones, or pavers that span the width of the drive. This will slow your eye down, and even lead it to the edges of the drive where you may have nice plantings or paths. Cluster large container plantings on either side of the garage door or build an arbor for vines above it to draw your immediate attention to something besides the door. And if your garage door is plain or worn, you might consider investing in a new door with windows or nice detailing. Don't go overboard, though—too much detailing will draw attention from the rest of the house.

Where space permits, a curving driveway is often more interesting. If laid out in a pleasing way, it will emphasize your house and landscape rather than your garage, carport, or parking area. If your lot slopes as well, you can decrease

▲ THIS SHORT DRIVEWAY makes the most of materials, but in an uncommon way—by including both whole and broken bricks. The result is both attractive and functional.

◀ STONES, PAVERS, OR CUT cobbles can also be placed in the center of a drive, replacing the old-fashioned grassy median strip. The materials require no upkeep but break up the pavement in a similar way.

Asphalt versus Concrete

Asphalt and concrete are the two most common materials for driveways in America. Asphalt is better suited to cold climates, concrete to hot climates. Either works well in moderate climates.

Asphalt is produced from petroleum and mixed with small stone particles. It is delivered hot to the site, dumped into a paving machine, spread in layers 4 to 8 inches deep, and then compacted with a heavy roller to create a smooth, firm, black surface. Both affordable and durable, it should last for many years. Asphalt is a good choice for cold climates, as it will withstand wide fluctuations in temperature and is especially resilient in extreme cold. Also, because it is black, it readily absorbs heat to help melt snow and ice. It is less suitable for areas of extreme heat because it softens and can easily be rutted or gouged. Asphalt drives will also dissolve or develop permanent soft spots if subjected to oil and gas spills. The look of asphalt can be improved by covering the surface with pea gravel in a layer of emulsion to help it blend in better with the surrounding landscape and to give it a longer-lasting finish.

Poured concrete is the best paving for driveways in warmer zones. It is slightly more expensive than asphalt, but is longer lasting if installed properly and can stand extreme heat. In cold climates, concrete is susceptible to cracking and spalling in winter's freeze-and-thaw cycles. Concrete has taken on a new look in recent years. It can be pigmented, stained with chemicals, topped with exposed aggregate, etched with acid, scored, pocked with salt, stamped, sandblasted, or coated with acrylic. It can be made to resemble bricks, stones, or pavers, or it can be combined with bricks, stones, or pavers to emphasize a street entrance or parking court. Used as edging or bands, it can accent and visually break up a large expanse of paving.

▲ **CONCRETE CAN BE STAMPED** to look more like brick—a nice detail at the street entry.

▲ CURVING DRIVEWAYS should
be generous in width for easy
maneuvering. This one has a
well-defined raised edge surrounded by mixed plantings.

the gradient by lengthening and curving your driveway. For
safety, comfort, and driving ease, driveways shouldn't have
more than a 12 percent grade (rise or fall of more than
12 feet in 100). On curves, a lower grade is preferred so cars
will have good traction in wet weather. Where a slope meets
a flat area, decrease the grade so vehicles do not scrape. At
the street, the grade should be no more than 6 percent;
where it meets a garage, it should be held to 4 percent.

When designing curving driveways, consider both the
approach to the house and the views along the way. Walk
the proposed course, and note anything that should be highlighted or screened. The curves of a driveway should have a
minimum centerline radius of 20 feet. And where fire trucks
would have to use the driveway to reach the house, curves
should have a minimum centerline radius of at least 50 feet.

If you have a level front yard with a depth of at least 30 feet and a width of at least 70 feet, a half-circle drive might be a good choice. The major advantage of a half-circle driveway is that it has both an entrance and an exit, so you never have to back out into traffic. Also, half-circle drives usually come quite close to the front door, convenient during stormy weather or for guests arriving for a party, and easier for people with limited mobility. And visually, an arcing driveway places the focus on the house instead of the garage. Since half-circle drives can be coupled with straight drives that run to a garage or parking area, adding a half circle is a good way to update an existing drive. You can also detail the half circle, or at least the section near the front door, with an alternate paving material or edging to help focus attention on your front entry. However, half circles tend to divide your front yard visually, and adding more paving materials creates more runoff for storm drains.

In larger front yards with a depth of 90 feet or more, you might consider making a full circle or looped driveway. Circles generally look best with formal or symmetrically designed homes, while loops are appropriate for informal settings. Circular and looped driveways can also have spurs for garage access or additional parking.

▲ A MODIFIED HALF-CIRCLE with a twist. This one is edged and banded to better integrate with the path to the front door. Guests park along this half-circle drive; access to the garage is through the far driveway spur.

CIRCLE DRIVES

Half-circle driveway

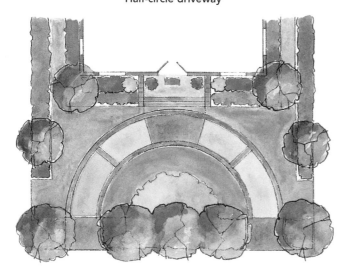

Loop driveway

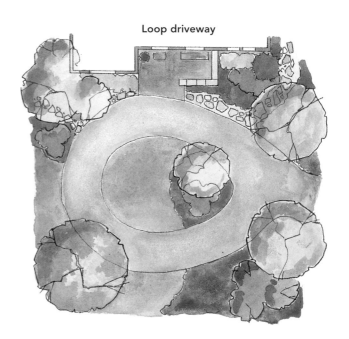

Parking Bays, Pull-Offs, and Parking Courts

A s a society, we've come to rely upon cars. We can't do the shopping, get to work, or take the kids to school without them. Households with three or more vehicles are common, yet few houses have garages to accommodate them all. Making matters worse, garages are often used as storage or work areas, which sometimes takes precedence over parking. As a result, our streets and driveways have become clogged with vehicles.

The simplest solution for increasing parking is adding a parking bay alongside a driveway. It can be placed either parallel or perpendicular to a driveway, or can be angled for

▼ A PEA-GRAVEL PAD creates additional parking without being obtrusive and allows water to drain freely into the soil beneath.

◀ NO GARAGE, BUT PLENTY of parking. This two-car slot, carved out of a front corner of the lot, takes up little space but gets the cars off the street. Because it was put on a lot with a sloped front yard, retaining walls and steps were added. The retaining wall also enabled the owners to create a level lawn.

several cars—much like what you might see in a parking lot (only without the painted stripes). Placed near a garage, a perpendicular parking bay can double as a turnaround space for cars backing out of the garage. In this case, the closest edge of the turnaround should be at least 22 feet from the face of the garage, with a turning radius of 10 feet. A single space should be approximately 20 feet long and 12 feet wide; a double space should be 22 feet wide. For a parallel parking bay, allow plenty of room to maneuver—about 25 feet long next to the driveway, tapering to 18 feet on the outside.

The constraints of a small yard challenge even the best designers when parking must be integrated in a plan. Even so, I've seen some wonderful solutions. When there's not room for a driveway, there is often enough space to pave a single or double parking space, or pull-off, along the side-walk or street. Just be sure to check your local codes first and obtain appropriate permits for cutting any curbs. Since this kind of off-street parking is very public, pay attention to design details and consider adding a low fence, wall, or hedge for screening (provided it doesn't block your view when backing out). If there really isn't room for off-street

ADDING A PARKING SPACE

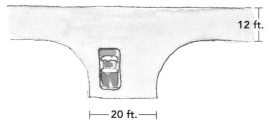

12 ft.

├── 20 ft. ──┤

Double turnaround along driveway

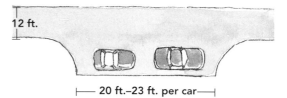

12 ft.

├── 20 ft.–23 ft. per car ──┤

Parallel parking space

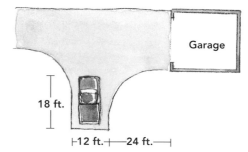

Garage

18 ft.

├12 ft.┼─── 24 ft. ──┤

Single turnaround near garage

Permeable Paving Surfaces

Permeable paving surfaces allow rainwater to seep back into the earth rather than run off into storm drains. This is especially important along driveways, because the oil, gas, and antifreeze that leak from cars are a significant source of water pollution. With a permeable surface, the soil acts as a filter, absorbing pollutants before the water percolates into the water table.

Gravel driveways are a natural choice for rural environments. Crushed gravel comes in several grades, or sizes, and varies slightly in color from one region to another. It is the most economical of all driveways to install, but new gravel must be spread regularly, and keeping weeds to a minimum can sometimes be a challenge. Though gravel is ideal for level lots, it's not a good choice where the grade exceeds 8 percent.

Pea gravel creates a beautiful surface that blends well into the surrounding landscape. Small stone that comes in a range of muted colors, it crunches subtly beneath car tires to announce the arrival of guests.

THIS PULL-OFF DOUBLES as a parking space and turnaround. It is edged in cut cobbles, paved in gravel, and somewhat screened from the house by a low hedge.

That beauty comes at a higher cost, though. Pea gravel must be replaced often, and recent studies show that the regular removal of gravel from rivers is detrimental to the environment.

Open-cell pavers are grids of high-density plastic or concrete set on a prepared base, filled with soil, and planted with a sturdy turf grass that can handle cars. Once the grass becomes established, the pavers blend almost seamlessly into the surrounding landscape, especially if that landscape features any lawn. Open-cell pavers provide a firm, level surface that won't settle into ruts. However, the turf grass requires water, fertilization, and routine care.

Pervious concrete and asphalt are fairly new to the scene but have tremendous potential for reducing excessive runoff. They offer a smooth, sturdy surface like traditional concrete and asphalt, but allow water to seep through to a crushed gravel base that acts as a water reservoir. These materials are stable on flat ground but are generally not recommended for steep grades.

OPEN-CELLED PAVERS can be planted with grass to create a permeable, environmentally friendly surface.

▲ DETAILS TRANSFORM a parking area into a parking court.
Here, a millstone, cut cobbles,
and stacked-stone retaining
wall enhance a utilitarian space.

► THIS LARGE PARKING AREA
was transformed into a parking
court with inset stones and soft
screening provided by low
shrubs and arbors.

parking, at least make sure that on-street parking has a clear,
level landing area. Sections of brick or stone make a welcoming pad for passengers getting out of their car.

It's important to integrate the parking into the landscape.
For visual interest and to reduce the apparent size of a driveway, consider paving parking areas with materials different
from those used on the driveway. Pea gravel and open-cell
pavers planted with grass will help parking areas blend into
the landscape; patterned paving will emphasize the landscape. Either approach can work as long as it harmonizes
with the house and landscape.

While a slab of concrete or a few yards of gravel make a
functional parking space, attention to detail can transform
that same space into a parking court. Parking courts,

Brick, Stone, and Pavers

Bricks, stones, and concrete pavers are classic paving materials that come in a wide range of colors, shapes, sizes, and textures. Styles are available to complement any house, and they can be dry-laid or mortared in an almost infinite range of patterns. Since they all require much hand labor, they are more costly than other driveway paving materials. But considering how long they last, and how much they add to the landscape, solid pavers are often worth the expense.

To give your driveway a pleasing look without breaking the bank, use bands or patterns of these higher-cost materials as accents in a base of treated concrete. Add a section of pavers at the street entry or near the front door of a half-circle driveway, or use them to create additional parking areas.

▲ OLDER DRIVEWAYS **can be easily widened by adding cut cobbles, bricks, pavers, or even stone turned on edge.**

because they are carefully designed and landscaped, have more flexibility in terms of their placement. A parking court can be placed either right at the house on a smaller or urban lot, or away from the house on a larger property. It should accommodate at least two cars with ample room for opening and closing doors—at least 24 feet wide by 19 feet deep.

By surrounding parking courts with freestanding or retaining walls, you can transform them into courtyard-like settings. They may also be accented with clipped evergreen hedges, container plantings, large urns, garden statuary, columns, arbors, or water features. Two or three different paving materials are typically used, and patterns are often set into the central area of the parking court. Millstones, if you can find them, also make an interesting centerpiece for a parking court.

Parking Does Double Duty

andscape architect Warren Simmonds made use of every square inch in this 25- by 35-foot space in Mill Valley, California. There's parking for one car, a tiny lawn, a patio for entertaining, and a small garden. To get that much into a lot this size required some creative thinking.

A swinging gate would have taken up nearly a quarter of the front yard. But by using a gate that rolls into a fence pocket, he was able to place the parking space closer to the street and add a patio next to the house. A small boxwood hedge provides screening between the patio and parking area. Yet the parking space,

▲ A SMALL NOOK SERVES AS A PATIO with seating for five. Plantings and a wall (which can be seen in the other photos) provide plenty of privacy, despite the close proximity of neighbors.

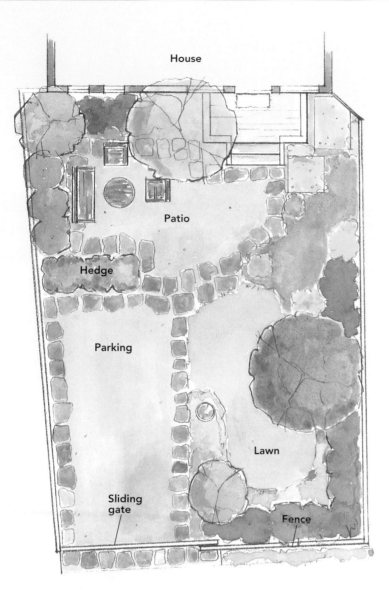

House

Patio

Hedge

Parking

Lawn

Sliding gate

Fence

▲ CLOSE QUARTERS call for creative solutions. A pull-in slot provides parking for one car. With a rolling pocket gate, the parking space can be placed close to the street instead of against the house.

because the materials match those in the patio, can easily double Deborah and Mark Lyon's space for entertaining when the car is parked on the street.

Shrubs soften the lines of the fence, and a small garden filled with roses and perennials brightens the yard through the growing season. A large tree provides a shady canopy and increases the garden's sense of privacy—even though neighboring houses are merely a few feet away.

▲ A LOW HEDGE separates the parking area from the patio, but matching paving means the parking space can be used for entertaining if the car is moved to the street.

Street Entries

Gateways are symbolic. They signify an entrance—whether to a ballpark, ranch, garden, or some other realm of existence. In the landscape, they can be functional or merely suggestive. Pillars, gates, wing walls, fences, mailboxes, cairns, and arches can all serve as gateways to let people know they've arrived at the right place. Planting beds can also mark a driveway entry, with or without the aid of structures.

Street-side gateways or entries are both diverse in design and multipurpose in function. In rural areas, gateways at the end of the drive help newcomers find your house, especially if it is hard to see from the road. A gateway sets the tone for the landscape style—be it formal, informal, or otherwise. Consider the metal arch over the gravel entry to a ranch, the cluster of brightly colored annuals by the mailbox of a country cottage, or the imposing stone walls and tall iron gate before an estate.

The most obvious entryway is the gate itself. Gates can be welcoming or austerely off-putting. Though many gates are designed strictly for decorative purposes and left open, others are installed for increased privacy, safety, or improved home security. They can be opened and closed manually or set on an automatic system. They can swing open or, where space is tight, slide into wall or fence pockets. When considering the height and placement of a gate, consult with your building department. Often there are setback requirements, and sometimes permits are required. Also, make sure gates or posts do not obscure the visibility of oncoming traffic. Landscaping around a gate will help tie it into the surrounding yard.

▲ THE SIMPLEST GATES can signal an entry.

▼ STONE PILLARS mark the gateway to this home, which has a long, winding driveway and can't be seen from the street. Simple wooden posts or a few sections of split-rail fencing would also serve this role well.

▲ CAIRNS MARK THE DRIVEWAY entrance and frame the view of the home. The casualness of these rock formations matches the simple pea-gravel drive.

Pillars, columns, or posts can also mark a driveway entrance. Often they are integrated with a fence or wall that surrounds a property. Other times, they are simply free-standing pillars placed on either side of the driveway. Stacked-stone pillars make a substantial marker. A matching pair of painted wood posts, especially when accompanied by short sections of picket fencing and colorful plantings, can create an elegant entry for a traditional home. Stone posts and a rustic wooden gate would suit a house in the woods or a cabin in the mountains. No matter what type of entry you create, don't forget to post your house numbers where they are clearly visible day and night. And when designing plantings, make sure you're not blocking your view of on-coming traffic.

5

Property Boundaries

▶ GATES CAN BE nicely detailed and offer a glimpse into the garden.

W e've all heard the adage, "Good fences make good neighbors" from a Robert Frost poem. But in truth, defining your property boundaries—whether with a fence, wall, hedge, patch of trees, or planting bed—is not so much about your neighbors as it is about you and how you wish to experience and use your front yard. There are as many reasons for defining your periphery as there are ways to do it—to increase privacy, frame pleasing views and screen unwanted ones, define the "walls" of a garden room, provide shelter from prevailing winds, buffer neighborhood noise, keep pets in or out of your yard, and prevent children from running into the street after a stray ball.

For homeowners with small lots, privacy is often a driving force behind enclosing a front yard. Without some sort of buffer, you can often hear your neighbors' conversations or even see into each other's homes. For total privacy, your best bets are tall, solid walls and fences with the pickets or boards spaced very tightly. A dense evergreen hedge will also do the trick, though on a narrow lot, it's important to remember that a hedge occupies much more space than a wall or fence. On larger lots, tall hedges or groves of trees can create a greater sense of privacy.

◀ PLANT BOTH SIDES of a fence or wall so your neighbors can enjoy the garden too. A 2- to 4-foot-deep border is all you need for some small shrubs, evergreen perennials, or creeping ground covers. This border is anchored by lavender, with a seasonal planting of nasturtiums at the corner.

Nothing will silence a busy street, but masonry walls—and to a lesser degree, hedges and fences—will absorb and reduce traffic noise. The higher the wall the better, because in a built-up area, sound bounces off hard surfaces and can come from many angles other than street level. But keep in mind that sounds will also bounce around inside a masonry wall, so consider softening sections of those walls with vines.

Not all enclosures are the same. You can screen a few areas along your property line with trees, build a high wall to create an enclosed courtyard, or install a low fence over which you can visit with passersby. The material, height, and opacity of your peripheral screening send a message to others about how you want to relate to them. Loose plantings, low walls, and widely spaced picket fences can be very inviting. Tall, solid walls and fences, as well as dense hedges, can be imposing. Even if you prefer your privacy, it's

▲ LOOSE PLANTINGS SCREEN utility boxes. Here, the utility box can scarcely be seen (lower left) amid the 'Otto Luyken' laurel. The low, shrubby plantings also provide an attractive, open boundary between the two homes. Closer to the house, taller plants like privet, crape myrtle, and river birch are used for screening.

▲ A SHEARED BEECH HEDGE defines a front-yard garden room. The low hedge and open arbor allow neighbors to take a peek at the plantings inside. Graceful ornamental grasses and striking perennials are placed between the hedge and sidewalk to create a "public" garden.

a good idea to send that message in a friendly way. After all, front yards are still considered semipublic areas and contribute to the overall character of a neighborhood. Leave a few feet between your wall, fence, or hedge and the sidewalk for a strip of flowering ground covers or perennials; soften walls or fences with vines; or add some small windows to walls and gates that offer a glimpse inside.

Boundary elements don't have to be high or solid to create a sense of enclosure. Something as simple as a cairn (a small mound of rocks) at each property corner can define your boundaries. A 3-foot wall will allow you to chat freely with neighbors while providing a backdrop for a flower bed. Also, you may choose to partition or screen only one or two sides of your yard, leaving the others open to the street or neighbors' yards.

If you live in a conservative neighborhood and are the first on your block to stake a claim to your front yard by defining your property boundaries, you might consider making changes gradually. Plantings are often more readily

Check Out Local Codes

Local codes and neighborhood covenants regarding walls, fences, and hedges vary. Such guidelines might address the height of walls, the distance a boundary must be placed from the street or curb, and any right-of-way granted to utilities and road crews. Some neighborhoods, in fact, ban any sort of street-side barrier. So before you spend your first nickel, contact your local planning office and homeowners' association, if you have one, to find out what's acceptable and what's not.

When you ask about setback distances, be sure to find out whether the setback is measured from the center of the street or the curb. And double-check the location of your property line—it may be further from the road than you think. Also verify whether the same

restrictions apply to hedges, walls, and fences. Often you can grow a hedge where you can't build a permanent structure.

Sometimes there's room for negotiation on codes. If you think you have a strong case, consider applying for a variance. In many places, applying for a variance to build a higher fence or to place it in the right-of-way is considered routine. The application might cost a few hundred dollars and take a few months, but could be worth the cost and effort. A variance is sometimes granted on a conditional basis. For instance, it might state that if the city decides to widen the street, your fence or wall will have to be removed. In that case, you'll simply have to decide whether it's worth the risk.

▲ A DRY STREAM along the periphery handles rainwater runoff efficiently and anchors a colorful perennial garden. In dry weather, it doubles as a garden path.

accepted than walls or fences. Start with a planting bed that runs 15 or 20 feet down the side of your property, perhaps extending from the corners of your house. Anchor this peninsula with a small flowering tree or large shrub, and surround it with a few smaller shrubs, well-behaved perennials, and creeping ground covers. You'll probably find that a few of your neighbors quickly follow suit, and in time, you'll feel more confident expanding the plantings or adding a low fence or wall.

Fences

Wooden fences have long been the screening of choice in America, and for good reason. Throughout much of the country, wood is readily available and therefore affordable. Fences are generally quicker and easier to build than walls, so labor costs are lower as well. And unlike hedges, which need time to grow, fences have immediate impact on the landscape.

Painted fences do need a fresh coat of color every four or five years. Stained fences can often go a bit longer but will look better with a coat from time to time. Wood can also be left to weather naturally, reducing the upkeep. Wooden

▼SCALLOPED PICKET FENCES are eye-catching. They can curve up or down and can be painted to match the color of the house.

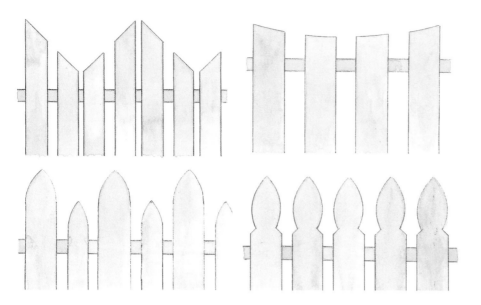

Picket fence style is determined by board width, spacing, and picket designs.

fences don't last forever, though. Over the years, pickets and posts may rot, become infested with termites, warp, or fall into general disrepair without regular attention. Still, for the money, they're an excellent form of screening and, with care, can last for many years.

Wood fences come in many styles. Picket fences, the most popular, are commonly found surrounding colonial and cottage homes. Split-rail, running-rail, and board-and-lattice fences are also popular. Of course, fences can be made from materials other than wood. Wrought iron is a favorite in places like New Orleans and Savannah. Bamboo suits oriental gardens and contemporary homes. And fences made of all sorts of metal—from copper and steel to yachting cables—are striking against postmodern architecture. Even chain-link fences, though most often relegated to backyards, can provide affordable and attractive fencing when covered in vines.

You can dress up a fence by mixing construction materials. The easiest way to do this is to build the posts from one material and the fence sections from another. You can also create low base walls from masonry materials, and top them with wood, iron, or metal fences. Just don't mix too many different types of materials.

Another way to dress up a fence is with a gate. Most gates are made from the same materials as the fence itself, though

Hoops Add Height to a Fence

A creative technique for increasing the height of a fence is to attach a series of hoops of bent No. 3 rebar to fence posts and train vines up and over them. If your local codes limit fence heights but not plantings, this *may* be a way to add height to your barrier—though you should verify this before adding the hoops. Even if you're restricted in height, extension hoops offer a way to maximize screening without building a high fence.

For good proportion, I like to increase the height of a fence by about half. On a 6-foot fence, for instance, I like to add another 3 feet (measured at the center point) with the hoops. And then to give the fence the perfect finishing touch, I plant flowering vines like climbing roses, jasmine, or honeysuckle along the fence posts and tie them loosely to the hoops as they grow.

▲ THOUGH HEAVY-DUTY materials were used to construct this fence, the openness of the pickets gives it an airy feeling. A small planting strip in front of the fence is filled with low-growing perennials.

▲ BOARD-AND-LATTICE FENCES offer privacy on a corner lot. This cedar fence is nicely detailed with custom lattice. Leaving spaces between the boards gives the fence an open, friendly feel, yet shrubs planted on the inside of the fence limit views within.

they don't have to be. Continuing the pattern of the fence in the gate is also common, but by creating a unique gate design with the fence materials, or even changing the materials themselves, you can call attention to the entry. As an alternative, consider building an arbor or arch over your entry—with or without a gate—and draping it with a fragrant climbing rose, favorite clematis, or other twining vine.

▲ A FENCE BOTH SCREENS the side yard and provides a solid backdrop for a mixed planting. A latticed window (lower left, next to gate) allows the family dog to keep an eye on front-yard activities.

▶ THIS PICKET FENCE curves inward at the corner to improve visibility for neighbors backing out of their driveway.

Walls give a look of permanence to a garden. When well constructed, they are, indeed, long-lasting structures. A solid brick or stone wall may age gracefully for hundreds of years—far outlasting the homeowners. The principal drawback to walls is their initial cost. Both the materials and labor are more expensive than those for fences and hedges. And except for low walls of stacked stone or structural block, you'll probably want to hire a mason, as tall walls require poured-concrete foundations and reinforcing bars. If cost is an issue, you might consider building a small section of wall in a prominent location and establishing remaining boundaries with other materials.

▼ GATES ARE GREAT places for personalization. Here, the owner placed a metal cutout of Kokopeli—a mythical figure of the Southwest said to spread music and good cheer —against sticks framed by wrought iron.

Brick and stone are among the most popular wall materials. Stone can be purchased as precisely cut rectangles, roughly quarried rocks, weathered fieldstones, rounded river stones, large ledge stones, and flat flagstones. Colors range from deep terra-cotta to dark gray; some stones even have a metallic sheen. While stone walls over 3 feet should be mortared, short walls may be either mortared or dry stacked. By contrast, all brick walls should be mortared for stability. They can be simply stacked, arranged in patterns, or laid in an open, latticelike fashion. And bricks come in a range of colors—from pale yellow to rusty red to charcoal gray—so you can choose a single color or mix several shades.

Still elegant, but more affordable, are stucco and structural-block walls. Stucco is a colored and textured finish applied over concrete block that can even be built up and rounded off to look like an adobe wall. Capstones or brick trim can add an attractive finishing touch to stucco walls. Structural blocks are oversized, hollow bricks in a wide variety of shapes,

▲ A BRICK WALL LAID in an open, lattice-like pattern uses fewer bricks and has a lighter feeling. This one has a curved profile, and the solid brick posts are capped with formed concrete finials.

▲ A STACKED-STONE WALL has a been-there-forever look—even if recently constructed. A low wooden gate matches the casual style of the wall.

◄ MIX MATERIALS TO CREATE a more interesting wall or fence. In the Southwest, rustic stick fencing looks good with adobe and stucco walls.

colors, and finishes that can be used to create single-width, freestanding walls.

An eye-catching gate works just as well with a wall as with a fence and is perhaps even more commonly used with a wall. But unlike fences, walls feature gates made of different materials. Heavy-duty, detailed wooden gates look good with just about any kind of masonry wall; wrought-iron gates are also a good choice. Because solid walls will block any light coming from your house, install some lighting near the gate so guests will feel welcome and you don't have to fumble with your keys in the dark. Arbors are also an option with walls, though they are seen less often. To balance the visual weight of a wall, arbors should be constructed from timbers at least 4 inches thick.

A Wooded Courtyard in the Pacific Northwest

The tall brick wall surrounding this Seattle home is so inviting that passing cars slow to admire it. The brick is nicely detailed—with an attractive cap and inset house numbers. The entry is recessed, with attractive lanterns and a wide brick path that leads from the street to the front door. The Craftsman-style gate is oversized and beautifully detailed, with inviting windows inset across the top. And the entire wall is set back a few feet from the sidewalk; this makes it feel less imposing and also creates a planting strip that has been filled with a lush mix of flowering perennials and shrubs—many of them fragrant. A separate yet equally inviting entrance provides access for family members and friends who park in the driveway. It has a matching gate, along with an arbor built from heavy timbers.

Designed by local landscape architect Keith Geller, the brick wall creates a quiet courtyard. But unlike most courtyards, which consist primarily of paved surfaces, this one features a woodland garden that captures the spirit of the Pacific Northwest. Winding paths of crushed granite make their way through this small forest and to the back yard. Evergreen trees offer additional screening and envelop the space with a sense of serenity. Japanese maples, rhododendrons, and an assortment of perennials accent the garden, while several small water features add to the calm and stillness of the courtyard. A bench allows one to sit and enjoy the setting.

What really makes this work is the attention paid to details. Note the way the bricks are laid in the curving path, the solid construction of the gate and arbor, the natural placement of plants, and the subtlety of the water features.

▶ A RECESSED WALL and gate signal the courtyard entry. The custom gate, brick cap, light fixture, and planting strip are all attractive details that make this privacy wall a pleasure to look at.

Choice Shrubs for Formal Hedges

Arborvitae (*Thuja* spp.)

Beech (*Fagus sylvatica*)

Black bamboo (*Phyllostachys nigra*)

Boxwood (*Buxus sempervirens*)

California wax myrtle (*Myrica californica*)

European hornbeam (*Carpinus betulus*)

Hemlock (*Tsuga* spp.)

Incense cedar (*Calocedrus decurrens*)

Japanese holly (*Ilex crenata*)

Laurustinus (*Viburnum tinus*)

Lavender (*Lavandula* spp.)

Leyland cypress (x *Cupressocyparis leylandii*)

Pittosporum spp.

Privet (*Ligustrum* spp.)

Wax myrtle (*Myrica cerifera*)

Yew (*Taxus* x *media*)

▲ BOXWOOD

▲ A SHEARED BOXWOOD hedge suits the formality of this brick colonial. It is kept medium height to echo the boxy shape of the house.

Evergreen plants that respond well to frequent shearing are the best choices for formal hedges. Needled or broad-leaved plants with smaller leaves are easiest to shear. Large-leaved evergreens have to be pruned by hand, as shears will simply clip the leaves in half, leaving the plants looking ragged. Clipped hedges need to look good from top to bottom, so taper them (narrower at the top than bottom) to expose all the branches to sunlight. Otherwise, the lower branches will thin, brown, and die out over the years. For ease of maintenance, keep formal hedges no more than 3 or 4 feet high. Plant in a single row, 1 to 2 feet apart. Planting closely allows the branches to intermingle, one of the distinguishing characteristics of a hedge.

Informal hedges are more laissez-faire, with plants allowed to grow into their natural shape and size. Informal hedges can be one species of evergreen or deciduous shrub, a mix of evergreen or deciduous shrubs, or a tapestry of

evergreen and deciduous shrubs. An evergreen hedge will provide solid, year-round screening. A mixed or deciduous hedge is less dense in winter, but offers seasonal interest with flowers, berries, and colorful foliage.

Shrubs in an informal hedge should be planted farther apart than the same shrubs would be in a formal, clipped hedge. Though the shrubs may be planted in a single row, they create a denser hedge when planted in a staggered row, 2 to 4 feet apart. Because this requires a bed width of at least 8 to 12 feet, staggered hedges are best suited to larger suburban and rural gardens. For a mixed hedge, plant individual shrub types in clusters of three to seven for a stronger visual effect, and repeat the clusters for continuity. One of the tricks to growing a mixed hedge is selecting plants that have similar cultural requirements and are compatible with one another. If one plant is considerably more aggressive than the others, it will soon overwhelm your planting.

Choice Shrubs for Informal Hedges

Alder buckthorn (*Rhamnus frangula* 'Columnaris')

Camellia (*Camellia* spp.)

Cherry and English laurel (*Prunus laurocerasus*)

Common myrtle (*Myrtus communis*)

Escallonia spp.

European cranberry bush (*Viburnum opulus*)

Flowering currant (*Ribes sangvineum*)

Flowering quince (*Chaenomeles* hybrids)

Forsythia x *intermedia*

Glossy abelia (*Abelia* x *grandiflora*)

Hedge maple (*Acer campestre*)

Japanese barberry (*Berberis thunbergii*)

Mock orange (*Philadelphus coronaries*)

Red tip (*Photinia* x *fraseri*)

Rose bay (*Nerium oleander*)

Russian olive (*Elaeagnus angustifolia*)

Rose of Sharon (*Hibiscus syriacus*)

Shrub roses (*Rosa* spp.)

Viburnum spp.

Weigela spp.

▲ BARBERRY

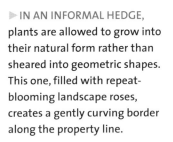

▶ IN AN INFORMAL HEDGE, plants are allowed to grow into their natural form rather than sheared into geometric shapes. This one, filled with repeat-blooming landscape roses, creates a gently curving border along the property line.

Periphery Plantings

As an alternative to hedges, mixed plantings may be used to mark your property boundary. Unlike hedges, which are composed strictly of shrubs, mixed plantings may include trees, shrubs, perennials, and other plants. And instead of being planted in rows, mixed plantings are usually placed in loose, curving island beds for a more natural look. Though the subject of plantings will be covered more thoroughly in Chapter 8, we'll take a brief look here at their use to delineate property boundaries.

One benefit of a mixed planting is the ease with which you can both screen unwanted views and preserve desirable views. Taller and broader plants can be grown for screening, and lower plantings can continue a bed while preserving a view. You can even leave gaps between two or more taller plantings, such as the limbs of trees, to frame especially inviting views.

▼ A LARGE, PARTIALLY WOODED lot deserves an attractive mixed planting along its border. This one includes an understory of dogwoods and azaleas.

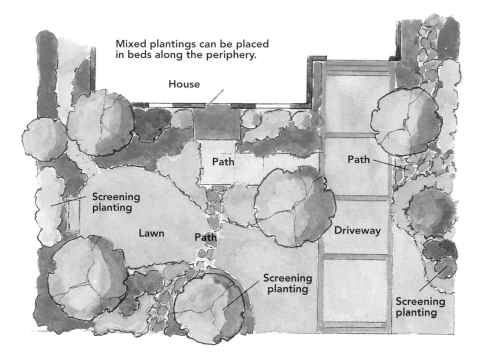

Mixed plantings can be placed in beds along the periphery.

House

Path

Path

Screening planting

Lawn

Path

Driveway

Screening planting

Screening planting

▲ MIXED PLANTINGS WORK In smaller spaces too, such as this narrow strip between neighboring driveways. Simply use smaller trees and shrubs, and plant them densely.

Mixed plantings can be low or high, open or dense, depending on whether you need solid screening or simply want to mark your periphery. You don't need a large area to exercise your horticultural muscle. A bed just 6 feet wide by 10 feet long has plenty of room for a small tree, a few low shrubs, and an assortment of perennials. Think about how the planting will look from all sides—for what your neighbor sees is just as important as what you see. Though all rules are meant to be broken at one time or another, it's a good idea to place the trees toward the middle of the bed, surround them with shrubs, and then use perennials, bulbs, and ground covers to fill around the edges. When you place your tallest plants slightly off center, your planting will look more natural.

If you are blessed with a wooded lot, think about leaving a buffer of trees between your yard and your neighbor's, or even between your house and the street.

◄ A WOODED FRONT YARD can be transformed into a shady destination. Clear the underbrush to create winding trails and sitting areas. Even though it's in a subdivision, this home feels more secluded.

A Cottage Garden for a Corner Lot

Bob McIntyre always wanted a house with a picket fence, and he finally got his wish. His house sits at an intersection in Palo Alto, California, where local codes restrict peripheral fences to 3 feet tall at corners and require a 2-foot setback from the sidewalk so oncoming vehicles are visible. He started with a 3-foot, curved-top picket fence and added an arbor where it wouldn't interfere with visibility. The setback left just enough space to plant a lavender border. Nasturtiums are tucked in at the corner, and roses

scramble up the arbor, making a colorful splash every summer. The fence and plantings have since spurred the creation of other boisterous front-yard gardens throughout the neighborhood.

Though the fence is low, it gives a sense of protection from the sidewalk and street. It is neighbor-friendly, allowing passersby to view the garden when they are out for an evening walk. The garden is laid out on an axis, with a brick main path and grassy side path. Each path has a focal point—a birdbath for the main path, and a bench

▲ A 3-FOOT-TALL PICKET FENCE set back 2 feet from the sidewalk offers privacy on this corner lot without obstructing views of oncoming traffic. And the bright, prolific plantings are a hallmark of cottage garden design.

▲ PATHS PLACED ON AXIS are surrounded with lush plantings, and a bench offers a place to sit in warm weather.

▶ NEAR THE FRONT DOOR, the entry area was extended with a small brick terrace. A window box, container plantings, and wicker chair make it inviting.

flanked by lemon trees for the side path. Bob often sits on the bench to read the paper and watch life in the neighborhood. We also built a small brick terrace near the front door, but the wicker chair there is more for looks than anything else. (Bob prefers sitting on the bench, which is further from the street.)

The garden is a riot of color all season long. The deep red roses Bob planted by the arbor are the queens of the garden in late spring, while masses of black-eyed Susans step up to the starring role in summer. They are tempered by wine-foliaged plants such as smokebush, New Zealand flax, and 'Chameleon' spurge. Cannas, dahlias, and lobelia jazz up the plantings with their bright red flowers, while window boxes, container plantings, and an herb garden bring life to the terrace.

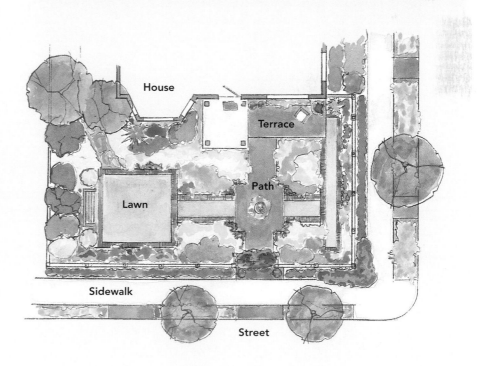

6

Foundation Plantings

▶ THIS NEAT AND TRIM foundation planting loosens up as the bed extends beyond the house.

Houses haven't always had foundation plantings. The practice of planting evergreen shrubs around the base of a house became popular when builders started using concrete block for foundations instead of brick or stone. Concrete block was cheaper and easier to install but wasn't very attractive. So foundation plantings as we know them evolved primarily as a way to hide part of the house.

Without foundation plantings, many houses would simply look like big boxes set down on a flat surface—what is sometimes called "plop architecture." Foundation plantings help soften that look, tying a house to the surrounding landscape and giving it a sense of belonging. Foundation plants can also help a house feel less imposing, especially large houses. Trees, shrubs, and vines break up broad expanses of wall and offer intimate details—such as the perfume of a rose or the delicate tracery of a Japanese maple leaf—that can be appreciated up close. Plants can draw your eye to a door, bay window, or other interesting architectural feature. And their greenery gives a sense of life and vitality to a house. In essence, foundation plantings can make a house more inviting.

◀ FOUNDATION PLANTINGS can be colorful. Start with flowering evergreen shrubs and then add deciduous shrubs, perennials, and annuals for additional seasonal color.

▲FOUNDATION PLANTINGS don't have to be evergreen or shrubby. This house is surrounded by upright grasses, mounding perennials, and spreading ground covers. Boulders are placed for accent, helping the home settle into its Rocky Mountain surroundings.

The act of placing plants around the base of a house is a little like dressing a person. Some homes can get away with a short skirt of plant material but most look best with a little more cover—perhaps a mix of larger shrubs and even a few trees. How we go about cloaking our homes depends a lot on their shape, size, and architectural style. Some are complemented by a casual arrangement of loose plantings; others are best suited to a tailored look—evenly trimmed hedges with matching architectural accessories.

Though it's common to simply plant a row of evergreens from one end of the house to the other, foundation plantings are more interesting if they feature a variety of plants—both evergreen and deciduous—and range in height from creeping ground covers to upright trees.

▲A SINGLE STRIKING PLANT, such as this white-flowering spirea, has the ability to unify a group of town houses or a neighborhood.

Evergreen Foundation Plants

PERENNIALS

African blue lily   *Agapanthus 'Storm Cloud'*
Big blue lily turf   *Liriope muscari*
Christmas fern   *Polysticum arostichoides*
Hellebore   *Helleborus* spp.
Japanese rush   *Acorus gramineus 'Ogon'*
Pheasant's tail grass   *Stipa arundinacea*

▲ *AGAPANTHUS*

SHRUBS

Chinese juniper   *Juniperus chinensis*
Common boxwood   *Buxus sempervirens*
Common camellia   *Camellia japonica*
Cherry laurel   *Prunus laurocerasus*
Heavenly bamboo   *Nandina domestica*
Japanese holly   *Ilex crenata 'Convexa'*
Japanese mock orange   *Pittosporum tobira 'Wheeler's Dwarf'*

Pieris   *Pieris 'Forest Flame'*
Rhododendron   *Rhododendron* spp.
Sweetbox   *Sarcococca hookeriana*

TREES

African fern pine   *Africarpus gracilior*
American arborvitae   *Thuja occidentalis*
Brazilian pepper tree   *Schinus terebinthifolius*
Bronze loquat   *Eriobotrya deflexa*
Columnar yew   *Taxus x media 'Hicksii'*
Nellie Stephens holly   *Ilex 'Nellie R. Stephens'*
New Zealand tea tree   *Leptospermum scoparium*
Sweet bay   *Laurus nobilis*
Sweet olive   *Osmanthus fragrans*

◄ NOT ALL HOUSES have foundations to hide. Sometimes low-growing ground covers like pachysandra are much more pleasing than shrubs. Deciduous trees with bright red berries like this crabapple are a pleasure to view from house windows and attract birds in winter.

Architectural Cues

Foundation plants should complement the style, lines, and scale of a house. Take a close look at your house to determine its overriding style. If the house is symmetric, plantings should match on either side of the door. As you move away from the center of the house, you can either continue to match the plantings or gradually introduce some variation. Overall, however, the plantings should be balanced. In addition to balance, most symmetric homes look best with geometrically arranged and neatly manicured plantings. That doesn't mean shearing shrubs into matching meatballs, but formal homes do benefit from an overall sense of uniformity.

Asymmetric houses offer more freedom in plant selection and placement. Balance still plays a role, but the rules have changed. Instead of simply balancing plantings with each other, you are sometimes balancing plantings with architectural features. For instance, if the chimney rises above the

▼ SYMMETRY CALLS For simplicity. Just match the plantings on either side of the house. Formal plantings of boxwood and topiaries are softened with cosmos and lavender.

Plantings accent and balance an asymmetrically designed house.

Matched plantings suit a symmetrically designed house.

roofline on one side of the house, a conifer planted on the other side that peaks just above the roofline would suggest a sense of balance. But rather than worry too much about creating balance, concentrate instead on establishing natural-looking mixed plantings that frame the house and highlight its architectural features.

Plants can also highlight the architectural lines of a house. A low sheared hedge along the base of a ranch-style house will emphasize its horizontal profile. Columnar trees placed at the corners will accent a tall, narrow house. Big boxwoods on either side of a front door will echo the mass of a boxy house. It is possible, however, to have too much of a good thing: For visual interest, include a few plants with contrasting shapes to break those same lines. Two small columnar plants on either side of the front door will break the strong horizontal lines of the ranch-style house. Several large, rounded, or horizontal shrubs beneath the windows of the tall house will bring your view back down to eye level. Clusters of differently shaped and sized plants at the corners of the boxy house will make it feel less overpowering.

Also remember to keep the scale of the house in mind when choosing plants. Tall trees may anchor a two-story house, but those same trees would dwarf a cottage. Here,

small ornamental trees would be a much better choice. Similarly, homes with several feet of exposed foundation need more massive foundation shrubs than homes built on slab with little or no exposed foundation.

Foundation plants can call attention to or play down the architectural features of a house. The most important architectural element to highlight is the front door. You can do this by placing slightly taller plants on either side of the stoop or landing. If the doorway and mantel are symmetric —matching lanterns or window panels on either side—the plantings immediately to either side of the door are usually matched, even if the house is asymmetric and the remaining foundation plantings are informal. Asymmetric doorways— those with a window panel or light fixture on just one side— can be treated either formally or informally. A combined approach can also be effective: Place a balanced, mixed planting on either side of the doorway but vary the plants in those groupings.

Plant form is as important as plant placement in creating focus on a doorway. Both plant height and shape are factors to be considered. Hard lines and strong form attract attention; softer shapes are less commanding. As a general rule, strong geometric forms are most appropriate for formal

Establishing Grade

For healthy plant growth and a dry basement, you need good drainage around the base of your house. If water tends to settle around the foundation rather than draining away from it, you can just about count on a moldy environment and a leaking or flooded basement in heavy rainfall. This excess moisture can also hurt plants. Soil that retains too much water prevents plant roots from absorbing oxygen—and this leads to root rot, which will harm and eventually kill many plants.

The soil line should be at least 6 inches below the base of the wall framing to prevent dampness and dry rot in your home. From there, the soil should slope steadily away from the house—a 5 percent grade for the first 6 feet is recommended. The runoff from gutters also needs to be directed away from the house. This water can be channeled down a slope where it can settle naturally into the soil, or into a swale or dry stream toward your neighborhood's storm-drainage system.

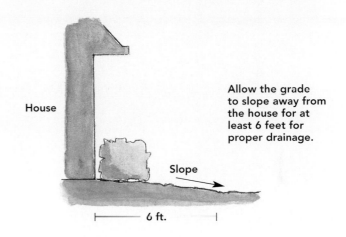

House

Allow the grade to slope away from the house for at least 6 feet for proper drainage.

Slope

6 ft.

Homes built on a slab foundation need only minimal foundation plantings.

homes, while softer shapes suit informal houses. In a formal setting, matching round or conical shrubs could be placed either side of the door, in most cases extending no more than three-quarters the height of the door. In an informal setting, something softer, and often taller, is nice. A small tree, such as a dogwood (*Cornus* spp.) or vine maple (*Acer circinatum*), could create a canopy over or near the doorway.

A climbing rose trained up and over the door, would also be a good choice.

Beyond the front door, the corners of a house usually demand the most attention. This is where your house meets the surrounding landscape, and plantings serve as a visual anchor. The traditional approach is to place tall evergreens at the corners. This softens the hard lines along the edges of your house. The key is giving those evergreens space to grow without rubbing against the walls and eaves. It's also possible to place taller plantings further away from the house, with only a low planting at the corner.

Foundation plantings can also point out special architectural details, such as a bay window or stacked-stone wall. A small stone wall, for example, can be framed along its base and sides, but a large wall might better serve as an attractive, textural backdrop for a striking specimen plant. *Azara*, which has a charming arching habit, glossy green leaves, and scented flowers in late winter and early spring, would be a good choice. So would an espaliered firethorn (*Pyracantha* spp.) or fruit tree.

To accent a bay window, you might simply bring a low ground cover planting or paving material up to the foundation wall. Taller plants on either side of the window would make a nice accent. If you prefer something lush, plant a low hedge at the base of the window, and train a climbing rose or other flowering vine up one angle of the bay. Bay windows, because they are so open and inviting, are especially suited for nearby floral displays, shrubs with winter berries, or trees with interesting foliage. If some screening is desired from indoors, consider planting a small tree, such as a crape myrtle (*Lagerstroemia* spp.) or Japanese maple (*Acer palmatum*), outside your bay window.

Not all houses need plants skirting their entire foundation. If you have a handsome brick or stone foundation, you might want to show it off in sections. Or if your home is built on a slab foundation, you may find some breaks in the plantings refreshing. Clustering plantings near doorways, corners, and other architectural features may be enough. But most of us have less-than-attractive foundations, and planting low shrubs beneath windows is a good way to screen them.

▲ FRAGRANCE IS A BONUS in foundation plantings, especially near an entry. This evergreen planting includes the herbs lavender, rosemary, germander, and thyme.

▶ TURN FOUNDATIONS INTO mixed borders—especially beneath windows where you can enjoy them from inside as well as outside. Just be sure to pay as much attention to plant form and foliage as you do to the fleeting flowers when making your selections.

A Foundation Renovation

When Anne and Dave Hall moved into their two-story colonial five years ago, the ground floor of the house was obscured by what the neighbors called "the mounds"— huge junipers that had outgrown their allotted space. While many homeowners would simply let them be—after all, tackling giant, prickly junipers can be daunting—the Halls bit the bullet and ripped them out.

Since Anne was new to gardening, she recruited designer Lisa Ravenholt to help her select replacement plants. Together, they came up with a striking combination— upright junipers for accent, a line of dwarf boxwood edging the front of the beds for year-round form and color, and a mix of evergreen and deciduous shrubs and perennials to fill in the middle. Roses, hydrangeas, and perennials brighten the

▲ **NOT-SO-TRADITIONAL FOUNDATION PLANTINGS** surround this traditional home. Dwarf boxwoods contribute a sense of formality, while looser plantings soften the composition. Taller plants frame the doorway and anchor the corners.

beds in spring and summer, while the lustrous red berries of heavenly bamboo add a splash of color in fall and winter. A saucer magnolia anchors the corner; as it grows, it will offer its lovely blossoms each spring. The clipped evergreens surrounding the looser plantings give the foundation planting a sense of exuberant order.

To keep their budget realistic, the Halls started with very small plants. But as you can see, they've filled in nicely in just five years. Starting small also allows plants to become well adapted to their conditions. A few plantings remained on the property—like the 20-year-old espaliered pear next to the garage. Unlike the ridiculed old junipers, the espalier has inspired many neighbors to have a go at creating their own. And now, perhaps, the new foundation plantings will be inspiration as well.

▲ INSTEAD OF BEING PLACED against the house, evergreen shrubs are put at the front of the bed to give this planting a sense of order.

◄ THIS 20-YEAR-OLD espaliered pear is a focal point in the front yard, flanking the house side of the detached garage.

Bed Layout

Foundation beds need not be straight and narrow; give yourself more space in which to plant. The easiest way to do this is to simply make existing foundation beds deeper—bringing them farther out from the house. In most cases, you can easily increase the depth by half, and often you can double it. If your existing foundation plants are in good shape, you can use them as a backdrop for other plantings. For instance, if you have a row of evergreen shrubs beneath your windows, you can add clusters of ornamental grasses, long-flowering perennials, and evergreen ground covers, along with seasonal bulbs and annuals, in front of them.

Instead of a straight border, you might give yours generous curves. Allow it to cross over paths and move out into the lawn. Curving beds are more suitable for clusters of shrubs and perennials and masses of ground covers. A bed that curves outward as it moves toward the corners of the house offers another benefit—especially for homes built on a central axis. You can plant formal rows of shrubs near the front door and against the house, but loosen up the plantings as you move away from the door by planting clusters of smaller shrubs or perennials in front of them.

Extend the foundation plantings in peninsula-like fashion from the corners of the house—like arms reaching out, embracing the yard. Once again, curve the beds to make them look more natural, and then fill them with mixed plantings—such as a dogwood surrounded by a cluster of azaleas and edged with perennials, spring bulbs, and ferns. To complete the design, place a stepping-stone path through

▲ THIS FOUNDATION BED CURVES GENTLY, which suits the natural surroundings well. Beds are filled with rhododendrons, azaleas, and other evergreen shrubs, as well as a few Japanese maples for leaf contrast and seasonal interest.

Cultural Conditions Unique to Foundations

Chances are, the soil surrounding the foundation of your house is considerably different from the soil elsewhere in your yard. That's because this area is excavated during construction, often backfilled with poor-quality soil, and then compacted. This creates a problem for plants that need to send their roots deep into the soil for nourishment. There is also a good chance that the soil around the base of your house is more alkaline because of leaching that occurs from cement foundations. The bottom line is that the soil around a foundation almost always needs to be loosened and amended before planting. Whether it is predominantly sand, clay, or some other base, it will benefit from compost worked in as deeply as possible. A soil test will provide guidelines for adjusting the nutrient content and pH.

The other thing to keep in mind with foundation plants is that, if placed beneath a deep eave, they may not receive the same amount of rainfall as the other plants in your garden. Either plant beyond the eave or consider installing a simple irrigation system to ensure that they receive ample moisture.

▲ THIS FOUNDATION BED has been expanded to serve as a focal point in the landscape. Colorful flowers can be easily seen through the bay window.

◄ CONSIDER EXPANDING your planting area by broadening foundation beds as they move away from the front door. To keep beds and lawns from starting a turf battle, edge your beds with brick or stone.

the bed for easy access to the side yard or a neighbor's home. These extended, peninsula-like foundation beds are an excellent way to integrate a house with the surrounding landscape and create a greater sense of privacy in a front yard.

Be sure to leave a little space between your plantings and your house, as well as a path to access this space. It's not much fun brushing branches aside every time you need to turn on the water, prune your shrubs, or wash your windows. Both your family and the utility meter readers will appreciate the gesture.

Three-Dimensional Plantings

All plants exhibit form. Some reach up, tall and branching; others remain low and creeping; some can even be pruned into tight geometric forms. Your goal is to have an interesting mix of shapes without going overboard—three or four distinct forms are usually sufficient.

Before you go shopping at the nursery, try thinking about plants as three-dimensional objects—boxes, cones, balls, and other shapes. As an exercise, get a small box shaped roughly like your house, and try placing objects in front of it as if they were foundation plants. Common items from the kitchen make excellent doubles for plants and help you think about their shape. Turn a catsup bottle into a conifer, an orange into a round shrub, a spaghetti box into a low

▼ COMBINE DIFFERENT plant shapes for visual contrast. No shrubs are naturally square, but boxwoods are round. Upright clumps of variegated lilyturf have a fountainlike habit, while this Japanese maple displays a horizontal spreading form.

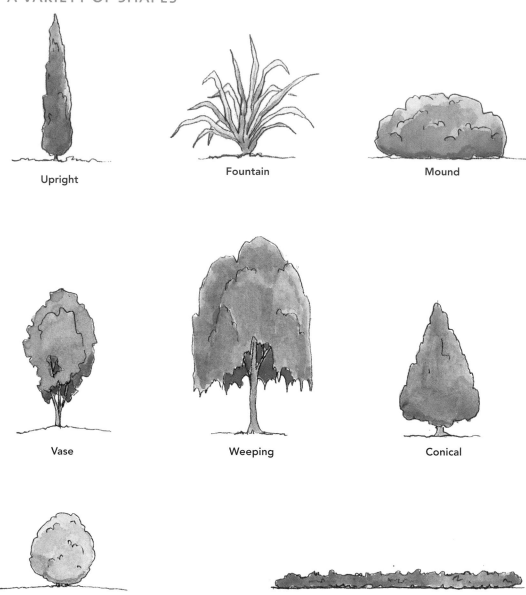

Upright

Fountain

Mound

Vase

Weeping

Conical

Round

Horizontal

hedge, and a wineglass into a tree. Move the objects around until you have a pleasing arrangement.

And finally, relate these shapes to plants. Some plants, such as hollies (*Ilex* spp.) and boxwood (*Buxus* spp.), look good pruned into spheres on either side of a stoop or sheared into rectangular hedges beneath a row of windows. Others, such as Italian cypress (*Cupressus sempervirens*) or 'Hicksii' yews (*Taxus* x *media* 'Hicksii'), have a naturally up-right, columnar form suited to house corners or framing doors. And still others have loose, informal forms that look

▲ DEEP BEDS OFFER PLENTY of planting opportunities. Grow taller trees or vines next to the house as a backdrop, and shorter plants toward the front edge next to the lawn. It's a good idea to include at least some evergreens for year-round structure.

▲ THIS FOUNDATION PLANTING includes two rows of evergreen shrubs. The rhododendrons at the back have a loose habit and large leaves, while the boxwoods in the front have small leaves and adapt easily to shaping or shearing.

good in clusters. Within each shape category there will always be many plants that offer a variety of texture, color, fragrance, and seasonal interest.

A key to creating interesting plantings is to plant dimensionally—that is, to consider the different layers available in the space. Applied to foundation plantings, you have the space against the house wall, the area on the ground, and that roughly triangular area between the two to work with.

It's this middle layer that we tend to think of as the shrub layer. This is the primary planting layer designed principally to complement the architecture of the house. Though evergreen shrubs will provide year-round color and structure, consider mixing in a few deciduous shrubs for their winter berries, spring flowers, or fall leaves.

Neat and Trim Traditional

If you walk through this quiet northern Georgia neighborhood in the evening, you're likely to see Marian or Gene Burch in their front yard. Because the yard is surrounded by mixed plantings with an assortment of trees and shrubs along the periphery, the front yard has a cozy, inviting feeling—though it's anything but small or secluded. They inherited most of the plantings from previous owners, but enjoy tucking in annuals for an extra splash of color and taking time to appreciate the landscape roses that bloom repeatedly throughout the summer along the driveway.

The house was built around five years ago, so the shrubs and trees in the foundation plantings haven't quite reached maturity. Even so, they have filled in nicely and do an admirable job connecting the house to the surrounding landscape. The designer used a mix of evergreen and deciduous trees—some with single trunks, and others

▲ FROM A DISTANCE, these foundation plantings look neat and trim—though they offer much more variety than a row of sheared evergreen shrubs.

THESE FOUNDATION plantings are layered, especially at the corners of the house—from trees and shrubs to low-growing perennials. Spirea adds a splash of color in summer.

that are multitrunked—to anchor the corners of the house and to provide shade near key windows. Shrubs, too, are a blend of deciduous and evergreen, and the spirea blooms for long periods in summer. There are other reasons the foundation plantings fit the house so well. First, though many different plants are used, most shrubs and perennials are planted in masses, and some of these masses are repeated in more than one location. And second, the layering from ornamental trees to shrubs, and then to perennials and the lawn, makes a smooth, natural transition.

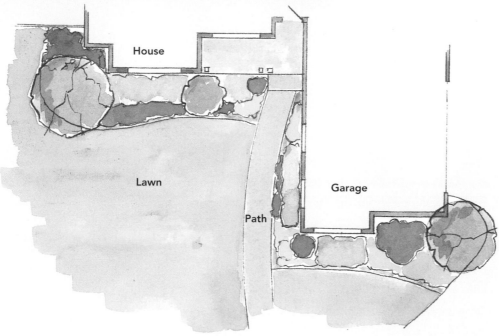

House

Lawn

Path

Garage

Deciduous Shrubs with Multiseason Interest

Azaleas	*Rhododendron* spp.	Meyer lilac	*Syringa meyeri*
Burning bush	*Euonymus alatus* 'Rudy Haag'	Purple beautyberry	*Callicarpa dichotoma*
Chinese snowball	*Viburnum macrocephalum*	Redtwig dogwood	*Cornus alba* 'Sibirica'
Dwarf forsythia	*Forsythia* 'Arnold Dwarf'	Rockspray cotoneaster	*Cotoneaster horizontalis*
Dwarf fothergilla	*Fothergilla major* 'Mount Airy'	Shrub roses	*Rosa* spp.
Hydrangeas	*Hydrangea* spp.	Snowmound spirea	*Spiraea nipponica* 'Snowmound'
Japanese barberry	*Berberis thunbergii*	Virginia sweetspire	*Itea virginica* 'Henry's Garnet'

The house façade offers an often-neglected planting opportunity. By planting something tall on or against a wall, you create a greater sense of depth in your foundation plantings and bring life to a space that is usually barren. A wall is the perfect backdrop for a tree with an interesting branching pattern, especially when you place low landscape lights in front of the tree to bathe it with light, casting interesting shadows on the wall behind. A wall is also an ideal surface for a climbing vine.

When it comes to foundation plantings, the ground plane is often overlooked as well. Bringing the bed out further, as previously mentioned, will give you more space to add an interesting ground-cover layer. To create strength in the bed line, edge it with flat stones or brick; this also makes it easier to mow the lawn. Evergreen ground covers, small ornamental grasses, geraniums (*Pelargonium* spp.), and all sorts of small, spreading, or clumping perennials can be planted in this area. Choose a bright-foliaged plant like Bowles' golden sedge (*Carex elata* 'Aurea') or Japanese rush (*Acorus gramineus* 'Ogon') to contrast with a darker evergreen backdrop. Select a bold-foliaged plant like *Hosta* or lambs' ears (*Stachys byzantina*) as a contrast to the lawn. Or add life to the plantings with clusters of feather reed grass (*Calamagrostis acutiflora*) that blow in even the gentlest of breezes.

▲ THE EASIEST WAY to improve a traditional foundation planting of a row of evergreen shrubs is to bring the bed out far enough to add a few perennials.

Plant Selection

Another key to creating an interesting planting bed is to include a variety of plant types—trees, shrubs, perennials, annuals, ground covers, and spring bulbs. When you vary the plant types, your foundation plantings will come to life and change with the seasons. Start with those that provide structure—a solid backdrop in any season, as well as defined shapes that relate to the lines and architectural features of the house. Evergreens are usually the best choices for these positions, but deciduous plants can also contribute structure, in winter as well as summer.

The easiest way to create visual interest is to add contrast in the garden, though too much contrast will just make your foundation plantings look busy. The secret to achieving the right balance is massing—grouping or clustering several of the same plants—and varying the size of those masses. Though single plants can be used, they are most often used for accent—perhaps at the doorway or house corner. Not every plant can be the star of the show; most will play supporting roles. Among the qualities to look for when selecting

▼ **DIFFERENT LEAF COLORS** provide visual interest—especially with the yellow-variegated hostas and burgundy-leaved coralbells. The lacy foliage of ferns also contrasts with the bold leaves of the hostas.

plants for a well-rounded foundation planting are contrasting

- **Leaf shapes and sizes**—from fine-needled to broad, ovate to palmate
- **Leaf textures**—from prickly to soft, coarse to smooth
- **Plant form**—from rounded or conical to sprawling or fountainlike
- **Height**—from ground-hugging to towering
- **Foliage color**—from dark, glossy green to pale green, and even variegated or colored leaves

Evergreens provide year-round structure, but deciduous plants help us celebrate seasonal changes. Both trees and shrubs may offer flowers, berries, and changing foliage through the seasons, and also good nesting sites for birds. Flowering bulbs, perennials, vines, and ground covers can offer almost continuous color and fragrance in the garden—even through winter if we select carefully.

Balance your plant choices so each season is represented. And give priority to plants that have multiseason interest, such as ornamental trees. In spring, they will display their lovely flowers; in summer, they provide shade from the hot sun. In fall, their changing leaves will brighten a nearby room with color. In winter, their bare branches allow sunshine to warm your house.

▲ SHOWCASE THE SEASONS. Fleabane and Jerusalem sage offer a profusion of flowers in summer; *Rosa glauca* showcases its pink flowers and burgundy foliage until replaced by orange-red hips in fall. Smokebush features both deeply colored leaves and smoky plumes. Dwarf evergreen boxwood gives this planting year-round structure.

Updating Existing Plantings

Whether you've inherited foundation plantings from a previous homeowner or just need to spruce up some mature plantings, it's a good idea to carry a checklist with you to the garden for evaluation. Here's what you'll need to look at:

- **Health**—Overall, how do the plants look? Are they full and vibrant, or do they look lean, as if struggling for sunlight? Does the foliage look healthy, or is it yellowing, diseased, or infested with pests? If the plantings look pretty healthy overall, are there individual plants that show less vigor?

- **Form**—Does the overall planting style suit the house? Do individual plants accent architectural features or serve some other role? Is there variety in form, or are all the plants the same shape and size?

- **Size**—Are the plants in scale with the house? Have some plants grown too large, perhaps covering up windows or blocking paths?

- **Texture and colors**—Do the plant colors harmonize with each other and with the house? Is there enough variety in foliage and flower color? Or perhaps too much variety?

Once you've completed your evaluation, you can begin to redesign your plantings and address the needs of individual plants. If, overall, your plantings are well designed but don't look very healthy, start with a soil test. You might discover that all you need is a good boost of chelated iron or some other nutrient. If it's not that, perhaps your plants are too sheltered and need more water, or maybe it's too shady, and you need to thin out the canopy of nearby trees. Seriously damaged or diseased plants should probably be removed, but

▲ VARIED FOLIAGE COLOR AND TEXTURE make all-evergreen plantings more interesting. Just be sure to select plants that mature at heights you consider acceptable in your foundation. Otherwise, you'll need to spend a lot of time with the pruning shears to keep them in shape.

whenever possible, try to salvage plants—either pruning them or moving them to a new location. Except with young plants, pruning is almost always easier than transplanting. In some cases, however, it's easier just to remove an existing plant and start fresh with another one that better suits the site.

If your problems are design-oriented, think about how you would create new plantings from scratch, and then see which existing plants might be adapted in some way to that plan. In many cases, you may just need to add plants for variety—working in a small tree or a few deciduous shrubs, extending the bedlines from the corner of the house, or making the beds deeper to add some clusters of smaller shrubs, perennials, and ground covers.

7

Ground Covers

▶ EDGING LAID A FOOT or more wide can double as a narrow garden path when the grass is wet.

When we think of ground covers for the residential landscape, we usually think of lawns. And for outdoor activities, lawns just might be the perfect surface. They're ideal for ball games, picnics, or a game of tag. They serve admirably as a spot for yard sales and garden parties. Babies take their first steps on cushioned lawns, and a few years later, can be seen sitting on those patches of grass blowing dandelions into the wind.

But lawns aren't, and shouldn't be, our only choice for ground covers. They are only suitable for sites that receive plenty of sunlight and climates with ample rainfall, and even there, they are quite demanding— just look at how much time and money we spend mowing, blowing, raking, weeding, aerating, dethatching, reseeding, patching, fertilizing, and treating lawns. A better model for front-yard landscaping is to use mown lawns where they can be enjoyed, admired, and easily maintained, and to cover other areas with lower-maintenance alternatives such as creeping evergreen perennials, masses of low-growing shrubs, mulches, and paved surfaces. In fact, these other ground covers can help set off a lawn, improving its overall looks and impact in the landscape.

Some of the most beautiful front yards are those with a combination of different ground covers. To decide which

◀ VARYING THE GROUND COVERS gives a yard a tapestry look that is very appealing. Here, a well-defined and edged lawn is surrounded by evergreen lilyturf, which both flowers and bears berries.

◀ CLEARLY DEFINING EDGES
makes lawns look much neater;
they're also easier to mow.

▶ PERIWINKLE GROWS EASILY
and spreads quickly to create a
solid mat beneath deciduous
trees. In spring, it is covered
with pale lavender flowers.

ground cover goes where, divide your yard into zones of
activity. For instance, you might have zones for high-impact
activities like touch football and playing with the family
dog, and zones for low-impact activities such as sitting on a
bench, playing quiet games, or dining with friends. You'll
have zones where you rarely, if ever, spend time, as well as
zones for circulation. Also, note areas with heavy shade or
full sun, or that are too steep to tend.

Lawns have the most uniform surface and can withstand
foot traffic. They're ideal for spaces devoted to high-impact
activities. Their fine texture and uniformity is also a nice
contrast to most other garden plants, so they are effective in
setting off a flower bed or border. Because most turf grasses
prefer full sun, lawns are not a good choice for shady areas,
such as beneath large trees or on the north side of a house.
While they require ample moisture, they don't like to have
their roots standing in water—so low-lying areas that tend
to puddle are best covered with something else. And finally,
because they have to be mowed regularly (weekly or more
often during their growing season), lawns are problematic
on steep slopes where mowing would be dangerous.

▲ PACHYSANDRA AND PERIWINKLE are both suited
to shade and can handle some sun. They are great
alternatives where lawn refuses to flourish, or
where the terrain makes it difficult to mow.

Other low-growing plants not only serve as alternatives to lawn in these trouble spots but can cover low-traffic areas—especially those along the periphery of your property. Small clumping plants and ornamental grasses are ideal for compact areas, while plants that spread quickly by long runners or stems are better for large areas. Shade-tolerant ground covers work well beneath trees or adjacent to a house. And mass plantings of low-growing shrubs can be striking in the landscape. Often, the best choice is a nonliving ground cover—mulch, chipped gravel, or other paving material. These are suited to high-traffic areas and spaces for dining and outdoor entertainment.

Before heading to the store for ground covers, think back to your site evaluation. What did you discover about your yard that will affect your ground cover selections? You'll also want to assess your maintenance and budget concerns. Here are some of the issues to think through:

• **Climate**—Most lawns and many plants need substantial water and are not good choices for drought-prone

GROUND-COVER ZONES

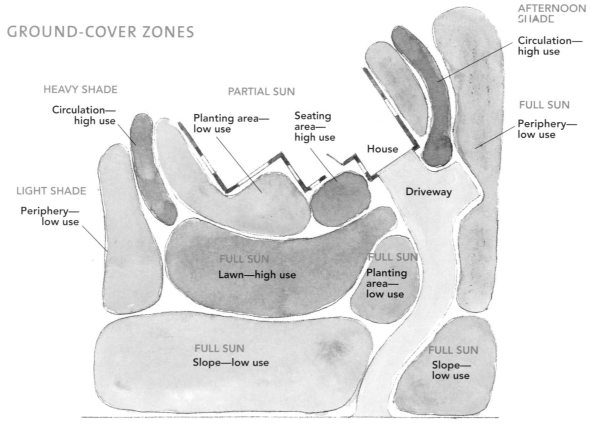

AFTERNOON SHADE
Circulation—high use

HEAVY SHADE
Circulation—high use

PARTIAL SUN
Planting area—low use

Seating area—high use

House

FULL SUN
Periphery—low use

LIGHT SHADE
Periphery—low use

Driveway

FULL SUN
Lawn—high use

FULL SUN
Planting area—low use

FULL SUN
Slope—low use

FULL SUN
Slope—low use

Simplicity in Design

Betty Ajay practices what she preaches. A landscape architect, she encourages the use of large masses of low-maintenance evergreen ground covers—especially in places where they can soften the heaviness of paving materials like stone and brick. It's an approach that results in clean, simple lines and reduced yard work. That's what you'll find at her Connecticut home as well as the homes of many of her clients.

For lots generous in size, lawn is the quickest and easiest way to cover ground where the natural vegetation has been removed. But Betty has significantly reduced the size of her lawn by planting large expanses of evergreen pachysandra and masses of low-growing hollies, and by creating large buffers of trees along the property's periphery. Although leaves must be raked out in the fall, the pachysandra requires little or no upkeep, and the shrubs only need occasional trimming.

The simplicity of Betty's approach to ground covers suits the clean lines of her house well. So does her front terrace, which spans the length of the main house. The gray flagstone blends naturally with the gray siding, and built-in planters filled with dwarf hollies offer an innovative alternative to railing—which would have significantly altered the look of the house. Wide, curving stone steps are edged in cobbles, also providing a comfortable approach to the house.

▲ **LAWN AND PACHYSANDRA** are the most prominent ground covers on this property. The curving edge of the pachysandra follows the gentle contours of the land.

▲ A WIDE TERRACE and broad steps balance the house shape and size. Planting beds were built into the terrace for shrubs, which (on low terraces only) eliminate the need for railings.

► LOW SHRUB MASSES are also used effectively as ground cover. These hollies have a naturally attractive horizontal habit that requires only occasional shaping.

climates. Consult your local nursery for the best plants for your climate, or choose from nonliving ground covers.

- **Sunlight**—Most lawns require full sun for healthy growth. Alternative ground covers are available for all kinds of light conditions.
- **Activities**—How you use a space, or even whether you use a space, has bearing on your choice of ground cover.
- **Soil conditions**—Before you make your selection, assess whether your soil is wet or dry, alkaline or acidic, and mostly clay, sand, or loam.
- **Maintenance**—Lawn is very high maintenance; most alternative ground covers require very little ongoing maintenance.
- **Budget**—Lawns are the least expensive ground cover to install but most expensive to maintain. Paved surfaces are just the opposite—expensive to install but with little or no ongoing maintenance costs. Mulches and evergreen ground covers fall somewhere in between.

▲ EDGING LAID FLUSH with the lawn plays three roles in the garden: It gives the lawn a clean, crisp edge; keeps grass out of the perennial borders; and makes mowing easier. In this garden, a second, upright edging adds an ornamental touch.

The sun-drenched view across an open lawn, especially in late spring and early summer, when lawns are at their best, is enchanting. Yet those that look best are not the endless lawns but those with definition: a broad, curving sweep of green set against a sunny border; a circle of lawn interrupted by the strong lines of a path or terrace; a rectangular patch surrounded by a picket fence; a wide, green path gently curving through a series of island beds. The secret to making a bigger impact with your lawn is making it smaller and more distinctive.

Especially nice are strong, voluptuous curves. Avoid making small, wiggly curves that are dwarfed by the immensity of the outdoors; what you want are deep dips and broad curves. Stretch out a sun-warmed garden hose to experiment with the lines. Run your lawn mower along those lines. If they are fun to follow, you've done a good job. If it's

Choosing the Right Grass

▲ THIS LAWN HAS A VERY DEFINITE curving shape complemented by gently rolling berms, or mounds. They give a front yard a sculpted feeling that is pleasing to the eye but may make it less suitable for games and activities.

When it comes to grasses, some like it hot, and others do not—so your first challenge is selecting a grass suitable to your climate. Cool-season grasses like bluegrasses (*Poa* spp.), perennial ryegrass (*Lolium perenne*), bents (*Agrostis* spp.), and fescues (*Festuca* spp.) grow throughout most of North America and are frequently sown as blends of several grass species for greater disease resistance. They thrive in moist, cool climates and will brown out during hot summer droughts if not watered. Fescues are the most cold tolerant, braving the cold winters of USDA Hardiness Zone 2.

Warm-season grasses like zoysia (*Zoysia* spp.), Bermuda (*Cynodon dactylon*), and St. Augustine (*Stenotaphrum secundatum*) are better suited to hot climates like Florida and southern California. St. Augustine grass is the most heat tolerant, growing happily even in Zone 10. Warm-season grasses grow in more moderate climates but will turn brown in cool weather. Because most warm-season grasses are creepers and do not mix well, they are typically sown as a single species.

Light conditions will also play a role in the grass you select. Most grasses prefer full sun, but some will tolerate moderate shade. Among cool-season grasses, look to the fescues. Chewings fescue (*Festuca rubra* var. *commutata*) and creeping red fescue (*Festuca rubra* var. *rubra*) are the most shade and drought tolerant. Some varieties of Kentucky bluegrass (*Poa pratensis*) are also shade tolerant. For warm-season grasses, St. Augustine grass is your best bet; it creates a dense turf in shaded landscapes. Bahia grass (*Paspalum notatum*) is also a good shade-tolerant choice for hot climates.

tough to cut, you've made the curves too tight. Geometric lawns work too, particularly in a formal landscape or a small, enclosed yard. If you've got a small patch of flat lawn, a square, rectangle, or other distinct shape might work best. If your lawn abuts a natural area, such as a meadow or woodland, a gentle curve is more appropriate for the border. Set the mower blade higher or mow this area less often to create a subtle transition.

To keep your lawn edges neat in refined areas, install a mowing strip. A border of brick, cobbles, or other material

Seed or Sod?

Lawn grasses are most often purchased as seed or sod—though not all grasses are sold in both forms. In fact, most mixed-species lawns are only available as seed. Which method you use for installation depends on availability, your needs, and your budget. Seeding is the least expensive method of installation and can be used to create a well-adapted, deep-rooted lawn. However, it may take up to a year for a seeded lawn to become firmly established, and you'll need to be diligent about weeding and watering during that year. Sod is considerably more expensive (costing up to 10 times more than seed) but can create a lush lawn the day it is installed and only needs a few weeks to establish roots. Sod is an excellent choice for small, formal patches of lawn in a front yard, while larger expanses are usually seeded.

will keep the grass in the lawn and any plantings in their place and, at the same time, simplify mowing. The mowing will go faster, and you'll rarely need to haul out the hand shears, weed trimmer, or edging tool. Though a 4-inch border will do, a more generous 10-inch border will allow lush perennials to spill out from the beds without getting nipped by a mower, and edging closer to 2 feet wide can double as a garden path. The key to installing edging is placing the material flush with the ground so the lawnmower wheel will run over it easily and cut all your grass at the same height.

There are many grasses to choose from, so don't just grab the first bag of seed you see at the nursery. Because grasses vary in durability and appearance, be sure to match the grass to your needs. For a small, formal lawn where appearance is important, you'll probably want to stick with a single species for its uniform appearance. Perennial ryegrass, red fescue, Kentucky bluegrass, Bermuda grass, and zoysia are all good choices. Though they look good, these grasses can't take heavy traffic and are more susceptible to disease. For high-impact areas where durability is more important than

▲ SMALL LAWNS can make a big impression. This lawn, just large enough for a game of croquet, sets off the perennial border beautifully.

good looks, choose among mixtures of perennial ryegrass and tall fescues for cool climates, and cultivars of St. Augustine grass for warm climates. These lawns won't look as uniform, but if you mix tough grasses, they should be able to stand much more wear and tear. An ecological option is to choose from seed mixes that include small herbaceous plants such as clover. Upon close inspection, they may look a little ragged, but they should adapt more readily to your conditions and provide a solid, sturdy ground cover.

When you're designing a lawn, it also pays to think about your watering needs and resources—especially if you live in a drought-prone area. Between erratic weather patterns and extensive development in so many cities, water rationing has become commonplace throughout much of the country—not just in the arid Southwest. For these reasons, it's a good idea to choose a drought-tolerant grass no matter where you live. Many of the fescues, in particular, have deep roots that seek out moisture in the soil and don't need to be watered as often.

▼ CURVED LAWNS look very natural. Go for deep dips and broad curves, not wiggly little lines. Flat lawns like this one are ideal for children's games.

Alternative Ground Covers

▲ THIS GARDENER HAS PLANTED a variety of ground covers in her yard. In addition to a central lawn and perennial beds, you'll find masses of ivy, mondo grass, blue-eyed grass, and pachysandra.

While lawns are the traditional ground cover favored throughout much of the country, more and more homeowners are discovering the benefits of alternative ground covers. Though they may cost more to install, they are much less expensive and considerably less time consuming to maintain. Planted in a mass, they create an evergreen canvas not all that different from grass when viewed from a distance. Because there are more varieties to choose from, they can be adapted to any site. And though most can't be walked on, you can create paths through them. Many have the added benefit of seasonal interest—with flowers, berries, or colorful foliage.

Many different types of plants are suitable to serve as ground covers. Depending on whether you want a uniform look or more of a tapestry, you may plant a single large mass of one ground cover, or smaller masses of several different ground covers. Your plantings can be a smooth, consistent texture, or a painterly composition of plants with different heights, colors, forms, and textures. Here are some of the different groups of plants to consider as massed ground covers:

- **Runners**—These plants spread by an extensive network of aboveground or underground runners. *Pachysandra terminalis,* which sends up new shoots and foliage from the root system, is a good example; many ferns also spread this way. Ivy (*Hedera* spp.) and periwinkle (*Vinca minor*) are both aboveground runners. If you brush the foliage aside, you will see the long stems and notice that they are sending out roots.

Evergreen Ground Covers

PROSTRATE

Cliff green	*Paxistima canbyi*
Creeping lilyturf	*Liriope spicata*
Japanese spurge	*Pachysandra terminalis*
Lesser periwinkle	*Vinca minor*
Mondo grass	*Ophiopogon japonicus*
Prostrate rosemary	*Rosmarinous officinalis* 'Irene'
Sargent juniper	*Juniperus sargentii* 'Glauca'
Snow in summer	*Cerastium tomentosum*
Sun rose	*Helianthemum nummularium*
Sweet violet	*Viola odorata*
Taiwan bramble	*Rubus pentalobus*
Wall germander	*Teucrium chamaedrys* 'Prostratum'

LOW GROWING (1 TO 2 FEET)

Blue Carpet juniper	*Juniperus squamata* 'Blue Carpet'
Creeping St. John's wort	*Hypericum calycinum*
Dwarf heavenly bamboo	*Nandina domestica* 'Harbor Dwarf'
Greater periwinkle	*Vinca major*
Heath	*Erica carnea*
Large blue fescue	*Festuca amethystina* 'Superba'
Point Reyes creeper	*Ceanothus gloriosus*
Sedges	*Carex* spp.
Sweet box	*Sarcococca hookeriana* var. *humilus*
Wintercreeper	*Euonymous fortunei*

MEDIUM HEIGHT (2 TO 3 FEET)

Australian Bluebell	*Sollya heterophylla*
Chinese juniper	*Juniperus chinensis* 'Saybrook Gold'
English lavender	*Lavandula angustifolia*
English yew	*Taxus baccata* 'Repandens'
French lavender	*Lavandula stoechas*
Leatherleaf sedge	*Carex buchananii*
Pheasant's tail grass	*Stipa arundinaceae*

◀ LILYTURF

- **Creepers**—These are slower-growing spreaders, such as thyme (*Thymus* spp.) and baby's tears (*Soleirolia soleirolii*), which create dense mats when they spread. They are good for smaller spaces and for filling in cracks between pavers.
- **Horizontal shrubs**—The best-known ground cover in this category is probably creeping juniper (*Juniperus horizontal-*

is), though creeping rosemary is also an excellent choice in moderate climates.

- **Clumping perennials**—Many low-growing perennials multiply rapidly and make a nice thick ground cover in just a few years. Daylilies (*Hemerocalis* spp.) are often used for this purpose.
- **Ornamental grasses and grass-like plants**—This is one of the broadest categories of ground covers. In addition to small grasses, there are sedges and grassy-looking plants like lilyturf (*Liriope* spp.) and pinks (*Dianthus* spp.).
- **Small, mounding shrubs**—Many shrubs make wonderful ground covers when planted in masses. Azaleas (*Rhododendron* spp.) are often planted this way in the South. Heaths (*Erica* spp.) and ground-cover roses (*Rosa* spp.) are good choices in other regions.

If your front yard is dominated by large hardwoods, it won't take long to discover that it's next to impossible to get grass to grow there and very difficult to plant anything large

▲ MOST DAYLILIES flower for only a few weeks in summer, but the strappy foliage makes an attractive ground cover for many months. Though not ever-green, daylilies do an admirable job of controlling erosion, even in winter.

▶ SEVERAL TYPES OF SHRUBS can be massed to create a tapestry-like ground cover. In most cases, you'll want to choose from shrubs that grow to 1 to 3 feet tall. Along the edges of your property, you may prefer something a little larger.

A Natural Collaboration

The lawn simply didn't work. According to landscape architect John Harper, the lawn in Dean Bates's and Shirl Handley's front yard "served no particular function, turned brown and patchy every summer, required frequent fertilization, and had to be reseeded each fall." Typical of those of many older Southern homes, this front lawn was competing with the substantial root system and shady canopy of a large old oak. And the oak was winning on all counts.

Though they presented a challenge to the lawn, the conditions created by the oak were ideal for the native wildflowers that bloom each spring throughout northern Georgia, and the ferns and shrubs that leaf out following the spring show. So rather than fight nature, John decided to work with it by planting native wildflowers and shrubs that change from season to season. And though it's the only lawnless front yard on the street, it looks perfectly natural because it blends in with the surrounding woodlands that fill many side yards and back yards.

In addition to filling the front yard with native plants, John also widened the

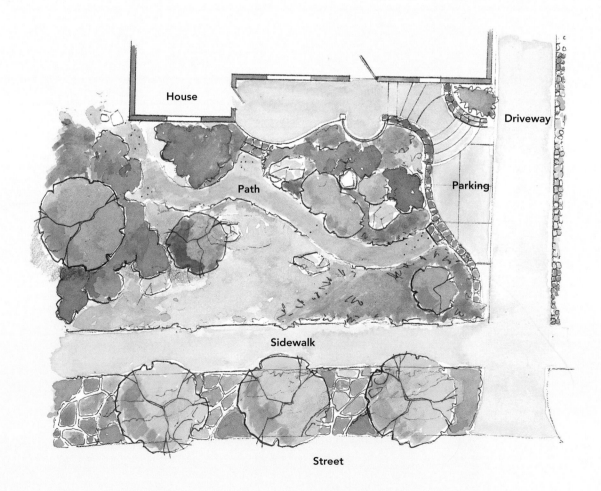

House

Driveway

Path

Parking

Sidewalk

Street

◀ THIS NO-LAWN LAND-
SCAPE draws its inspiration
from nature. In place of
evergreen masses, plantings
are diversified and include
mostly natives. It's an
approach that works exceed-
ingly well beneath huge old
shade trees.

▼ BEFORE THE LANDSCAPE
renovation, the entry was
much smaller; maintaining
a good-looking lawn was a
constant battle.

narrow driveway with stone cobbles and
redesigned the front entry (when they dis-
covered the front porch was dilapidated).
This new entry is much more inviting and

accessible than the old one. It features
curving stacked-stone walls, broad flagstone steps, custom wrought-iron railings,
and built-in path lighting.

▲ MANY PROSTRATE COTONEASTERS (foreground) make good ground covers for open hillsides; look for varieties that are evergreen and spreading. Given plenty of sun, most evergreen cotoneasters will produce a good crop of berries for the birds.

beneath many trees. Some homeowners choose to let nature provide its own ground cover and simply thin out plants that become too weedy. Another approach is to plant native species especially suited to these conditions and allow them to spread at their own pace. Though you might cover this area with a mass of plants, such as spreading ferns, it is often easier and more natural looking to plant a mix of under-story trees, shrubs, and perennial ground covers.Plantings here will be slower to take root and spread but can be surrounded with mulch, which will look nice and help keep the weeds down.

Nonliving
Ground Covers

Not all ground has to be covered with plants—whether lawns, evergreen ground covers, or garden plants. In fact, some of the most functional spaces in the front yard are paved—paths, driveways, parking, terraces, patios, and courtyards. These last three, in particular, are excellent ways to make use of your front yard and reduce the size of your lawn. But since both paving materials and seating areas have been covered extensively in other chapters, we'll focus here on two other commonly used nonliving ground covers: gravel and mulch.

In hot, arid regions of the country, where extensive use of lawns or evergreen ground covers is impractical, finely chipped gravel is often the ground cover of choice. It keeps the soil cooler and helps to retain the little moisture there even in the heat of summer. Many drought-tolerant plants like cacti, succulents, and desert wildflowers enjoy growing

▼ IN SPACES THAT are hard to mow or that could be used for activities, paving is an alternative ground cover. Though it is often an excellent choice, keep in mind that paving increases the flow of runoff into drainage systems while it reduces the amount of water absorbed by the soil for plants.

in ground covered in a light layer of chipped gravel. It does not break down, so except for the gravel that gets kicked up over the years, it shouldn't have to be replaced or replenished. It comes in a variety of hues, from brown and buff to gray and terra-cotta, so it can be coordinated with your home and surrounding landscape.

Another nonliving ground cover is mulch. Technically, most mulch was once living, but whether pine needles, ground bark, or cocoa hulls, it has reached a point of decay. And that's precisely why mulch makes a good ground cover. It is a natural material, so it blends into the landscape almost seamlessly. And as it slowly breaks down, it nourishes the soil beneath. The only drawback is that it has to be replaced periodically. Because pine straw breaks down easily, you may need to spread fresh bales each spring or fall. A thick layer of hardwood mulch or bark chips, however, may only need to be replenished every few years.

Mulches make good transitional ground covers. If you have an area you'd eventually like to plant, simply cover it with mulch until you have the time and money for the

▲PINE NEEDLES ARE ANOTHER good ground-cover mulch. They spread easily and mat down quickly for a clean, smooth surface. Here, they help control erosion on this bank while the ivy gets established.

Ground-Cover Mulches

Mulches vary from one part of the country to another based on what can be most easily and affordably attained. Of course, not all mulches used in the garden are suitable for use as front-yard ground covers. Wheat straw, for instance, is great for a vegetable garden but looks messy as a ground cover. The following mulches are commonly available and make excellent ground covers:

Cocoa bean hulls—A dark, attractive mulch that smells a bit like chocolate when stepped on.

Hardwood mulches—The bark and clippings of different kinds of hardwood trees are ground or shredded into easily spreadable mulch. They vary in color, fragrance, and consistency. Because hardwood mulch causes nitrogen to be tied up temporarily, you may need to add some nitrogen to the soil if you plant in this area.

Pine straw—Needles from pine trees, most readily available in the South, are raked and sold by the bale.

Pine bark—Sold as nuggets or mini-nuggets, depending on the size of the chips, and chosen based on their appearance. The nuggets are larger and coarser; the mini-nuggets, a bit more refined, break down faster.

▲ MULCHES CAN COVER patches of ground. They are especially useful in areas designated for mixed beds or other ground covers that won't be planted for a year or two. The ground bark in this landscape provides a low-cost, low-maintenance ground cover. As it breaks down, it will enrich the soil below.

project. By then, the soil will be enriched and easy to plant. (Conversely, if you had planted the area in grass, you'd have to remove the sod and amend the soil.) If your space is small, you can buy mulch by the bag or bale at any garden center, nursery, or home center. If you're planning to cover a larger area, consider buying it by the truckload. As long as you can back the truck up near the area to be mulched, it's quicker and easier to spread in bulk, it costs less, and you're not left with lots of plastic bags to place in the trash.

8

Plantings

▶ TRAILING ROSEMARY **cascades over a retaining wall beneath a steep slope.**

Front yards need not be limited to lawns, foundation beds, and hedges. They are also ideal places for beds, borders, and woodland groves. Such mixed plantings can be placed beside paths and driveways or along the periphery, or they may dominate your front yard. Plantings can be as simple as a few annuals planted beneath a lamppost, or as elaborate as a fenced cottage garden. Mixed plantings with evergreen trees and shrubs can be placed to screen views or buffer wind. A woodland grove is a wonderful low-maintenance way to reduce the size of your lawn and create a habitat for small wildlife. Perennial borders planted against a fence or evergreen hedge will add a splash of color throughout the growing season. And a series of gently curving island beds can transform your front yard into a strolling garden.

Front yards of all shapes and sizes are suitable for plantings. The types you choose will be determined by the style of your house, what is considered acceptable in your neighborhood, your native environment, and how much time you wish to spend tending the plantings. While some need very little care after planting, others require regular attention—especially during the growing season.

◀ ISLAND BEDS WITH GRACEFULLY **curving edges float in a sea of lawn. They can be filled with small trees, shrubs, perennials, annuals, and bulbs.**

In fact, ongoing care for plantings is much more important in a front yard than in a back yard. While we might "let things go" a little in the back yard when we travel or get busy with other activities, it's best to keep a front yard looking reasonably neat at all times. In winter, when you may not spend time in your back yard, you still come and go daily through your front yard, and it remains on view for your neighbors. So think carefully about the maintenance requirements of the plants you select, as well as their seasons of interest. Disease-resistant, repeat-blooming landscape roses that need little pruning, for instance, make much more sense than leggy, disease-prone Hybrid Tea roses that bloom for only a short period of time—no matter how beautiful their blossoms. And while fast-growing trees such as Bradford pear (*Pyrus calleryana* 'Bradford') and Leyland cypress (x *Cupressocyparis leylandii*) may make an impact in the landscape in only a few years, they tend to have weak wood that may snap under the weight of snow and ice or in high winds.

▲ THIS POCKET PLANTING OF FERNS, ivies, and geraniums has long-season good looks. Except for occasional watering and the removal of spent flowers, it requires little care.

◄ RETAINING WALLS MAKE excellent backdrops for borders and offer a creative solution for steep yards. This one includes several levels and puts plants at eye level.

► HERBS AND GRASSES are low-maintenance plantings; once established, they should need little supplemental water in most climates. Grasses should be cut back once a year—usually in early spring before they begin putting out new growth. Some herbs appreciate a little light pruning from time to time, which promotes bushy growth.

Drip for Dry Spells

Ideally, the plants we place in a garden should be able to survive on natural rainfall. But most new plantings need a full growing season to become established—especially if they are planted in spring or summer—and long periods of drought will stress even the toughest of plants. Drip irrigation systems are the most efficient way to meet a garden's supplementary watering needs. They should be designed and installed when you create your beds, before the plants go in.

Drip system technology has improved greatly over the past decade. Emitters last longer, hoses are more resistant to wear and tear, and sensors can now detect soil moisture levels so the systems turn on only when needed (which is important considering how taxed many municipal water systems are due to burgeoning growth). A simple drip system can be easily attached to a hose bib and installed in an afternoon. No glue is required—just screw, push, or snap the parts together like tinker toys. You can run feeder lines to individual plants, or use evenly spaced emitter lines to spread the water throughout a bed.

Clean Lines Complement a Craftsman Home

David Ketchum loves to garden but wanted some help redesigning the front yard to suit his recently renovated Craftsman home. Because the house had such strong lines, similarly strong lines were needed in the yard. We started by giving the lawn a distinct shape and well-defined edging—a bluestone mowing strip wide enough to double as a path in wet weather. The lawn is slightly domed in the middle for drainage and looks like an emerald cushion, begging to be sat or walked upon. The driveways and paths were edged with brick, which widened them, toned down the concrete, and added color to the hardscape.

▲ A SMALL BUT WELL-DEFINED and neatly manicured lawn sets off planting beds. Container plantings accent the entry.

◄ PLANTING BEDS WERE PLACED around the periphery and in the sidewalk strip. The plantings are fairly low, so neighbors get a sense of passing through a garden when they walk down the street.

◄RANDOM PIECES of blue-stone create a wide edging that doubles as a narrow garden path when the grass is wet.

We created a plant palette to complement the pale, moss-green stucco walls—including wine-foliaged barberries, a light-green 'Sango-kaku' Japanese maple, and the evergreen, orange-brown pheasant's tail grass as foundation plants. Chartreuse-foliaged hostas and creeping jenny add a bright note, and purple-flowered rhododendrons, bellflowers, 'Salome' daffodils, and asters offer varied color through the seasons. The beds surrounding the yard were planted in layers—from low-growing ground covers to small, ornamental trees—to take advantage of the limited space and to better tie the house to the land.

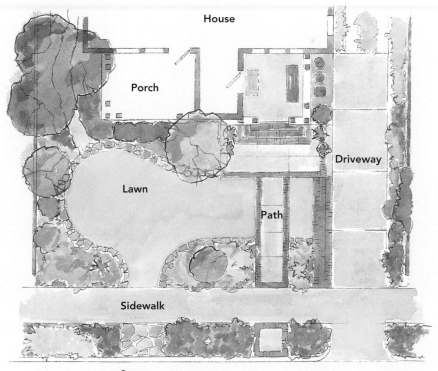

House

Porch

Lawn

Driveway

Path

Sidewalk

Street

Beds and Borders

Island beds and borders are the highlight of any garden. Though beds and borders may contain the same plants, the way they are viewed and therefore designed differs considerably. Borders are most often long and narrow, with a wall, fence, or hedge as a backdrop. Steep slopes, where retaining walls are used to create flat terraces, are also excellent places for borders. In contrast, island beds are freestanding—sometimes geometric in design, other times more naturalistic, with graceful curves. They can be placed just about anywhere in the yard—floating in the lawn, surrounding a mailbox or lamppost, along the periphery, or near a path, terrace, or driveway. Borders are viewed principally from the front, while island beds are visible from all sides. Even if a planting borders a driveway or path, it should be designed as an island bed since it doesn't have a solid backdrop.

▲ ISLAND BEDS, even if they border a driveway, should be designed for view from all sides. This one has an asymmetric arrangement anchored by a dwarf pine.

◄ A BORDER HAS A BACKDROP, and a fence serves admirably in that role. Make your beds 2 to 4 feet deep so you can include a variety of plants but can still reach to the back to deadhead spent flowers.

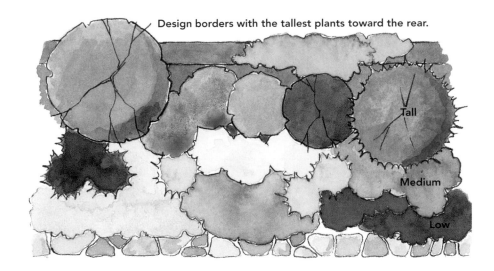

Design borders with the tallest plants toward the rear.

Tall

Medium

Low

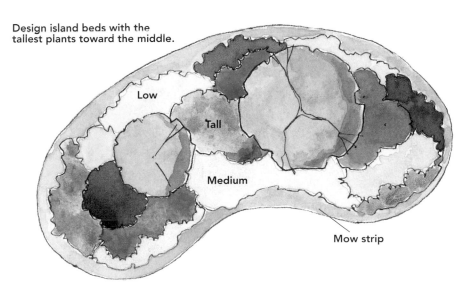

Design island beds with the tallest plants toward the middle.

Low

Tall

Medium

Mow strip

Borders are designed so the tallest plants are placed toward the back, the shortest are in the front along the edge (and along the sides, if they are exposed), and the mid-height plants fill in the middle. This allows you to see all the plants and ensures that they receive adequate sunlight. But follow this rule loosely, as you don't want your border to look as ordered as a school picture. One way to break the routine is to place tall "see-through" plants toward the front of your border to create a veil of foliage or flowers through which you can see the rest of the garden. The tall *Verbena bonariensis*, which holds small clusters of purple blossoms high on erect stems, is a good example. So are many ornamental grasses.

Island beds, because they are viewed differently and do not have a backdrop, are usually designed with the tallest

Long-blooming Perennials

Black-eyed Susans	*Rudbeckia fulgida*
Bloody cranesbill	*Geranium sanguineum*
Catmint	*Nepeta* x *faassenii*
Indigo spires salvia	*Salvia pratensis* 'Indigo Spires'
Joe Pye weed	*Eupatorium fistulosum* 'Gateway'
Lenten rose	*Helleborus orientalis*
Mexican tarragon	*Tagetes lucida*
Pineapple sage	*Salvia elegans* 'Scarlet Pineapple'
Purple coneflower	*Echinacea purpurea*
Rose vervain	*Verbena* 'Homestead Purple'
Russian sage	*Perovskia atriplicifolia*
Shrub verbena	*Lantana camara* cultivars
Speedwell	*Veronica* 'Sunny Border Blue'
Spurge	*Euphorbia characias* ssp. *wulfenii*
Stella de Oro daylilies	*Hemerocallis* 'Stella de Oro'
Stonecrop	*Sedum* 'Herbsfreude'
Tickseed	*Coreopsis* 'Moonbeam'

▲ RUSSIAN SAGE AND PURPLE CONEFLOWER

plants toward the middle, the smallest along the edge, and the medium-sized filler plants in between. In most cases, the tallest plants should not be placed dead center but slightly off-center or more toward one end of the border. If you have an irregularly shaped, curving border, place the tallest plant toward the wider end and work your design out from that starting point. To use an island bed as screening near the street or along a property boundary, you can create a berm—or mounded planting bed—in which to place the plants. This will raise the plantings an extra foot or two. Berms are also a good alternative if you have unusually difficult soil, as you don't have to dig as deep to amend the existing soil.

Beyond these basic design approaches, island beds and borders are otherwise very much alike. Both need to be narrow enough so you can reach into them to deadhead, prune, and tend plants (about 4 feet for a border and 8 feet for an island bed), or else they should include narrow stepping-

▲ BORDERS, WHETHER CURVING or straight, look nice around the periphery and edged with lawn. This one is layered in a naturalistic style—from canopy and understory trees to flowering shrubs and an assortment of perennials with contrasting foliage.

▲ THIS FRONT-YARD GARDEN Includes a mix of clumping evergreens, upright bulbs, bold-foliaged annuals, and long-flowering perennials for a scene that changes through the seasons.

▲ THE YELLOW FLOWERS of Jerusalem artichoke are echoed in the yellow-variegated foliage of nearby plants.

stone or mulch paths to keep you from stepping on plants or compacting the soil. If placed near the street, beds usually look best set back about 5 or 6 feet—both for better viewing and for safety when tending.

You can anchor beds and borders with shrubs or small, ornamental trees; add clusters of perennials; accent them with seasonal bulbs; and fill in any gaps with annuals (especially during the first few years, before the larger plants have reached full size). Keep in mind that flowers can be fleeting, so plants should be selected as much for their form and foliage as their blossoms (if not more so). And for those flowers, repeat bloomers or plants with a long season of bloom—six to eight weeks instead of just a few days—should play a leading role in the garden. For year-round interest, consider including some evergreens in your beds and borders. In regions with long winters, you may even want evergreens to dominate your plantings.

Seasonal changes make a garden more interesting and help you attune yourself to the cycles of life. Use a mix of plants to make a splash at different times of the year. Celebrate the arrival of spring with ferns that unfurl gracefully and bulbs that won't be deterred by a late-season cold snap. Usher in summer with a burst of flowers and bold, colorful foliage. Settle into fall with muted grasses, perennials with interesting seed heads, and shrubs with colorful stems or peeling bark. For the stillness of winter, select shrubs with bright berries or ornamental trees with graceful branching patterns.

Though entire books have been written about the art of planting design, the basics are really quite simple. All plants have shape, size, leaf form, texture, and color. Within any garden setting, you can make individual plants stand out by contrasting those elements. And you can make the individuals work together as a whole by repeating those elements. For instance, try placing smooth leaves next to coarse or

hairy ones; large-leaved plants next to those with delicate or finely-cut foliage; tall, upright plants next to low, mounding ones; purple flowers next to yellow ones; burgundy foliage next to chartreuse foliage. But in doing so, repeat the individual plants, shapes, sizes, colors, or combinations throughout your bed or border for continuity. Clustering plants in small masses—say three, five, or seven of the same plant—also works and is easier to maintain. You can repeat the masses throughout the bed for unity.

Color is the most complex of the design elements. In addition to creating contrast with colors, you can achieve color harmonies by combining flowers that are very similar in hue. For instance, flowers in different shades of purple and pink are lovely together and create a soothing atmosphere. When designing color harmonies, contrasting colors (used with restraint) can provide an occasional accent in the garden. To purple and pink you might add a splash of yellow. Color schemes can also be based on the degree of color saturation—selecting a base color that runs the gamut from pastel to electric. And finally, white, gray-green, and silver are considered blending colors—they go with almost any

Plants with Striking Foliage

Adam's needle	*Yucca filamentosa*
Bowles' golden sedge	*Carex elata 'Aurea'*
Bronze fennel	*Foeniculum vulgare*
Cardoon	*Cynara cardunculus*
Century plant	*Agave americana*
Coralbells	*Heuchera micrantha* var. *diversifolia* 'Palace Purple'
Ethiopian banana	*Ensete ventricosum*
Gunnera	*Gunnera manicata*
Indian shot	*Canna 'Tropicana'*
New Zealand flax	*Phormium tenax*
Purple sage	*Salvia officinalis* 'Purpurascens'
Rodgersia	*Rodgersia podophylla*
Sea holly	*Eryngium giganteum*
Smokebush	*Cotinus coggygria* 'Royal Purple'
Southern catalpa	*Catalpa bignonioides 'Aurea'*
Spurge	*Euphorbia characias* ssp. *wulfenii*

▲ HOSTA, ZONAL GERANIUM, AND FERN

colors and make nice transitions if you are shifting your color scheme slightly from one section of the border to another. That said, you should use white with restraint in a colored garden, as white draws the eye more readily than any color and will quickly dominate your planting.

When evaluating color schemes, start by taking a look at your house. If it has painted details such as shutters, doors, or trim, or even distinctively colored brick, stone, or stucco, make sure your planting scheme complements these colors. If that's not an issue, then simply start with your favorite flower color and add a contrasting color, one or two harmonious colors, or different shades of that favorite color to create a color scheme.

Container Gardens

Container plantings look great flanking a front door, marking a path, or clustered in a courtyard. And if you do have beds and borders, you can use containers as a focal point or to fill a temporary gap.

There are many types of containers—pots of all shapes and sizes, square and rectangular box planters, window boxes, hanging baskets, and even recycled objects like buckets or crates. Like other garden ornaments, containers exist to suit the style of any garden. No matter what kind you choose, keep in mind that bigger is usually better. That's because large pots hold more soil and moisture and therefore need to be watered and fertilized less often. Of course, you can almost always find a perfect place for a small pot filled with a few succulents, and small pots can be moved

▼ CREATE GARDEN vignettes with container plantings. This cluster of containers and ornaments highlights the side-yard entry.

around more easily if weight is a concern. Make sure your pots have holes in the bottom and are filled with loose potting soil so they will drain easily. Consider placing feet or trays beneath your pots so they won't rot the wood or stain the concrete beneath them when water seeps out of the bottom.

The nice thing about container plantings is how easily they can be changed from season to season. Simply pull out the old plants and put in something new. If they were annuals, throw them on the compost pile. Just about any plant will grow in a pot—though plants with long taproots can be troublesome. Give them the same kind of light you would if you were growing them in the garden. Beneath a porch, you'll need shade plants. On an open, south-facing stoop or terrace, select sun-loving plants.

Container plantings are very versatile. You can grow just one plant in a pot or combine several plants in a single large pot. You can cluster several pots together in an asymmetric arrangement, line the steps leading to your door, or place matching container plantings on either side of a door. Combine plants the same way you would in the garden—contrasting plant shapes, sizes, leaf forms, colors, and textures for visual punch. If placing more than one plant in a pot, planter or window box, try positioning a distinctive plant with an upright habit toward the middle, a few trailing plants along the edges, and perhaps some mounding plants in between.

▲ BIG POTS AND ARCHITECTURAL PLANTS make a strong impression. In this case, the bold and colorful foliage draws your eye to the front door. Also, big pots don't have to be watered as often as small pots.

▶ WINDOW BOXES are an excellent way to bring plantings closer to eye level. Choose the largest box your window can support and fill it with a mix of upright, mounding, and trailing plants for best effect.

Cottage Gardens

A passion for gardening and a cottage, bungalow, or beach house are the ingredients for a cottage garden. Cottage gardeners tend to throw convention to the wind—eliminating lawns and foundation plantings, and replacing them with a plethora of plants and lots of personality.

First and foremost, a cottage garden is small. In addition, a cottage garden is generally characterized by a low enclosure—no more than 3 or 4 feet high—within which you'll find an abundance of flowers. Intersecting paths run through most cottage gardens, as much for access to all sides of planting beds as for circulation. Plantings run the gamut from herbs, vegetables, and flowers to native plants or even something a

▼ COTTAGE GARDENS are often surrounded by low fences and almost always contain a profusion of flowers. This gardener has a passion for Old Garden roses.

▲ IN THIS COTTAGE GARDEN, the emphasis is more on foliage than flower, but it still overflows with abundance. The widely spaced pickets give the garden an open, inviting look, while evergreen shrubs provide a dark background for interior plantings. Vines scramble up and over everything—the fence, arbor, and front entry.

little more refined—such as sheared boxwood anchoring the corners of beds. Overall, however, the planting style is almost always loose and colorful, with lots of old-fashioned annuals and biennials like hollyhocks (*Alcea rosea*), foxgloves (*Digitalis purpurea*), and cosmos (*Cosmos bipinnatus*).

Beyond the prolific plantings, it's personalization that most characterizes cottage gardens. Though hardscaping is usually minimal, ornamentation is not. Chairs and benches, birdhouses and birdbaths, window boxes and colorful containers—even sculpture, found art, and folk art—are common elements. These ornamental elements reflect the architectural style of the house, regional aesthetics, and the personality of the homeowners. They are fun, eclectic, and often fanciful.

Most of the plants in cottage gardens are herbaceous, so they die back to the ground in winter. That's one of the reasons a low enclosure is important; it keeps the front yard looking good even in winter. A few evergreens, such as the boxwoods previously mentioned, along with evergreen herbs like rosemary (*Rosmarinus officinalis*), germander (*Teucrium chamaedrys*), and lavender (*Lavandula* spp.), can also add winter interest. And cool-weather annuals like pansies (*Viola* x *wittrockiana*) or vegetables such as kale, cabbage, or chard can be tucked in for a splash of color.

A Plantsman's Showcase

When Thomas Vetter bought his home, there was no garden, a concrete path stopped short of the street, and the house had little personality. What a difference a porch, some paint, and a gardener can make!

Over the years, Thomas has transformed an ordinary lot into a gardener's showcase—beautifully designed and with a stunning collection of plants. His design philosophy is

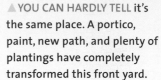 YOU CAN HARDLY TELL it's the same place. A portico, paint, new path, and plenty of plantings have completely transformed this front yard.

◄ A MASTER PLANTSMAN is at work in this garden, combining plants for their year-round good looks. Yellow is the predominant color; burgundy and lavender are used for accent.

◀ DECORATIVE ITEMS are common in cottage gardens. This one serves as a focal point in a planting bed.

straightforward: "Pick plants that have good structure and then include a mix of them throughout the garden." He also places more emphasis on a plant's foliage than its flowers. And because he wants the garden to look good year-round, he often tests plants in pots for a year to see how they perform before placing them in the ground. From bare branches that catch the lightest snow of winter to upright corymbs of flower heads to flushes of golden foliage, this garden is eye-catching in every season.

He started by designing wide berms that surround the yard and are filled with excellent soil for his plants. Only a small patch of lawn remains, but it sets off his planting beds nicely. He also removed the concrete path and, instead, ran a path of bricks and pavers from the driveway to the front door. The concrete was recycled to create an artful path leading from the front yard, through an arbor, to a side-yard garden.

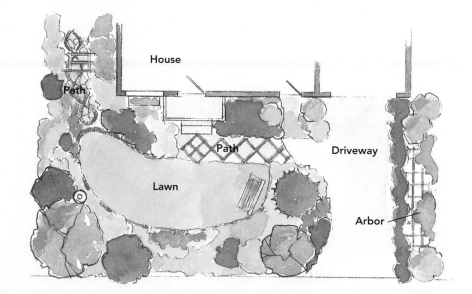

House

Path

Path

Driveway

Lawn

Arbor

Woodland Groves

Trees are valued in the landscape for many reasons. Originally, they were planted in front yards to provide nuts and fruits. But as front yards have evolved from working areas to more ornamental spaces, their role has changed. Today, trees are more often planted for their sheer beauty, screening, and shade. Near windows, deciduous trees can offer shade in summer and allow sunlight in winter. Along your periphery, a cluster of evergreen trees can screen unwanted views, buffer wind or noise, and increase your sense of privacy. In mixed borders, they can enhance your garden in every season. And planted as a small grove or

▼ A GROVE OF CANOPY TREES underplanted with azaleas and shade-tolerant perennials creates a nice woodland setting in this front yard. An alluring main path winds between the grove and house.

▲ TALL EVERGREENS PROVIDE dense screening between neighbors, while a redbud offers an inviting overhead canopy for this bench. Redbuds flower in spring and display their flattened pods in summer.

woodland, they can create a natural, low-maintenance setting that attracts birds and other small wildlife.

Groves of trees are especially nice along the side and front periphery. A grouping of evergreens will form a dense screen, while deciduous trees create a loose, more open buffer. For a natural-looking stand, consider planting one or two species in a random manner—perhaps with trees of different sizes and ages. Slender, multitrunked trees such as birches (*Betula* spp.) are especially suited to small groves, and they are lovely surrounded by lawn or underplanted with an evergreen ground cover and spring bulbs. If you're planting along a property line, keep the ultimate spread of your trees in mind. In most places, your neighbors can cut any limbs that encroach their property—whether near the ground or hanging above. Road and utility crews also have the right to trim any trees within their right of way, so be

Trees for Shade and Beauty

Crape myrtle	*Lagerstroemia* spp.
Eastern redbud	*Cercis canadensis*
Fringe tree	*Chionanthus virginicus*
Honeylocust	*Gleditsia triacanthus* 'Sunburst'
Japanese snowbell	*Styrax japonicus*
Kousa dogwood	*Cornus kousa*
Olive	*Olea europaea*
Maidenhair tree	*Ginko biloba* 'Autumn Gold'
Palo verde	*Parkinsonia florida*
Paper-bark maple	*Acer griseum*
Queen palm	*Syagrus romazoffiana*
River birch	*Betula nigra* 'Heritage'
Saucer magnolia	*Magnolia* x *soulangeana*
Sourwood	*Oxydendrum arboreum*
Yoshino cherry	*Prunus* x *yedoensis*

▲ JAPANESE SNOWBELL

sure your trees won't hang out into the street or grow up into power, cable, or telephone lines.

Similarly, if planting shade trees close to your house—whether as a specimen planting in a bed or border or as a cluster of trees—think about the trees' mature size before digging your holes. You don't want outstretched limbs to brush against the siding or hang over the roof. In most cases, it's best for only the very edge of the tree canopy to reach the roof. Though it may not shade your roof, it will still shade your windows. Select trees with deep roots rather than shallow, spreading roots, and plant them a generous distance from your house foundation, driveway, and paths. And if you have a sewage drain field in your front yard, avoid planting any trees in this area—as the roots will penetrate and damage the drain pipes.

▲ THIS ALLÉE OF TREES was recently planted along a path leading from the front to side yards. It will grow to form a lovely canopy overhead and provide subtle screening between these two areas of the yard.

If you live in a region noted for its woodlands and have a moderate-sized to large front yard, consider leaving or establishing a natural woodland area. Unlike a grove, which has a slightly manicured look, woodlands are much more natural, with a mix of canopy trees, understory trees and shrubs, and small shrubs, perennials, and ground covers. If planted with mostly native species, this area will blend in with the surrounding natural landscape and more or less take care of itself over the years.

9

Lighting

▶ LIGHTING CAN CREATE drama in the garden. Here, the shadows are as eye-catching as the subject.

M ost homes have porch lights and perhaps a lamppost along a path or floodlight near the garage. But landscape lighting can be so much more. It not only makes finding and approaching your house easier and safer after dark but can extend the hours you spend outdoors and create a warm, inviting environment.

Effective outdoor lighting is subtle, not bold. In most cases, less (or at least less intensive) is more. You need just enough light to move around safely—not enough to read a book or work at a computer. Unlike indoors, where you have walls to reflect and even out the light, bright lights can be harsh set against the night sky. When you light an area, you draw attention to it and away from other areas. For this reason, it's best not to light your entire yard.

The light intensity of individual fixtures will vary throughout the landscape depending on the distance between the light and the subject, the surface the light falls upon (dark surfaces absorb light, while light surfaces reflect light), the ambience you wish to create, and the relationship between the various lights in the landscape. The brightest lights should draw your eyes to

◀ LIGHTING SERVES MULTIPLE ROLES in the landscape. Recessed lights over the front entry are functional; spotlights on the water feature create a dramatic focal point; subtle tea lights hung on the overhead canopy help create atmosphere.

▲ THOUGH THE LIGHTS on these gateposts are principally functional, they are also artistic— echoing the grid used on the iron fence.

focal points in the landscape, while lower lights will create mood or meet basic safety needs.

There are two basic forms of landscape lighting: functional and accent. Functional lighting is just that—lighting that allows you to function safely in an area after dark. It includes lighting for paths and steps so you can traverse them safely, as well as for more general needs, such as illuminating entries, courtyards, parking courts, or terraces. The second type of lighting highlights architectural features of your home, garden ornaments, trees, and other special plantings. In other words, it is used to create mood rather than to help you do anything or go anywhere.

Turn the Lights Out

Studies have shown that plants, like people, perform their best if they get a good night's rest in complete darkness. So turn out the lights when you don't need them. It will save on your power bill, too.

The Scoop on DIY Kits

In recent years, many do-it-yourself outdoor lighting kits have been introduced. Most are reasonably easy to install and provide an affordable option for basic safety lighting needs, such as lighting a path or steps. However, the types and styles of fixtures are limited, their range (the distance they can be run from a house) is short, and their capacity is limited. Outdoor fixtures take a lot of abuse, and because of the way they are installed (both wires and fixtures are above ground), do-it-yourself fixtures and wiring are especially subject to wear and tear. And finally, even though these are low-voltage fixtures, they must still be handled with care. Bulbs can get hot enough to burn. If your needs are limited and you feel comfortable handling electrical projects, a lighting kit from a home center may be exactly what you need. For more durable or extensive lighting customized to your landscaping needs, consider contacting a lighting designer.

◄ THIS WOOD-AND-COPPER LANTERN marks THE driveway entrance and lights a sitting wall that is a favorite gathering place for neighbors in the evening.

Rather than delving into watts, spots, and electrical engineering, we're going to look at landscape lighting from a general design viewpoint: what you can light, why you should light it, and, in general, what form of lighting best suits each situation. This way, you can better evaluate your needs and communicate them to a lighting professional.

Though landscape lighting can be installed in mature landscapes, the ideal time to tackle electrical jobs is when you're building your home, installing a new landscape, or renovating an existing one. That's because it often requires digging holes and trenches, and some of the most attractive and durable lighting fixtures are actually built into steps, paths, and walls (though there are alternatives as well). Even if it requires a little groundwork, lighting can dramatically change the look of your home after dark and is well worth the effort.

▶ WALL-MOUNTED downlights showcase a collection of neatly trimmed dwarf boxwoods in containers as well as shed light on this staircase. Because it is a whole flight of steps rather than just a few, multiple lights were required for adequate coverage.

Lighting Maintenance

Maintaining outdoor lights is a little more involved than maintaining most indoor lights. To begin with, the fixtures are exposed to the elements. Dirt and leaves get lodged in ground fixtures, and high winds (as well as arborists) can knock tree lights out of position. Many fixtures—like those hung in trees or hidden behind shrubs—are hard to reach when it's time to change them, which is recom-

mended at least every two years. And replacement parts, including the lamps or bulbs, are not always easy to find. For this reason, you might wish to discuss an ongoing maintenance plan with your lighting designer. Consider having someone familiar with your landscape lighting inspect it at least annually to replace bulbs, adjust fixtures, and repair any damaged parts.

Lighting Paths, Steps, and Driveways

The most important role of lighting is that of safety, and your top priority should be lighting paths and steps. This includes the steps leading down from your porch or stoop; the path and steps leading to the street, driveway, or parking court; and any other paths or steps used at night. Often we assume that porch lights or lampposts provide sufficient light on nearby steps, and sometimes they do. But remember that when you walk out your front door, you are most often going from a brightly lit area into darkness, and eyes need time to adjust. Extra lights on steps and along the path will help.

When lighting paths and steps, you want relatively even-spaced lights that shed their light down and out, not up. Because beams lose intensity the farther away they are from their source, it is important to overlap the beams of lights placed alongside a path to create an evenly lit surface. For a narrow path, lights along one side are usually sufficient. For paths wider than 4 feet, lights on both side will do a better job.

For steps, the best approach is to place lights at both the top and bottom of the flight, and on both sides—regardless of width. If the steps are long, you may need interim lights along the way as well. If there are only two or three steps, a single light with good beam spread placed next to the middle step may do, though two or more lights on steps are almost always preferable.

Though path lights—fixtures raised anywhere from a few inches to a foot or more on posts and designed to cast light down and out on a path—are the most common means of lighting paths and steps, they aren't the only option. Downlights placed high in trees are often used, especially if there is a broader area to be lit—such as a courtyard or surrounding plantings—though these should never be the sole lights for steps. And many fixtures can be built into retaining walls and steps—such as tread lights and sidelights—making

▼ ON SMALL LOTS, a lamppost is often all that is needed to light the way. This one doubles as a support for a climbing rose.

▲ DOWNLIGHTS HUNG IN THE ARBOR and in trees illuminate steps and the courtyard. Lighting is also used to highlight garden sculpture.

▲ THOUGH DRIVEWAY LIGHTS are rarely needed, this one helps highlight where to turn into the drive from the street. It also helps those pulling in to avoid driving over plantings.

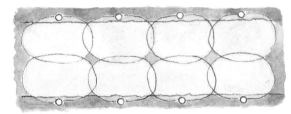

Beams should overlap slightly for even lighting on paths.

them much less obtrusive in the landscape, and somewhat less subject to wear and tear. You can even set filtered-glass blocks in a sidewalk and light them from below to gently illuminate the way.

Most driveway lights are more annoying than useful. Placing path lights along a driveway tends to make it look like an airstrip and will call attention to it, rather than to your house. Besides, you should be able to see just fine with the headlights on your car. There are times, however, when driveway lights make sense. If a driveway is unusually difficult to maneuver, perhaps because it is very narrow or has tight curves or because there is a steep drop-off along the shoulder, lighting can improve safety. And supplemental lighting helps in turnarounds, where you would be relying only on your car's backup lights, which are considerably dimmer than headlights. And finally, if your driveway doubles as the path to your front door for guests, some path lights will be appreciated.

Lighting Entries and Activity Areas

When you look at your front yard at night, the brightest area should be your front door. However, that doesn't mean it should be the harshest light. In fact, soft lights are the most pleasing—frosted bulbs and milky glass in fixtures are much easier on the eyes and create a warmer, more inviting mood. You can choose from overhead, recessed lights built into the porch ceiling or portico, hanging lanterns, or coach lamps placed on one or both sides of a door. Though spotlights placed in the yard to shine on an entry will certainly illuminate it, they tend to create glare, making it difficult for people to see, and so are best used to highlight other architectural features.

Activity zones like parking bays, courtyards, and terraces also need to be lit. In parking areas, soft lighting makes it easier to get in and out of a car, gather your belongings, and manage things like gifts or groceries. Traditional hardware-store floodlights are functional but offer little ambience. Instead, consider placing softer downlights in trees, on the garage, or against the house to illuminate a parking area. They can even be placed on automatic switches that sense the approach of a vehicle or person. Path lights, a lamppost, or lantern can mark the point where the path leads from the parking area to the door.

▲ SCONCES OR COACH LAMPS can be placed on either side of a door or on the outside of a portico. This one is as attractive as it is useful and coordinates with the color of the shutters.

Enchanting after Dark

◄▲THIS FOUNTAIN IS LIT principally from an overhead angle for drama. It casts a deep shadow on the ground. Accent lighting draws attention to the fountain and vine-covered trellis, while downlights hung in trees provide even lighting on the terrace floor.

Mavin and Pete Howley live on a beautiful wooded lot beneath the graceful canopy of several large native California oaks. Without supplemental lighting, the entry to their home would indeed be very dark.

The entry garden, designed by Suzman Design Associates, includes a flagstone path that widens into a terrace, a shade garden, and a lovely tiered fountain that serves as the focal point of the entry. Lighting designer Anna Kondolf was called in to highlight these features so the garden could be enjoyed after dark.

Because it was a fairly complex project, she used a variety of lighting techniques. Downlights are hung in the trees for general illumination—to light the way from the parking area to the front door and in the terraced area. Some were placed to provide even illumination; others were installed above limbs to cast interesting shadows on the ground. Uplights were buried in the ground to highlight the dramatic branches of the oaks; spotlights were used to accent smaller ornamental trees and the fountain. And finally, path lights were used on side paths that run to the kitchen door and a side-yard garden. Together, these lights offer a whole new way of viewing the garden.

▲UPLIGHTING HIGHLIGHTS tree branches, while downlighting through tree branches casts interesting shadows on the ground.

▲ BOTH GENERAL AND ACCENT lighting illuminate this deck, courtyard, and garden. Downlights hung from trees shed light on broad areas, while uplights call attention to the sculptural qualities of trees.

Courtyards and terraces may require more than one type of lighting. Most important is the general lighting, which again, can best be provided by downlights. However, you may also need some task lighting for a dining table, seating area, or barbecue grill. This too is most often supplied by downlights, but may be brighter or more directional. For a table, you might consider candles or perhaps an interesting lantern hanging from a tree limb or arbor. Accent lighting is also frequently used in courtyards or terraces.

Accent
Lighting

ccent lighting is the creative element of landscape lighting. It can be used to suggest mood or high-light focal points in the landscape. Focal points are often garden ornamentation such as sculpture, statuary, or water features, but they can be architectural features, such as stacked-stone walls or special plantings—perhaps a box-wood parterre or trees with interesting branching patterns. Though you want to emphasize these elements in the land-scape, they should not be illuminated more brightly than your front door. In fact, accent lighting is often most effec-tive when it is very subtle.

It is within this category of lighting that you will find the greatest variety of fixtures and lighting techniques. Floodlights can be used to "wash" a wall or object with light, often casting interesting shadows behind it. One effective technique is to "graze" a wall with light from an angle to emphasize its texture.

To highlight sculpture, statuary, fountains, or other ornamental objects, consider using several spotlights (which are more direction-al than floodlights). The number of lights you use and where you place them will vary the effect dramatically. A single light on a sculpture could create dramatic shadows; adding more lights would soften and reduce the shadows. If the sculpture is lit from behind, a silhouette would be created; if lit from the front, interesting shadows could be cast on a background wall; if lit from above, the shadows are cast on the ground; and if lit from all sides, shadows could be greatly reduced or eliminated.

▼ ACCENT LIGHTING CALLS
attention to key plantings, a water feature, a nicely detailed gate, a large sculptural pot, and metal sculptures of birds ready to take flight.

Uplight a tree by shining one or two spotlights into the branches.

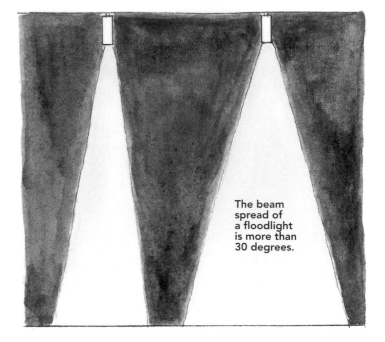

The beam spread of a floodlight is more than 30 degrees.

Uplights can be placed on or in the ground and directed up into trees to highlight their branches, which is especially effective with deciduous trees in winter. Downlights can be placed in trees to cast shadows of the branches on the ground. Installed near large, ornamental grasses, lights can emphasize subtle movements in the night garden.

Most water features look spectacular illuminated at night. Soft, general lighting will allow them to be seen while also blending them into the surrounding landscape. Spot lighting will call attention to water features and make them stand out. Waterproof lights inside a water feature are the most dramatic of all; they highlight the water itself.

In most cases, you want to see the object you are lighting and not the lights themselves. The exception would be specialty lights such candles, torches, and tea lights. Tea lights—tiny white lights on strings that can be hung along arbors, arches, eaves, and canopies, or wrapped around trees and shrubs—have become especially popular. They are similar to the lights we string up during the holidays but are made specifically for long-term outdoor use and can brighten a landscape any time of year.

Keep the Holidays Bright

Holiday lights are a booming business in America, and most of it falls into the do-it-yourself category with strings and swags of lights that can be hung from your house or wrapped around trees. As wonderful as these holiday lights are, most of the lights you buy at a drug or discount store can pose a fire hazard when left outdoors permanently. The wires and connections are not made to withstand the weather, and parts will rust from one holiday season to the next. Enjoy the season and then bring your lights in after the celebration is over. For a more permanent display, consider professional-grade tea lights designed for long-term outdoor wear and tear.

WATER CAN BE ILLUMINATED in many ways—from inside a water feature, for example, or by casting light upon the water feature. A spotlight shines toward the waterspout on this one, pulling out the rich color of the painted wall, highlighting the water as it splashes into the pool and calling attention to the sculptural figure overlooking the pool.

THIS COURTYARD can be viewed from the living room window. Cross-lighting on the dolphin water feature casts interesting shadows on the masonry wall behind.

SOME FORMS OF LIGHTING are solely for drama, like this torch that highlights a recessed entry.

10

The Inviting Backyard

Backyards are no longer just large expanses of lawn. They increasingly encompass a wide range of inviting spaces designed for recreation and relaxation.

At the heart of this transition is our desire to spend more time at home with family and friends and to make the most of the space we have—both indoors and out. While fresh air compels us to head outside, technology also plays a key role in our ability to spend more time outdoors. Advances in outdoor lighting make backyards more accessible and inviting after dark. New types of patio heaters and fireplaces comfortably extend the outdoor season. Designs for outdoor kitchens transform backyard barbecues into gourmet feasts. Construction innovations make pools and spas more affordable. And the development of durable, weather-resistant materials for furniture and fabrics continues to enhance the style and comfort of outdoor furnishings.

Successful backyard design, however, involves much more than adding appliances or accessories. It's best approached as part of the overall home-design process—one that addresses the relationship between indoor and outdoor spaces.

◀ START PLANNING A BACKYARD with simple, affordable, and creative ideas. This setting has all the ingredients of an inviting outdoor room: shade, a sense of enclosure, style, easy access to the kitchen, a view from the living room, and a place to eat, work, or converse.

EXPAND YOUR LIVING SPACE

A home's living space can be doubled by making the most of a backyard. After all, many backyards have a greater footprint than the house itself. And you can creatively transform even the tiniest of spaces into inviting outdoor rooms that beckon use in all but the coolest of seasons.

Inside our homes, there are rooms we gather in and rooms we escape to for relaxation. Outdoors, we need those same kinds of spaces. Porches, decks, patios, and pools make excellent gathering places. In fact, we can design multiple spaces for various types of get-togethers—perhaps a cozy patio for a romantic dinner, a comfortable deck for family meals, and a generous-sized terrace for hosting a crowd. When families entertain outdoors, it's ideal to have separate spaces for the parents to visit while the kids play with friends. Escapes can be as simple

▲ TERRACING INCREASES THE USABLE AREA in a sloped yard by creating two or more level surfaces for gathering spaces, play spaces, or gardens. The terracing in this backyard formed two gathering places, as well as opportunities for built-in seating and raised garden beds.

OUTDOOR LIVING AND RECREATIONAL SPACES

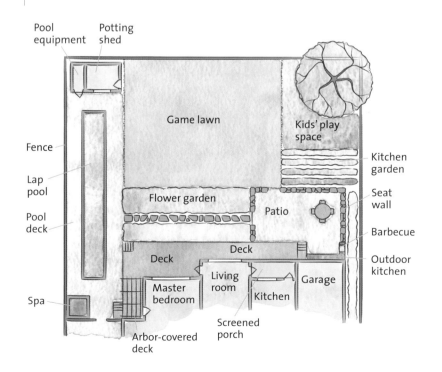

Pool equipment
Potting shed
Game lawn
Kids' play space
Fence
Kitchen garden
Lap pool
Flower garden
Patio
Seat wall
Pool deck
Barbecue
Deck
Deck
Outdoor kitchen
Master bedroom
Living room
Garage
Kitchen
Spa
Screened porch
Arbor-covered deck

as a hammock strung between two trees and a fort for young children or as elaborate as a freestanding studio for an artist and potting shed for an avid gardener.

The Indoor-Outdoor Connection

The most frequently used spaces are those that visually and physically bridge the gap between indoors and out. These spaces are seen through interior windows and doors. From outdoors, they connect to the house in the form of porches, decks, and patios. These intermediate—or transitional—spaces are among the most inviting because the house provides a sense of security and amenities are always nearby.

When porches, decks, and patios are planned as integral elements of a new or renovated home, they can be designed to

▶ RICH WOOD SURFACES, wool blankets, and a blazing fire lend a sense of warmth to this porch. Compared with the open deck at the end of the house, which offers enticing views of the lake, the covered and furnished porch provides an intimate gathering space.

◀ THIS OUTDOOR ROOM was created by an interior decorator who treated the patio as she would have a living room. Decorative accents adorn the wall and tables, chairs are arranged in conversational groupings, and brick warms the floor as a rug might indoors.

create indoor-outdoor transitions that are so subtle they blur the line where the house ends and the landscape begins. For continuity between spaces, construction materials should echo those of the house; decorating themes and colors can easily carry over outside from interior rooms.

These intermediate spaces should also relate in a functional way to adjacent rooms. For example, an outdoor dining area is most conveniently located just beyond the kitchen door. A larger outdoor space for entertaining should flow easily from a living room or family room. A secret-garden patio just large enough for two is ideally located outside a master bedroom.

Vary the Spaces

As you move farther away from the house, spaces tend to become more casual—sometimes relating more to the surrounding landscape than to the house. Throughout the yard, spaces should vary in shape, size, and character. Relaxing spaces, for instance, should feature comfortable chairs and lounges, while dining areas need sturdy tables and outdoor cooking amenities; both should be positioned for afternoon shade in hot climates. Children's play spaces require soft landing surfaces, while areas for entertaining large crowds call for

▲▲A HAMMOCK in a secluded corner of the yard offers a place of quiet refuge after a long week. Be sure to hang a hammock between two trees or build a sturdy arbor, like this one, for support. In hot climates, remember to choose a shady spot.

▼THE CAREFUL COORDINATION of materials between the living room and patio results in a near-seamless transition from indoors to outdoors. Matching floor tiles, modular design features, and metallic finishes pull the rooms together, while the large glass sliding doors eliminate any remaining visual barriers between the spaces.

smooth surfaces than can be easily negotiated in dim light or with drinks in hand. Design some areas for sitting or lounging, others for standing or strolling, and one or more for activity, especially if you have children.

CREATE YOUR OWN DOMAIN

Unlike many front yards, which are semi-public spaces shared with neighbors, backyards can be personal spaces where you are free to express your own sense of style and way of living. But even with more design options, you'll feel most comfortable with a little privacy built into your backyard.

▲ THESE TWO MASSIVE MASONRY WALLS serve multiple purposes: They screen unwanted views of the neighbor's house, help define one side of the outdoor room, and add a striking focal point against the green landscape—much like a bright painting on a dark wall.

◄ ON SMALL LOTS, fences take up very little space and can be detailed with stylized posts, pickets, and gates to give a space character. The pickets in the weathered fence and white gate are spaced just wide enough to let in light and air without losing privacy.

For added privacy, wooden fences are quick, easy, and affordable to install. However, there are other ways to achieve seclusion. Masonry walls, hedges, mixed plantings, vine-covered trellises, and outbuildings also help enclose a backyard. Although the periphery of the backyard is the logical place for an enclosure, screening gathering spaces that are located close to the house makes them feel cozy and protected, while making the yard appear more expansive.

To create personal, private backyard domains, involve each member of the household in the planning process. Everyone will have different opinions and needs, but there's room in every backyard to include a special space or unique feature for all. (And don't forget that pets need their outdoor spaces, too.) Start by brainstorming or creating a wish list. Chances are, there will be more on the list than can be accomplished, but priorities will emerge as plans develop, and the backyard will begin to fall into shape.

START BY DIVIDING SPACES

Sometimes, the biggest challenge is just getting started. A tiny backyard plot can feel hopelessly limiting, while a large expanse of lawn can appear daunting. In each case, the best approach is to begin by dividing the space.

In tight spaces, it's important to make every inch count. A composition of several cozy areas has a way of feeling much larger than a single medium-sized space. And if there's not room to divide, simply laying out paths, patios, or lawns diagonally or along an S-curve makes a yard appear bigger by allowing it to unfold gradually

▲ THIS STUDIO and small, adjacent lawn are encircled by dense plantings, which lend privacy to the setting. A series of four double glass doors along one wall of the studio allow the room to be flooded with natural light.

rather than in a single glance. Paying close attention to details, such as paving materials or plant combinations, also makes a small space seem larger, as it takes longer to visually absorb all of the elements.

Division works on a larger scale, too. Divide expansive properties into smaller, functional spaces so they appear more inviting and manageable. When you are planning your backyard spaces, identify areas for cooking, dining, entertaining, gardening, swimming, or playing ball, and determine how much space is required for each. Also, be sure to define areas that you wish to leave in their natural state—such as meadows or woodland groves.

It takes time to implement the plans for an entire backyard, so tackle one area at a time, and don't be surprised if it takes a period of several years to finish the project. Start with areas closest to the house because you can see them from indoors and because they will be used most frequently. Also address any urgent outdoor needs up front—such as storage or play spaces for children.

▲ WITH A SPA, SWIMMING POOL, outdoor kitchen, large lawn, woods, and multiple seating areas, everyone in this family can be outdoors at the same time without feeling crowded. The pool is positioned for maximum sun exposure, while umbrellas provide shady areas to beat the heat.

DIVIDING BACKYARD SPACES

LARGE YARDS

Divide large yards into manageable, inviting spaces focused on particular activities.

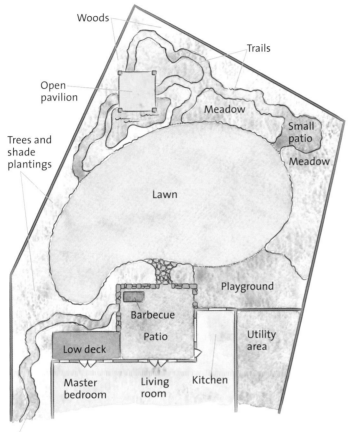

Woods
Trails
Open pavilion
Meadow
Small patio
Trees and shade plantings
Meadow
Lawn
Playground
Barbecue
Patio
Utility area
Low deck
Master bedroom
Living room
Kitchen
Side yard access

SMALL YARDS

Define areas in a small yard to create cozy yet functional spaces.

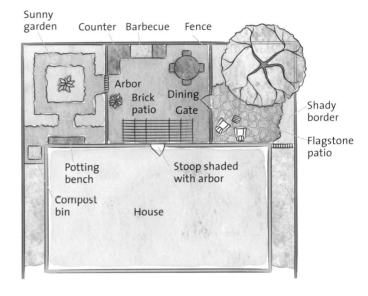

Sunny garden
Counter
Barbecue
Fence
Arbor
Brick patio
Dining
Gate
Shady border
Flagstone patio
Potting bench
Stoop shaded with arbor
Compost bin
House

◄ SEATING LEDGES built into these walls allow the center of this patio to be left open for entertaining larger crowds. The kids have room to play, too, with a large lawn adjacent to the home playground equipment.

▲ WHEN SUBDIVIDING A YARD, individual areas can be defined with walls and fences or by simply changing the materials underfoot. Both strategies are used in this landscape, which includes a fence, pea-gravel garden paths, a flagstone patio, and a mulched area near the oyster-shell bocce-ball court along the periphery.

▲ THIS SMALL, URBAN BACKYARD in San Francisco features five separate areas, each located on a different level. In addition to the central courtyard, upper garden, and lower courtyard shown here, there is a sunken dining patio near the kitchen and a deck off the living room.

Define and Connect Spaces

Regardless of size, backyard spaces should be clearly defined and conveniently connected. This may be as simple as changing the paving materials when one space transitions into another—such as stepping from a flagstone patio onto a lawn. However, building a low seating wall around a patio or adding a step between two areas will distinguish the spaces from one another without taking away from the open feeling. To make spaces feel cozier, build 4-ft. to 6-ft.-high walls between them.

To avoid revealing a backyard all at once and to create inviting destinations, conceal distant spaces partially or entirely from view and prolong the experience of getting there—perhaps with a narrow path that meanders through a garden area. By varying the size of spaces and the degree to which they are open or enclosed, you can create a series of outdoor areas appropriate for numerous activities, for changing numbers of people, and for enjoying at different times of the day and night.

▲ THIS BACKYARD is less than 25 ft. deep, so the space was divided vertically—with decks extending from each level of the house—to create more livable space. As a result, everyone in the family can find a quiet place to escape.

COLLABORATE WITH NATURE

Nature is a great collaborator in the design process. By taking advantage of your backyard's existing natural features and considering the impact of your decisions on the greater landscape, you can create beautiful and healthy environments.

If you are creating a backyard from scratch while building a new house, preserving existing trees during construction will provide shade and screening, which will reduce a home's heating bills. When redesigning an existing backyard, opting for permeable surfaces, such as dry-laid stone, pea gravel, or mulch, will allow rainwater to soak into the ground rather than run off into drainage ditches. Choosing fuel-efficient outdoor grills and building patio

▲ WHO NEEDS A LAWN when you have woods? During construction, the builders were careful to leave as many trees surrounding this house as possible. With the stone, wood, and twig building materials, the house looks like it has emerged naturally from the surrounding landscape.

◀ LAWNS PLAY an important role in the landscape but require time and resources to keep them looking good. Make a strong visual statement by creating lawns only as large as needed and defining them with hedges, patios, or edging materials.

▲ UNCUT AREAS beyond the mown lawn reduce yard work, provide a home for animals, and create a stunning view. Meadows and broad swaths of tall grasses also make a natural transition between a kept yard and woodland buffer.

floors or fences and decks with recycled or ecologically harvested materials conserve natural resources. Building low-emission outdoor fireplaces or choosing alternative fuels for fireplaces also helps protect the earth's ozone layer.

By replacing sections of lawn with mixed plantings, you can help restore lost habitats for birds, butterflies, and toads. A mix of native and well-adapted plants will reduce the need for supplementary water and fertilizer. All of this requires planning, but by planting with ecology in mind, you'll ultimately have more time to spend relaxing in your backyard.

▼ THIS HOUSE is only blocks away from Atlanta's skyscrapers, but you'd never know it. By preserving the mature oaks, eliminating the lawn, and planting native shrubs and perennials, this backyard feels more like it's located on the side of a secluded mountain. With the addition of a pond, the entire environment provides an ideal habitat for birds.

11

Dining and Relaxing

When planning outdoor rooms, take design cues from your home's indoor spaces. By designing a porch, patio, deck, pavilion, or casual seating area with the same attention given to an indoor room, you can create a place to gather with your family, to entertain friends, or to escape to after a long day at work.

An outdoor room can have a floor, walls, a ceiling, comfortable furnishings, and decorative accents just like your living room, dining room, or kitchen. An exterior space may even be similar to an indoor room in shape, size, and furniture arrangement. However, when deciding what type of structures and furnishings to include in an outdoor room, keep in mind the changing quality and amount of light, the fluctuating temperatures and weather patterns, the sounds of nature and neighborhoods, and the life cycle of the landscape.

One or more areas designed for open-air living enhance any backyard. Start by positioning a gathering space—especially one designed for dining—close to the house for convenience. Add areas with comfortable seating in both the sun and shade, and provide a porch, awning, or other structure for shelter from sudden rainstorms. Use walls, fences, or hedges to increase privacy. Place plants adjacent to stone, brick, concrete, or wood to soften the hard surfaces. Finally, use container plantings, water features, or outdoor sculpture to provide the finishing touches to an outdoor room.

Under the Shelter of a Porch or Portico

ORCHES, PORTICOS, VERANDAS, LOGGIAS, AND BALCONIES are all sheltered outdoor spaces connected to a house. These in-between spaces are spots in which to enjoy fresh air and the surrounding landscape without leaving the comfort and security of home. Because it is sheltered, a covered room gets more use than other outdoor spaces, especially if it is tucked into a cozy nook or corner of the house for protection from prevailing winds. An outdoor fireplace makes a roofed space even cozier and more inviting during chilly evenings.

A screened porch keeps bugs at bay and increases privacy, while an open porch heightens the awareness of being outdoors. Because of its close proximity to the interior of a house, a porch is a place to begin and end each day, to serve meals, and for children's play, especially when appropriately furnished. Furnishings for a porch can be as simple as a couple of rocking chairs or as elaborate as a room full of sofas, tables, chests, rugs, and lamps, depending on what types of activities are planned for the space.

◄ THE VAULTED CEILING of this porch adds height and makes the space feel like it is open to the surrounding woods. Materials such as natural wood shingles and exposed beams blend the structure into the setting.

◄ KEEP BEAUTIFUL—or uninviting—views in mind when determining the location for a new porch. This porch looks out onto a stone patio and natural, woodland setting. While considering the scenery, remember that eastern views catch the sunrise and western views capture the sunset.

▼ BROAD STEPS THAT RUN THE WIDTH of the porch create an almost seamless flow of space between the interior, porch, and patio of this home. Placing the outdoor dining area on the covered porch makes it convenient to the kitchen.

► A SCREENED PORCH often doubles as a dining room in pleasant weather, expanding a home's living space. In moderate climates, a screened porch can be used nine months of the year. This porch's dining area has floor-to-ceiling screening to bring in more of the outdoors.

▶ BY PLACING SKYLIGHTS in a porch roof like this one, the sunlight brightens the porch and the adjacent interior room. In warm climates, an eastern exposure prevents the rooms from overheating in the afternoon. In cool climates, a southern exposure warms up the space during the day.

◀ MOST PORCHES ARE BUILT against one or more walls of a house. This porch, however, is separated from the house by a breezeway, allowing the porch to have screens on all four sides. In inclement weather, sliding doors drawn along two sides of the porch protect the space from wind and blowing rain.

Sprucing Up a Stoop

A STOOP OR LANDING—the area just beyond the back door—provides the "formal" connection between a house and the backyard. No matter how tiny a stoop might be, it should be a pleasant place to pass through or perhaps to pause for a few moments to sit on a bench or step to pet the dog or watch the setting sun.

▼THIS BACKDOOR STOOP was transformed into a small deck with steps wrapping around the corners. The deck has room for a couple of chairs, a simple bench, and container plantings. The arbor around the door helps frame the rear entry.

▲A CURVED, BRICK LANDING, a Spanish-style wood-and-tile overhang, and a custom-designed contemporary screen door with colorful matching trim give this small stoop character. A multicolored collection of pots and plants adds the finishing touch.

▶THIS SHALLOW BUT LONG SHELTERED ENTRY is enhanced with a built-in bench for seating. The bench provides a spot to pull off muddy boots before entering the house, visit with pets, or escape a sudden shower.

► A BREEZEWAY is a passageway, but it can also serve as a porchlike gathering space with the addition of a few comfortable chairs. This space catches the slightest breezes, but a ceiling fan adds character and keeps the air circulating on still days.

▼ A PORCH GETS LOTS OF TRAFFIC because it is a transitional area used to go in and out of a house. The rocking chairs on this back porch are invitations to pause and enjoy the view. A table and chairs tucked into the corner encourage a longer stay.

▼ PORCH SWINGS are traditionally hung with chains. This one is attached to the porch roof with marine-grade white rope, which blends in better with the surrounding coastal architecture and beach furniture. It also eliminates the squeaking associated with chains.

▶ INDOOR FURNITURE suits a multipurpose, all-weather porch. A game table quickly converts for dining. Casual chests, freestanding country closets, and bookcases store games, toys, table linens, and throws. A sofa doubles as an extra bed in warm weather.

▲ EXPOSED WOOD ON PORCH FLOORS takes a beating from sun, rain, and wind, so rot-resistant wood or composite decking material is essential. Pressure-treated pine, Douglas fir, cedar, redwood, mahogany, and tropical hardwoods all weather well and require minimal care.

Anatomy of an Outdoor Room

Though it's helpful to compare outdoor and indoor rooms during the backyard planning stage, the materials used to create each type of space differ. For example, outdoor flooring materials have to stand up to weather. Also, fewer surfaces are covered with solid, impervious materials. Here are ideas to help you create an indoor, roomlike setting outdoors.

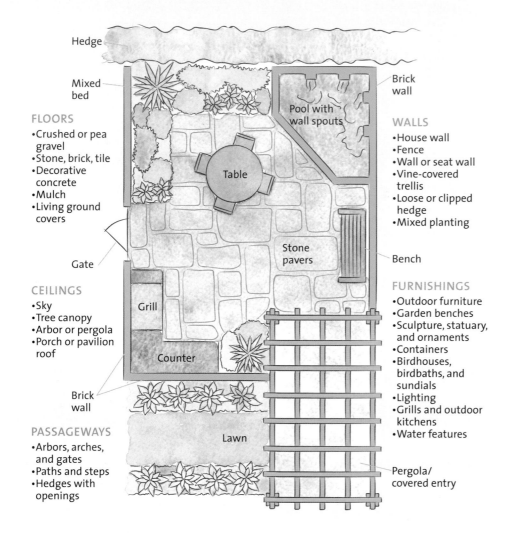

Hedge

Mixed bed

FLOORS
- Crushed or pea gravel
- Stone, brick, tile
- Decorative concrete
- Mulch
- Living ground covers

Gate

CEILINGS
- Sky
- Tree canopy
- Arbor or pergola
- Porch or pavilion roof

Brick wall

PASSAGEWAYS
- Arbors, arches, and gates
- Paths and steps
- Hedges with openings

Table

Grill

Counter

Lawn

Brick wall

Pool with wall spouts

Stone pavers

WALLS
- House wall
- Fence
- Wall or seat wall
- Vine-covered trellis
- Loose or clipped hedge
- Mixed planting

Bench

FURNISHINGS
- Outdoor furniture
- Garden benches
- Sculpture, statuary, and ornaments
- Containers
- Birdhouses, birdbaths, and sundials
- Lighting
- Grills and outdoor kitchens
- Water features

Pergola/covered entry

▲ THE ARCHITECTURAL ELEMENTS of a house influence porch details. Here, custom railings with round posts and finials mimic an interior staircase and add a touch of elegance to the back porch. The closely spaced pickets safely enclose the area. The columns and railings are painted white to match the house trim, helping to tie the structure more closely to the house.

▲A PORCH SHOULD MEASURE
a minimum of 6 ft. wide. Anything narrower starts to feel cramped and out of scale with the house. An 8-ft. to 12-ft.-wide porch easily accommodates a hammock, a group of chairs, or a small dining table.

▶A WRAPAROUND PORCH has room for a variety of sunny and shady spaces to suit different times of the day. This cozy seating area nestled in the corner of the porch is private so it won't be interrupted by passersby.

▶THE WELL-DEFINED SEATING AREA on this back porch creates a room within a room. This sitting room is delineated by corner drapes, as well as by a narrowed passageway created by box planters. A light fixture is centered in the ceiling above the furniture.

◄ THIS PORCH is regularly used for relaxing and dining because it is adjacent to the kitchen. The high, vaulted roofline and custom railings give the porch character, while a skylight helps brighten the space.

▼ WOOD IS THE TRADITIONAL flooring for porches, but cut stone, flagstone, and tile are also appropriate weather-resistant materials. They are cool underfoot, making them ideal in warm climates or on porches with strong sun exposure.

▲ EVEN THOUGH THIS PORTICO receives ample natural light, light fixtures extend the hours of outdoor enjoyment, creating a space that can be used day or night. A chandelier provides ambient lighting, while a wall sconce increases visibility along one side. Uplights accent the palms to create a striking focal point in the corner.

▶ THE TILE FLOORING and seating area of this outdoor space extends beyond the roof of the portico to form a subtle transition between the house and landscape. A fireplace adds warmth on cool nights.

Warming Up an Outdoor Room

A RADIANT FLOOR HEATING SYSTEM can be used outdoors to warm up porches, porticos, and even pool decks. The system utilizes a series of water-filled cables laid on top of subflooring, covered with a thin layer of concrete or other substrate, and then topped with flooring materials such as wood, tile, flagstone, or decorative concrete. Unlike traditional heating systems, which warm the air, a radiant floor heating system concentrates heat in the floor, where it radiates warmth safely and efficiently to bare feet. Even the furniture will be warmed by heat coming up from the floor.

A Dream Deck

OME HOMES HAVE DRAMATIC OCEAN OR MOUNTAIN VISTAS, but most homeowners are content with views of backyard gardens, small groves of trees, or emerald patches of lawn. Overlooking backyard views and open to the sky, a deck offers a sense of freedom and expansiveness from a protected position near the house. Although a deck is usually attached to one or more walls of a house, it provides a greater sense of connection to the landscape because it is uncovered. It can be located off one or more rooms, wrap around a house, or cascade down a hillside in a series of multilevel platforms that can create varied areas for relaxing, gathering, cooking, or dining.

▶ DECKS PERCHED HIGH above the yard serve as promontories—offering expansive views while maintaining a comfortable connection with the house. The sloping hillside and partial enclosure (on three sides) of these decks accentuate their role as promontories.

◄COPPER PICKETS and a pineapple finial dress up this red-wood deck. Lattice screens the neighbor's house from view, while a beam trellis provides a strong support for vines. Together, these elements frame a view of an old oak tree.

▼THIS LOW DECK is located just beyond the kitchen, making it a convenient spot for meals. It is built just above ground level, eliminating the need for railings. A perennial border provides a buffer between the deck and steep hillside that leads to the lake below.

▶ THE ROUND TABLE, box planter, chair backs, and railing echo the curve of this deck. The deck extends out from the house, much like a dock into a harbor, to bring the dining area closer to the water's edge.

◀ A DECK WITHOUT RAILINGS offers unobstructed views to the surrounding landscape. In some municipalities, a deck without railings is permitted as long as it isn't more than 36 in. off the ground. In other municipalities, railings may be required for decks that are 18 in., 20 in., or 30 in. off the ground. Be sure to check local codes before designing and building a deck.

Materials Planning Pays Off

BEFORE DESIGNING A DECK, it's smart to check the available sizes, bulk quantities, and pricing of wood planks used for flooring. Because wood availability and pricing fluctuates, you may want to look at several board sizes. Most wood planks are sold as 8-ft., 10-ft., 12-ft., or 16-ft. boards, and 12-ft. boards are often the least expensive to buy per running foot. Overall deck lengths in multiples of 8 ft., 10 ft., or 12 ft. will result in the least amount of waste; a 12-ft., 24-ft., or 36-ft.-long deck that uses 12-ft. boards could be the most cost efficient to build.

▼THIS DECK HELPS unite the house with the surrounding landscape by extending far into the yard and gently cascading down the gradual slope. Rough-hewn benches, which double as low deck railings, give the deck a natural, woodsy look.

▲A DISTINCTIVE RAILING—which includes the posts and pickets, as well as caps and finials—can give a deck personality. These "twig" railings and oversized wooden posts visually connect the deck with the home's rustic architecture, while framing the view of the lake.

◄ SEATING CAN BE positioned many ways on a deck. Here, chairs face out to the view. They could also be clustered in several conversation groups or pulled up around a table. A single chair off by itself provides a contemplative space.

▲ IF THE VIEW from a deck is to a lower area, such as this garden, consider railings that enhance the view. Wrought iron replaces the usual wooden pickets in this railing, creating a sturdy structure without restricting the view.

◀ THIS BROAD, TIERED DECK features both upper and lower gathering spaces—one for dining and the other for sunbathing. The two spaces are connected to each other and the house by a transitional landing and stairs. Built-in planter boxes and custom railings give the spaces color and character and help tie all the elements together.

A DISTINCTIVE DECK DRAIN

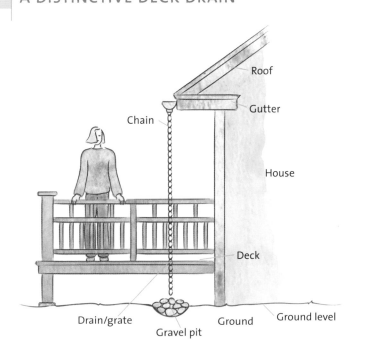

▲ INSTEAD OF A TRADITIONAL DOWNSPOUT, a large chain hanging from the eaves is used to direct the water from the gutter to the ground. An iron drain cover allows the water to pass through the deck's surface. Spacing between planks prevents water from accumulating on the deck.

Dining and Relaxing | 217

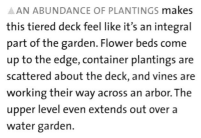
▲AN ABUNDANCE OF PLANTINGS makes this tiered deck feel like it's an integral part of the garden. Flower beds come up to the edge, container plantings are scattered about the deck, and vines are working their way across an arbor. The upper level even extends out over a water garden.

▶THIS HOME FEATURES two small decks: a private space off the upstairs bedroom and a lower deck off the main floor for entertaining and dining. Laying boards on a diagonal alters the perspective on the lower deck, making it look larger than it is.

Room to Dine Comfortably

THERE ARE SOME GUIDELINES ON HOW MANY **people** an outdoor table will accommodate and how it will fit into your backyard space. A 26-in. round bistro table will seat two, a 48-in. round or square table will seat four to six, and a 36-in. by 72-in. rectangular table will seat up to eight. Side chairs average 17 in. wide and deep, while armchairs run closer to 24 in. wide and deep.

Although tables tend to stay put, chairs are often pushed in and out, and even shuffled about a space. A good rule of thumb for a cozy yet comfortable space is the width or length of the table plus at least 3 ft. on each side. That provides ample room for getting in and out of chairs and space for someone to slide by for serving or clearing dishes. For a more open feeling or greater flexibility in the arrangement of furniture, allow extra room. If there are steps nearby, be sure to leave at least 5 ft. between the table and steps for safety.

▲ DECKS THAT EXTEND from upper floors offer bird's-eye views of backyard landscapes. This deck features cut-stone flooring that matches the pool edging below. The sturdy railings complement the architecture of the house.

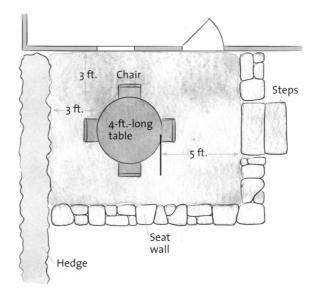

▶ DECKS AND PATIOS surround this house. A small upper deck provides a quiet place to sit outside the living room. A large mid-level deck features an outdoor kitchen and space for entertaining. A lower patio provides a casual place for relaxing near the family room.

▼ A DECK DOESN'T HAVE TO BE attached to a house. This low, freestanding deck offers a destination in the landscape. Regardless of where a deck is built, the flooring should be raised at least 6 in. off the ground to provide adequate ventilation and help prevent rot.

◄ BUILT-IN SEATING can be installed along the outside edge of a deck or placed against the house, as shown here. Built-in benches provide casual seating and can help accommodate a crowd when entertaining.

▼ DECKS SUIT HOUSES on steep hillsides. This one has a deck that wraps around the house, extends toward the edge of the property, and then cascades down steps to a stone patio and small lawn. The configuration makes the yard more accessible and inviting.

◄ STAINLESS-STEEL CABLE PORCH RAILINGS complement the contemporary architecture of this beach house. The cable is noncorrosive and may be attached to wood, carbon-steel pipe, structural tubing, or stainless-steel posts.

A Patio and Terrace Link to the Landscape

▼THIS TERRACE is built close to the ground, but the low wall provides a sense of enclosure and offers additional seating. The wall is constructed with a fieldstone base and flagstone cap; the terrace is built from oversized slabs of the same fieldstone.

APATIO OR TERRACE is a paved outdoor area that frequently links the indoors and out. Although the terms are used interchangeably, terrace refers more specifically to a "shelf" on a sloping site. The flooring may echo a home's interior materials, as in the case of matching tile, brick, or decorative concrete, or it may more closely relate to the natural environment, as with stone or pea gravel. Walls formed by the house, freestanding masonry walls, fences, hedges, or mixed plantings help create a greater sense of privacy and coziness around a patio or terrace. Its roof may be an arbor, a canopy of trees, or left open to the sky. A patio or terrace can be made more livable with a fireplace, outdoor kitchen, comfortable seating, and outdoor lighting. Plants placed along the edge of a patio or terrace connect the space to the surrounding landscape.

◄THIS SMALL FLAGSTONE PATIO is enclosed on all sides—either by the house, stone walls, or a water feature—to create an intimate space for an alfresco dinner. Colorful lanterns hang from a rustic arbor, adding a decorative touch and illuminating the space after dark.

▲ THE DESIGN AND MATERIALS of this small stone patio unite the home and the landscape. The patio flows from the back door and across the stream into the yard. The
stones in the patio, pillars, steps, and water feature all match in color for a uniform
appearance, although they vary in shape, size, and cut.

Creating Inviting Side Yard Transitions

THE SIDE YARD IS ONE OF THE MOST NEGLECTED SPACES in a residential landscape. When it's tucked between two houses, the sliver of yard can be dark and narrow. On a larger lot, it is often little more than an unused expanse of lawn or woods.

Most often, a side yard is a passageway that connects the front yard and backyard—although, if backyard space is limited, it might double as an outdoor room. Because a side yard is exposed to the street and neighboring house, the key to making it inviting is to create privacy. Erecting a fence or wall on a narrow lot will do the job. Adding a pergola overhead will enhance the sense of passage and screen views from the neighbor's upstairs rooms. In a spacious side yard, hedges, trees, or mixed plantings of perennials, grasses, shrubs, and trees along the periphery will provide desired screening.

An arbor or gate placed near the front of the house makes the path through the side yard more inviting. Plantings give the passageway more visual texture. Adding a focal point—such as a sculpture or water feature—at the far end of the side yard's path will draw you into the space.

▲ THIS GRAY-STAINED PERGOLA creates an inviting passageway through a narrow side yard while increasing privacy for the homeowners. Without the evergreen-vine-draped crosspieces, neighbors in their upstairs bedrooms could see into the downstairs rooms of this house.

▶ THIS SMALL, INFORMAL PATIO of dry-laid, rounded cobblestone was designed for the homeowners' enjoyment. A larger patio with smoother flooring and additional seating would be more suitable for entertaining.

▼ MOST PATIOS are built adjacent to a house. This one was built a short stroll away—against a retaining wall along the edge of the lawn where it can be viewed from indoors. It is accompanied by a bench and fishpond.

▲ BRICK FLOORS are perfect for small spaces, where they can be laid in myriad patterns without looking busy. When covering large expanses of ground, brick tends to look busy unless other paving materials with broader surfaces—such as stone or concrete—are mixed into the design.

RAISED SEATING AREAS are more comfortable when they are protected and private. The stone retaining wall and side walls that wrap around the table and bench make this small patio feel even more intimate.

A TERRACE WITH a random shape and irregular edges, like this one, is less formal than a geometrically designed space. Here, mounded plantings and large boulders create a gradual transition into the land-scape, making the patio feel as if it naturally grew out of the space.

▼ PLACE FURNITURE FAR ENOUGH away from doors so that the traffic flow remains uninterrupted, even on small patios like this one. Chairs clustered in corners also feel cozier than similar groupings in the middle of a patio.

▲ AN L- OR U-SHAPED HOUSE creates lots of opportunities for patios. This patio connects interior rooms and serves as a pass-through, increasing overall traffic and activity in the space. The homeowners gain additional privacy and protection from windy weather because the walls of the house partially screen the patio.

▲ A SUNKEN PATIO like the one just beyond this basement door is cozy and private. The surrounding stacked-stone retaining walls and juniper groundcovers prevent soil erosion on the sloped site. The walls also add texture and a feeling of warmth to the seating area.

▶ A WALL OF PLANTS provides privacy around this brick patio, making it a comfortable space for a casual family dinner. Colorful tropical plants such as bananas, gingers, hibiscus, and coleus mingle among trees and shrubs to obscure views and establish boundaries.

Expressive Materials Make a Difference

SPECIAL MATERIALS used in small doses can upgrade your backyard into a one-of-a-kind oasis. For example, a tiny gathering space can be made into a unique spot when you focus on the details. It's a place to splurge on distinctive paving materials, favorite plants, or the perfect chair.

Mixing and matching materials is another effective way to add expressive materials to the landscape. Build a picket fence atop a low stone wall, or combine stone and brick in a path. Seek out materials with unique qualities, such as textured tile or colorful river cobbles, or combine materials with contrasting textures and colors such as red brick and bluestone pavers.

▼THIS PORCH AND PATIO occupy neighboring spaces with similar views yet are very different places. One is sheltered against the house and under a roof; the other is spacious and exposed to the elements. They are separated by boulders, grassy plantings, and a change in elevation.

▲BUCKETS OF PEBBLES and a few bags of concrete mix are the tools landscape designer Jeffrey Bale uses to turn a patio floor into a work of art. Patience, creativity, and elbow grease are all that's needed to create inexpensive pebble-and-tile mosaics like this one.

▲ON THIS HILLSIDE, terracing is used to connect a series of outdoor rooms. The transition between the two patios is marked by an opening in a trellised wall, a narrowing of the steps, and step materials that differ from the paving surfaces.

▲ CLUSTERED POTS help define a dining area on this raised patio. The white spikes of gayfeather in the foreground and distance mark corners of this outdoor room, while foliage plants offer long-season good looks.

▲ THE SOOTHING SOUND of water encourages relaxation. The trickling fountain in this backyard serves as a focal point and creates an inviting getaway. The edging around the pool provides a place for the owners' daughter to watch and feed the fish.

▶ CITY DWELLERS often transform rooftops into terraces filled with container plantings. Rooftops can be ideal spots to grow herbs and vegetables, perfect accompaniments to alfresco dining. Shrubs and small trees are also appropriate container plantings, as long as they are secured to withstand windy days.

Planting Pockets
Soften Paving

THE HARD SURFACES AND EDGES of stone or brick patio floors look softer with the addition of plantings. Greenery that sprawls as it grows will naturally conceal corners and edges of hard flooring. There's another planting method that gives a patio an even more custom look: Remove some brick, stone, or tile pavers in a defined or random pattern in and about the patio. Doing this will expose soil-filled pockets for plantings.

Though planting pockets can be as narrow as the ½-in. crack between two pavers, most plants will appreciate an amended planting pocket that is at least 1 ft. wide. Compact shrubs and trees can be tucked into pockets that are 2 ft. to 3 ft. wide.

▼THIS ARBOR-COVERED TERRACE has a captivating water feature that runs its length. A recirculating runnel, or channel of water, flows across the terrace, tumbles down the steps, and spills into a fishpond below.

▶ THIS CURVED TERRACE protrudes into the yard and adjoins a portico and raised patio. The terrace serves both as a transition to the lawn and as a gathering space for dining and entertaining. Terracotta tile, which is only durable in moderate climates, visually connects the three spaces.

▲ EVEN ON A GENTLE SLOPE, a patio can ease the grade change from the house to the lawn. The patio shown here is located just beyond the kitchen, where it serves as a convenient spot for parents to watch their young children play nearby.

◀ TALL, SCULPTURAL PILLARS create a grand entrance to this raised patio. Raising a patio slightly above the surrounding grade calls special attention to the seating area.

Showcasing Outdoor Art

A COURTYARD OR PATIO is an intimate space in which to showcase outdoor art. A single piece of art will make a stronger statement than multiple pieces that compete for attention, although collections can be showcased effectively by limiting the number of pieces that are seen from any given location. Some sculptural pieces are meant to stand alone as the focal point on a patch of lawn or in the center of a courtyard. Other pieces of art stand out with a backdrop of plantings.

The type of plantings you use to highlight a piece of art will be determined by the object's material and shape. Plants with intricate foliage create a sharp contrast with bold, smooth surfaces. Ornamental grasses envelop architectural artifacts or sculpture with well-defined edges in a soft setting. Mounding plants hide the base of sculptures, allowing the eye to focus on the art's expressive qualities.

Choose a meaningful spot for outdoor art. Place a contemporary sculpture, mobile, found object, architectural artifact, or more traditional cast-stone statuary where it serves as a focal point along a wall, at the end of a path, in a border, or at the center of a formal garden. For maximum benefit, place an object where it is visible from an indoor room as well.

▲ SOFT PLANTINGS on this patio complement the carved-stone faces and granite-ball fountain. The sculptures are located just beyond the back door, where they can be enjoyed from both indoors and out.

◄ THE KEY TO COMBINING STONES is to strike a balance between contrast and uniformity. The smooth-surfaced, cut-granite pavers on this patio differ in texture and style from the random stone used in the walls, yet they are similar in color. Both look at home in this New England landscape.

▼THIS SMALL PATIO is laid in several brick patterns and utilizes odd-sized remainders—an approach reminiscent of the brickbat paving used in Colonial Williamsburg or the clinker brick paving from the Arts and Crafts era. This carefree style suits the rustic charm of the cottage.

▲PATIOS CAN BE DESTINATIONS placed away from the house. This patio, just large enough for a table and chairs, is tucked into a hillside next to a recirculating waterfall and pond, offering a relaxing escape with a view of the house.

▼CREEPING THYME, Corsican mint, small sedums, and blue star creeper thrive even when tucked between the dry-laid, random flagstone pavers on this sunken patio. They can all handle light foot traffic, and the thyme and mint release a sweet fragrance when stepped upon.

▲THE PATIO IS SEAMLESSLY built into the curving path that winds through this Florida backyard. The brick edging creates a sense of fluidity and motion in a small space, and the canopy of trees provides shady relief on warm days.

Outdoor Rooms on a Budget

An inviting gathering space doesn't have to break the bank. Start small and expand or upgrade as funds allow. Here are a few ideas for keeping costs down:

- Place outdoor rooms near the house to take advantage of shared conveniences such as kitchens, baths, lighting, and stereo systems.
- If supplemental lighting is required, look into easy-to-install solar lighting kits, utilize oil lanterns, or bring out the candles.
- Cook over a freestanding charcoal or gas grill, or build your own fire pit.
- Create walls from plants or stock fencing materials. Quick-growing vines will cover inexpensive fencing materials.
- Go eclectic—gather rustic furnishings from flea markets and antique malls. A fresh coat of paint will do wonders for worn furniture.
- Convert an antique tub, ceramic pot, or wood trough into a water feature.
- Warm up your surroundings with a portable fire pit or chiminea.
- Keep construction simple. It's easy to spread crushed gravel yourself, for example. Accent gravel floors with sections of irregular flagstone or cobblestone edging.

▲ A TWIG OR BAMBOO FENCE covered with fast-growing vines makes quick and inexpensive screening. This type of structure will last several years. At that time, it can either be rebuilt, or a more permanent fence can be constructed.

▶ THIS PATIO IS PAVED with bricks that radiate out from a central point in a circular pattern, ringed by a boxwood hedge, and accented with a round dining table. The repetition of circular elements creates a sense of unity and formality in the landscape.

▲ FLAGSTONE CAN BE LAID in multiple ways in the same yard. It is mortared and edged in brick on the patio and adjacent path. On connecting paths, it is dry-laid with a random edge. In the garden, it is used for steps along a gravel path.

▶ THIS ASYMMETRICAL PATIO calls attention to itself because of the random pattern of its stone flooring. The pattern and light color of the stone provide a dramatic contrast to the surrounding plantings.

▶ THIS BROAD, STONE PATIO breaks up an expanse of lawn. Positioned in an open area, the space is suitable for a party, outdoor wedding, or other social event. The retaining wall handles overflow seating.

▶ NOT ALL PATIOS are spacious enough for large gatherings or even for lingering very long. The white café table and chairs anchoring this petite patio simply offer a spot to pause while exploring the garden.

Getting Creative with Concrete

CONSIDER CONCRETE for the look of stone, brick, or tile without the cost. Stamped and stained, concrete bears a remarkable resemblance to other masonry materials. Although concrete still comes in the ubiquitous gray, it is also available in an array of colors, textures, and finishes. It can be mixed with aggregate, tinted with stain, brushed with sand, or stamped into patterns. It can be precast, polished, and laid like cut stone. Concrete can also be formed into interlocking block pavers and arranged into patterns. In cold climates where concrete is less commonly used, special reinforcements added to the concrete help eliminate heaving during the winter.

▼ THIS SMALL PATIO, which is tucked into a hillside, is paved in dry-laid, cut-granite cobblestones and hugged by evergreen shrubs and ground covers to create a calm, cozy space.

▲ THIS PATIO is designed as a series of broad steps on a gentle slope. What makes this design so successful is the mix of paving materials with contrasting textures, the addition of a water feature, and the selective use of upright pergolas.

▲ PATIOS AND PLANTING BEDS are good alternatives to lawn—especially in small backyards where space is at a premium. Eliminating the lawn reduces routine maintenance chores, and mixed plantings with small ornamental trees, shrubs, and perennials keep the backyard interesting throughout the seasons.

▶ CONTAINER PLANTS can be easily used to spruce up a patio and give color to large expanses of wall space. The large pots on the patio just beyond the back door of this New Orleans home hold citrus trees, bamboo, and a water garden with papyrus.

WATER FEATURES

▶THIS RUNNEL draws visitors from the upper deck to the lower garden as they follow the water across the patio and down the steps. The water is then transported back up to the small fountain on the deck, where it begins its journey again.

▼GRADE CHANGES in a landscape offer excellent opportunities for creating water features with cascades or waterfalls. This 3-ft. cascade is enhanced by the contrast in shape and size of the large, rough-tumbled, rectangular stones and the smaller, round, river-washed stones.

▼THIS SMALL FISHPOND is edged with stones and filled with water lilies, water lettuce, and papyrus. It includes a softly gurgling urn fountain. Both the moving water and fish help keep mosquitoes at bay, yet birds still find the pond attractive.

▼ALTHOUGH THE WATER is recirculated from the pond by a pump, this small water feature looks and sounds like a spring because water trickles out from beneath the stones. The rough, mossy stones enhance the natural-looking setting.

◄WALL FOUNTAINS come in all shapes, sizes, and styles and can be built into freestanding or retaining walls. The sound of the water splashing into the pool below is determined by the volume of water trickling out of the fountain, the distance the water falls, and the depth of the pool.

OUTDOOR FURNITURE

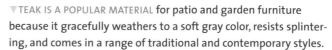
◀ OUTDOOR TABLES come in nearly as many shapes and sizes as indoor tables, seating from 2 to 12 people. Some have hideaway leaves to adjust the length. Others fold up easily so they can be stored for winter.

▼ TEAK IS A POPULAR MATERIAL for patio and garden furniture because it gracefully weathers to a soft gray color, resists splintering, and comes in a range of traditional and contemporary styles.

▲ THE SAME CARE SHOULD BE GIVEN to choosing outdoor chairs as given to selecting interior furniture, and comfort is a top priority. Select from among cushioned armchairs, side chairs, sofas, chairs with ottomans, and lounges, as well as garden benches, gliders, rockers, and porch swings.

New Furniture Choices

FURNITURE MANUFACTURERS **have responded to our increased passion for decorating outdoor rooms with stylish furniture made from a variety of materials.** In addition to teak, red cedar, molded plastic, and wrought iron—which have long been outdoor favorites—choices for outdoor furniture now include cast aluminum, galvanized metal dipped in a zinc bath, rust-resistant steel with an enamel finish, faux wicker, and exotic woods. All furnishings can be made more comfortable with the addition of fast-drying, water- and mildew-resistant cushions, which come in an infinite range of colors and styles.

▲ PATIO FURNITURE is formed from many different materials. Metal chairs, such as these, are among the strongest, most durable options and include steel, cast iron, wrought iron, and galvanized aluminum. Each of these metals can be painted, zinc-dipped, or treated with a polyester top coat to prevent rust.

▶ WATER- AND MILDEW-RESISTANT cushions add style and comfort to outdoor furnishings. Cushion fabrics come in a wide range of colors and patterns and can be coordinated with indoor décor, an outdoor decorating theme, or plants and garden accessories.

BUILT-IN SEATING

▶ALTHOUGH THIS RUSTIC STONE BENCH IS CONSTRUCTED more for visual interest than for comfort, it is quite functional. It helps retain a steep bank, while providing a casual place to pause for a special view or to set tools when working in the garden.

▼A BUILT-IN BENCH can be a practical alternative to a deck railing. It increases seating in a small space to help accommodate a crowd. With some ingenuity and a few hinges for doors, the space beneath the seats can convert into outdoor storage space.

▼ THIS CURVED STONE SEATING is built to last. Cushions soften the stone, and slabs built higher than the seating are used as end tables. The bench, with its backdrop of exotic greenery, is the focal point of this backyard patio.

Building a Wall at Sitting Height

ALOW WALL SERVES MANY ROLES. It can define the edge of a patio or terrace, create a sense of enclosure without making a space feel "closed in," and provide extra seating without taking up additional space. To make the wall comfortable for sitting, build it 14 in. to 16 in. high and at least 12 in. wide. For masonry walls, make sure the cap (top piece) is a smooth surface that won't snag clothing. A cap in a contrasting material from the wall, such as bluestone on brick or stucco, will add a distinct look to a backyard.

▼ A WALL AROUND A PATIO can double as seating as long as it has a reasonably smooth surface and is built at a comfortable sitting height. The board that sits atop this masonry retaining wall carves out a spot for a quiet break next to a garden stream.

▲ THE HEAVY WOODEN BENCH built into a nook along this retaining wall also serves as the base of a pergola. The structure is draped in vines, creating a cool place to enjoy the surrounding garden.

A Peaceful Courtyard

THE CONFIGURATION OF A COURTYARD makes it an inherently quiet, secluded place. Though it may be open to the sky, a courtyard is enclosed on three or more sides, creating a gathering space that is protected by the house and surrounding walls. In some cases, it may even serve as a passageway between rooms of the house.

When designing a courtyard, it's important to include a shady spot for the seating—perhaps beneath a tree, umbrella, or an eyebrow arbor attached to the house. By providing a glimpse of the views beyond the courtyard through a gate, window, or gap in the courtyard wall, the area will feel more spacious. And finally, the addition of vines, planting pockets, or raised or container plantings will soften the look of hard surfaces around the courtyard.

▲ MANY TREES WILL ADAPT to the confines of a courtyard and, once established, provide an overhead canopy of shade and shelter. Trees commonly grown along sidewalks—such as star magnolias, redbuds, and pollarded sycamores—are good choices for courtyards.

◀ THIS NEW ORLEANS-STYLE HOME features French doors and full-length glass windows that open onto a courtyard. The large expanse of glass makes the interior rooms brighter and the courtyard seem larger than it would if surrounded by solid walls.

▼THE WINDOWLIKE OPENING in this brightly colored gate helps open up an otherwise enclosed backyard space, expanding views and improving cross-ventilation. Similar openings can also be built into masonry walls, framed in fences, and cut out of dense hedges.

◄DETAILS CAN MAKE A BIG difference in a small space. The stone pattern in this small courtyard might look busy if it were used in a large space. Here, it has the same effect as a throw rug or runner used to accent a room.

▲BRIGHT COLORS suit courtyards—especially those surrounded by tall walls or buildings that tend to make the spaces shady. Not only will bright colors feel more cheerful, they will also reflect more natural light around the courtyard than dark colors, which simply absorb light.

▶CLINGING VINES, such as climbing hydrangea or Boston ivy, will soften a brick or concrete wall. Climbing roses, twining vines, and vines with tendrils need additional support and occasional guidance, which can be provided by a trellis mounted an inch or two from the wall.

Designing a Wall or Fence

WALLS AND FENCES serve many roles in the landscape. They separate spaces, create privacy, add a vertical accent where needed, and provide a backdrop for colorful plantings. They can also frame special views, screen unwanted ones, and help buffer neighborhood noise.

Walls are built as low as 1 ft. high, while fences can be built as high as 8 ft. They may be made from wood, brick, stone, interlocking blocks, or stucco. Their height and design are meant to send a clear message. For example, a low, painted fence with widely spaced pickets encourages friendly conversation. A tall, solid masonry wall indicates a desire for privacy.

Openings, such as windows and doorways, can enhance a fence or wall. Arbors, arches, and posts can frame a doorway, offering a glimpse beyond, while a gate adds character to a wall or fence.

To give a wall color and texture, think about what kind of material will give you the intended result. A stacked-stone wall has a rough surface and natural finish. A brick, block, or stucco wall has a course texture and comes in a variety of colors. Wood fences may have smooth or rough surfaces and can be painted or stained in any imaginable color.

▲THIS COURTYARD, which is anchored by a tall, masonry retaining wall, was designed to create an inviting backyard space on a large, sloping lot. It includes a pea-gravel sitting area, a small lawn, fountain, and 3-ft.-deep flower borders.

▲IN SMALL COURTYARDS surrounded by tall walls, plants will help reduce the noise that bounces off hard surfaces. Grow vines on walls, build raised flower beds, create planting pockets, or add containers and window boxes filled with favorite plants to soften sounds.

Cooking Out

THE OUTDOOR KITCHEN IS THE ULTIMATE LUXURY AND CONVENIENCE in outdoor living. Not only does it keep the heat out of the house in summertime, but having an outdoor cooking area also reduces the number of trips made to the indoor kitchen. As a result, more time can be spent enjoying the outdoors.

The grill is at the heart of an outdoor kitchen. Freestanding grills are popular, affordable, and available in a wide range of styles. A fully equipped outdoor kitchen, however, can transform the backyard barbecue into a gourmet gathering. Today's grills feature optional smoker boxes, side burners, rotisseries, woks, warming racks, and more. Weatherproof kitchen cabinets serve as host to bar sinks, beer taps, compact refrigerators, and storage drawers. Outdoor outlets offer a convenient place to plug in lights, radios, and blenders. Durable, all-weather countertops make serving a convenience and may be designed as counter seating with pull-up stools.

▼ TO KEEP SMOKE OUT of guests' eyes, place a grill away from seating areas and on the downwind side of a patio and deck. This grill is positioned along one side of a deck and under an open-roofed structure to help define and enclose the space.

▲ A GENEROUS LENGTH of counter space flanks this oversized grill to make serving a crowd easy. It is built against a wall of the house under several sconces used to illuminate the counter space and grill at night.

▶ THIS BARBECUE COUNTER has wood siding and is painted to match the house. The 13-ft.-long counter includes a 30-in.-long grill, dual side burners, an under-counter refrigerator, a stainless-steel sink, storage drawers, and an electrical outlet. The doors beneath the sink and grill give homeowners access to appliances and storage.

Choosing the Right Grill

IF YOU HAVEN'T SHOPPED FOR A GRILL IN A WHILE, you're in for a surprise. Before heading for the hearth and patio store, home center, or hardware store, beef up your knowledge of grill features:

- **PORTABILITY:** Some units are easy to move; others are heavy, permanently connected to gas lines, or built into counters.

- **FUEL:** Charcoal grills give food a smoky flavor, but it takes time to build a hot fire. Gas grills are easy to light and offer greater control over temperature. Charcoal grills with gas starters offer the best of both. Electric grills are environmentally friendly and easy to clean. And infra-red grills radiate heat at very high temperatures, which makes searing meats a snap.

- **BTU:** British Thermal Units are a measure of heat energy. Most average-sized grills with two burners should have 30,000 to 50,000 BTU. If you live in a cold region of the country, a grill with higher BTU may work more efficiently. (In moderate climates, you'll just use more fuel with a higher BTU grill.)

- **ACCESSORIES:** Accessory choices include side burners, smoker boxes, warming racks, rotisseries, woks, lights, carts, cabinetry, and more.

- **PRICING:** Prices range from less than $100 for a small portable grill to as much as $10,000 for a top-of-the-line grill with all the bells and whistles.

◄ PROFESSIONAL-QUALITY, free-standing grills offer more grilling space and options than small, portable grills but are more affordable and occupy less space than custom-built outdoor kitchens. This 36-in. stainless-steel grill has a 12-in. dual side burner for simmering sauces, steaming vegetables, and cooking rice.

◄ A TRADITIONAL WOOD-BURNING OVEN—which has its roots in Italy—has been custom designed and built for this pizza lover and outdoor chef. The oven reaches temperatures exceeding 400 degrees and can also be used for baking breads, roasting vegetables, and cooking meat dishes.

▲ THIS ADOBE-STYLE PATIO features a raised fire pit—topped with river cobbles for a decorative accent—used to warm up the space. Like most fire pits, it can be fitted with a grill for cooking. Dry-wood storage is conveniently located nearby.

◄ BARBECUE GRILL UNITS can be dropped in or slid into stone walls. This drop-in unit is built into a mortared, fieldstone retaining wall. It includes a side burner, warming rack, and a countertop made from bluestone. A slide-in unit would feature stainless-steel storage beneath the grill.

▶ THIS PAVILION has plenty of space to entertain with room for a grill, ancillary outdoor appliances, counter space, and storage. The bar arrangement enables the chef to converse with guests while preparing a meal.

▼ THESE HORNOS, or adobe bread ovens, are modeled after those used by Native Americans throughout the Southwest. Today, hornos are built from sun-dried, mud bricks that are either handmade or purchased at an adobe brickyard, and then bonded together with mud mortar.

◀ THIS OUTDOOR KITCHEN features a drop-in gas grill and bar sink, plus several storage drawers and cabinets built into the brick wall. It is located beneath the shelter of a portico, where it is protected from the rain but exposed enough to let the smoke escape from the dining space.

▲ A GRILL located on an interior wall of a pavilion needs a hood to vent smoke away from the enclosed space. This grill has a copper hood and matching wall sconces that will acquire a verdigris patina as they age.

◄ THIS CHARCOAL GRILL is built at the end of a swimming-pool deck and has flanking brick-and-bluestone walls for additional seating. The adjustable rack inside the grill can be dropped for small fires during family dinners and raised for large fires when hosting pool-side parties.

▶ THIS WRAPAROUND KITCHEN surrounds the chef with counter space, making it easy to serve drinks and meals to many guests at once. The umbrella provides shelter for guests and food. The gas lamp illuminates the cooking and eating areas after dark.

▲ THIS L-SHAPED COUNTER creates convenient grilling and serving areas that accommodate counter-style or buffet-style dining. L-shaped counters are the outdoor equivalent of the efficient "work triangle" often used to design indoor kitchens.

▶ LIGHTING IS AN IMPORTANT ASPECT of outdoor kitchen design. Chefs need to see when the food is finished cooking, and guests like to see what they are being served. The owners of this grill mounted a small spotlight on the fence to shine directly onto the cooking surface.

Building an Outdoor Kitchen

WHEN PLANNING AN OUTDOOR KITCHEN, consider how accessible it will be to water, gas, and electricity. An outdoor kitchen placed against one wall of a house makes it easier to tap into utilities. As an added benefit, a roof overhang will help shelter outdoor appliances.

You'll probably want to hire a professional to do this kind of work, but here are a few things to consider. A kitchen built in a location far away from the house will involve digging trenches for supply lines. Check with your municipality regarding building codes for the required distance between gas and power lines. Be sure to ask if you need one or two separate trenches to accommodate the lines.

For a bar sink, refrigerator, and icemaker, plan on adding a cold-water line. Hot-water lines are rarely needed outdoors unless you plan to add a dishwasher. Remember to install adequate waste-water drainage for sinks and refrigerators.

◄ YOU CAN CREATE outdoor kitchens using a wide range of appliances. This kitchen includes a five-burner gas grill, double and single side burners, storage drawers, and a refrigerator. Other common amenities include bar sinks and warming drawers.

Keeping Warm

WHAT BETTER WAY IS THERE TO CREATE AMBIENCE than with the warm glow of an outdoor hearth? A fireplace knocks off the chill in northern or high-altitude regions where summer evenings are cool and in warmer climates where outdoor living is enjoyed well into the winter. A fire pit, fire dish, luminaria, or chiminea will warm up a small area of the outdoors. For a bolder aesthetic statement or more warmth, install a manufactured or custom-built fireplace of brick, stone, tile, or stucco, and accent it with an attractive mantel. Another option for warming an outdoor area is a patio heater, which comes in floor, tabletop, and wall-mounted models. Safe fuel options for outdoor hearths run the gamut from wood and manufactured logs to propane, natural gas, and proprietary gels, which vary in cost and portability.

◄ A STACKED-STONE CHIMNEY looks at home on the exterior wall of this traditional house. The outdoor fireplace is a welcome surprise. A single chimney can support an indoor and an outdoor fireplace as long as separate flues are used for safety and drawing efficiency.

◄ THIS OUTDOOR-ROOM arrangement offers the best of both worlds—the shelter and warmth of a partially enclosed structure with a built-in fireplace, and the bright, open space of an adjoining patio. The tile flooring ties both areas together.

▲ AN OUTDOOR FIREPLACE with gas-burning logs helps relieve the chill of frosty mornings and nippy evenings beneath this backyard pavilion. Today's gas logs produce yellow flames that resemble those created by real wood.

◄ WHEN PLANNING FOR AN OUTDOOR FIREPLACE, keep in mind the space needed for firewood. In addition to easily accessible stacks of dry, seasoned wood, it is convenient to have a small, sheltered bin for wood within an arm's reach of the fire.

▲FIRE PITS are traditionally placed in the center of an outdoor area to create inviting social spaces for larger groups. Several sides of this fire pit are surrounded with seating to accommodate many guests.

▲▲A FIREPLACE creates a special ambiance in an outdoor room. The yellow flames of a fire add visual—and physical—warmth to this covered space, while recessed ceiling fixtures provide overhead light.

◀THE LARGER SCALE of an outdoor space differs from an indoor room. That is why this heavy, oversized fireplace fits in so well against a hillside. A smaller fireplace would be a better choice underneath a pavilion and a portico.

▲ THIS MASONRY FIREPLACE is constructed beyond the footprint of the portico, leaving plenty of room under the roof for dining or gathering around the large wooden table. A chimney diverts smoke away from the seating area.

▲ DRY-WOOD STORAGE can be built alongside the fireplace or into a nearby structure, such as this stacked-stone retaining wall. A masonry structure for wood storage is best because it won't be damaged by termites or other pests that may be attracted to firewood.

Burning Wood Responsibly

BURNING WOOD GENERATES EMISSIONS that may contribute to air pollution. To reduce the impact on the environment, build small, hot fires with dry, well-seasoned hardwood. Seasoned hardwood (dried for six months or longer to reduce the moisture content) is easy to light and burns long and efficiently. Consider burning manufactured logs or use alternative heating options such as pellet stoves, fireplace inserts, and EPA-certified clean-burning fireplaces. Also, be sure to use a chimney to raise the point at which the smoke releases. This will keep gathering spaces and neighboring yards free from smoke.

► THIS WOOD-BURNING FIRE PIT—reminiscent of a campground fireplace—is surrounded by a small stone patio and a rustic stone bench. Plantings on one side of the patio help screen the fire from prevailing winds.

▼ THE MATERIALS used to build this freestanding fireplace and chimney match those of the patio flooring, surrounding stone walls, and pergola posts. The raised hearth offers a convenient place to sit and warm up by the fire.

► THIS HEARTH AND SEAT WALL are built with the same stone and at the same height to keep the look uniform and to define the space without blocking views. The area beneath this raised hearth has a clever storage space for firewood.

▲ PREFABRICATED OUTDOOR FIREPLACES—delivered by truck or trailer and easily installed—come in a wide range of styles, finishes, and sizes, making it easy to match the fireplace to your outdoor decor. This traditional brick version has gas-burning logs.

▼ THIS PLAIN, CONCRETE-BLOCK outdoor fireplace was faced with flagstone to achieve the warmth and beauty of a traditional, more costly, and labor-intensive stacked-stone fireplace. The stone provides a striking yet natural contrast to the wooden deck.

▲ A RAISED FIRE PIT can be constructed from stone, brick, tile, or stucco. This pit features a base of round cobbles capped with flagstone that match the stone used on the pergola posts, patio flooring, and outdoor kitchen.

Adding a Garden Structure

GARDEN STRUCTURES—whether arbors, pergolas, gazebos, or pavilions—make ideal settings for inviting outdoor rooms. Because most are designed as destinations, they serve as focal points in the landscape. Arbors and pergolas (extended arbors) are the simplest to construct because they have posts and an open framework overhead that beg to be draped in vines. The octagonal gazebo or larger, rectangular pavilion is also built with posts but has a solid roof overhead. Whether roofed or simply covered with vines, each structure offers a shady retreat for the backyard.

A structure as simple as a garden bench beneath an arbor or as elaborate as an outdoor kitchen, living room, and dining area incorporated into a generously sized pavilion creates a comfortable, inviting space. Sometimes, an arbor or a pergola is attached to a house—so it can provide shade for a patio, deck, or courtyard, as well as for the adjacent interior room. Although these structures are often made out of wood, they also come in other materials such as iron or copper or feature the addition of solid posts made out of brick, stacked stone, stucco, or concrete.

▲ A RAISED STRUCTURE built over a water feature has the feeling of a boardwalk or dock. This design brings the water closer to the sitting area. Also, by making this water seem to disappear beneath the structure, the stream appears to be larger than it is.

◄ A SIMPLE BENCH is transformed into a thronelike sitting area with the addition of a decorative arbor, brick flooring, and canopy of climbing roses. It protrudes slightly into the lawn, making it a place of importance in the landscape.

▲ THIS PAVILION is a commanding element in the landscape because it is positioned at the end of a path. The fence that frames the path is painted in the same colors as the pavilion.

▶ AN INTRICATELY DESIGNED ARBOR can be a reflection of special architectural details in a home. This Japanese-style arbor features openings with window boxes that have been planted in addition to curved details, which are echoed in the picnic table and benches.

▼ THIS PAVILION is built on a steep slope near a small waterfall and stream, creating an observation platform. It is constructed of redwood timbers with built-in seating and a copper roof.

THIS PERGOLA is built on a patio near a back door and functions like a porch because it provides a sheltered space next to the house. It can be covered with vines to increase shade, soften the wooden surfaces, and add a splash of color.

A RUSTIC STRUCTURE, like this gazebo, slips seamlessly into a woodland setting. The gazebo is constructed with rot-resistant black locust posts and rhododendron branch railings. The rhododendron branches will have a longer life span if they are treated with a sealer every other year.

GARDEN STRUCTURES like this pergola should be designed with both the house and landscape in mind. In most cases, posts and beams should be similar in size to those on the house. However, oversized materials are called for against an expansive backdrop like this lake.

▲ THIS PERGOLA is the centerpiece of the backyard. It serves as a gathering place and marks the intersection of several paths that pass between the columns and lead to ornamental and kitchen gardens, a play area, and the house.

▶ LIGHT COLORS in a landscape always catch the eye first; that is why this painted white arbor stands out in contrast to the surrounding greenery. The arbor is a dominant element in the yard, so special attention was given to the design of the columns and ornate top.

◀ AN OPEN GARDEN STRUCTURE, such as this gazebo, feels cozier when it is placed against a solid backdrop of plantings. If an outdoor structure is located in too open a space, it may feel exposed. If it is set against other structures, it may look too busy.

Positioning a Gazebo

A GAZEBO IS A SUBSTANTIAL STRUCTURE best suited to larger landscapes, and its positioning will affect how it is used. Placed close to the house or a pool, it will be used frequently for dining and gathering. Farther from the house, it serves as a getaway or destination for special occasions. Position a gazebo so it can be seen from indoors or from a special point in the yard—perhaps at the end of a winding path or as the only vertical element in a sweeping border. A gazebo placed high on a hillside will offer expansive views of the surrounding landscape.

◀ THE WATER'S EDGE is always a favorite gathering space. By building seating along the sides of this pergola, it still functions as a passageway and frames a view of the pond. The structure is also large enough to accommodate a table and chairs to use on special occasions.

BUILDING A PERGOLA against a tall stone, brick, or stucco retaining wall—especially one that forms a corner nook—creates a secluded and protected spot. The vines that are scrambling along the overhead beams enhance the pergola's sense of enclosure.

ENCLOSING AN ARBOR on one side forms a comfortable and protected spot for a bench. This arbor, located along the edge of a lawn, becomes a focal point in the yard and a place from which to view activities.

▶ A GAZEBO is often placed along the periphery of a property where it becomes a destination and focal point. Tucked away in the backyard, this gazebo looks out over the curving borders of a woodland garden filled with tulips and daffodils in early spring.

▼ THIS ARBOR is tucked into a border of mixed plantings, where it becomes an integral part of the garden. Colorful container plantings enclose the open sides of the arbor, while bougainvillea scrambles up the sides and over the top.

Striking Vines for Arbors and Pergolas

WHEN CHOOSING A VINE, think beyond the flower colors. Select a vine with handsome foliage, fragrant flowers, or fall berries. Make sure the mature vine suits the size and stability of the structure. Here are a few praiseworthy vines for an arbor or pergola:

- American wisteria (*Wisteria frutescens* 'Amethyst Falls')
- Bougainvillea (*Bougainvillea spp.*)
- Carolina jessamine (*Gelsemium sempervirens*)
- Clematis (*Clematis spp.*)
- Climbing hydrangea (*Hydrangea petiolaris*)
- Climbing roses (*Rosa spp.*)
- Fiveleaf akebia (*Akebia quintata*)
- Golden hops (*Humulus lupulus* 'Aurea')
- Grape (*Vitis spp.*)
- Jasmine (*Jasminum polyanthum*)
- Porcelain berry (*Ampelopsis brevipedunculata*)
- Trumpet creeper (*Campsis radicans*)
- Virginia creeper (*Parthenocissus quinquefolia*)

▲ SCREENING A GAZEBO can significantly increase its use and enjoyment while keeping out pesky insects. If electricity is available, adding a ceiling fan will keep the gnats away and cool things off on a muggy afternoon.

▲ CLIMBING ROSES that stretch from 12 ft. to 30 ft. in length make ideal choices for arbors and pergolas. Since roses are not true climbers, but instead grasp onto supports with hooks (thorns), give them direction by loosely tying them to posts or trellises.

▶ THE CONCRETE COLUMNS on this gazebo have a traditional appearance. Other materials such as wood, lightweight resin, metal, fiberglass, and cast stone are often used for arbor and pergola columns because they are durable and weather resistant. Overhead beams on most gazebos, such as this one, are built from pressure-treated or naturally rot-resistant lumber.

▼ THIS CONTEMPORARY STRUCTURE, with a central gathering area, two passageways, and a peaked roof, was specifically designed to support a large, rambling rose. Roses are this gardener's preference, but wisteria, trumpet vine, and other large vines would also emphasize the unique shape of this structure.

Creating a Casual Seating Area

IT'S EASIER TO ESTABLISH CASUAL SEATING AREAS throughout the landscape than it
is to plan a fully furnished outdoor room. Yet casual spaces can be just as
inviting and are adaptable to any landscape and budget. All that's needed are
a few comfortable chairs arranged on an open lawn, beneath the shade of an old
tree, in a clearing in the woods, or on a knoll overlooking a favorite view. Create
several seating areas—each with its own unique character—to enjoy at different
times of day. For a quiet escape, set a garden bench in a small clearing surrounded
by plants. For a comfortable place to watch the kids play, place a few lounge
chairs along the edge of the lawn. To stimulate conversation, gather a circle of
Adirondack chairs near a water feature. The more casual the seating area, the
more inviting it will be.

▼ A PROMONTORY in the residential
landscape is a prime outdoor seating
area because it often overlooks a
meadow, field, garden, pond, or hill.
A sunrise or sunset is more compelling
when viewed from a promontory.

▲ WHEN POSITIONED AT THE END of a path, a bench has drawing power. Not only does the path lead directly to it, but the bench also beckons to passersby to sit and relax. A small water feature makes this sitting area even more inviting.

◀ EVERYONE NEEDS a peaceful, secluded place to escape to from time to time. A quiet spot along a woodland path or adjacent to a pond or stream is the best spot for contemplation and reflection. Even a simple bench, such as this stone slab, invites a pause for a meditative moment.

▲ A SIMPLE, OCTAGONAL tree bench is easy to build and lasts for years. The homeowners set their tools here while working in the garden and occasionally, when they have a chance, sit under the tree to watch the birds.

▶ A FEW DRY-LAID FLAGSTONES edged by golden creeping Jenny and creeping thyme make this patio look like a natural part of the surrounding garden. When the thyme is stepped on, it releases a sweet fragrance.

◀ A COUPLE OF CHAIRS, an occasional table, and an umbrella create a casual seating area on a corner of this lawn. The furniture is sturdy enough so it won't blow over on windy days yet light enough to be moved when the lawn is mowed.

▶ THIS SMALL SEATING AREA is tucked into a corner of the garden. It measures just 5 ft. wide, but it is large enough for a café table and two chairs, creating a quiet spot to enjoy an afternoon cup of tea, write a letter, or take a short lunch break.

◀ A TREE WITH A BROAD canopy of leaves offers a shady seating area along the loosely defined edge of this backyard. The heavy, rustic-style table and benches blend in with their surroundings. Cushions make the seating more comfortable.

▶A SWING HANGING FROM A TREE, an arbor, or a porch will create a romantic seating area for two. Leave a few feet of unobstructed space in front of and behind the swing to allow for movement. For stability, a swing needs to be anchored by sturdy supports.

▼THE ADDITION OF A HAMMOCK in the backyard provides a spot to nap. It is also a fun piece of outdoor furniture that will occupy children for hours. String it between two trees or mount it on sturdy posts.

▲THE PERFECT SPOT for an afternoon nap, this outdoor bed also provides a colorful accent to the garden. A plastic, zippered mattress bag protects the mattress during an unexpected shower. Quick-drying fabrics designed for outdoor use will resist fading from prolonged sun exposure.

Council Rings with a Modern Twist

COUNCIL RINGS CONJURE UP MEMORIES—campers gathered in a circle around a campfire to sing songs, tell stories, and roast marshmallows. Although the origins of council rings are rooted in Viking and Native American traditions, noted 20th-century landscape architect Jens Jensen is credited with the modern version of the council ring. His signature design features circular seating walls made of native stone, often placed in woodland clearings.

A council ring is a magical gathering space in the landscape, especially on a secluded mountain property or in a rustic retreat. A simple council ring can be created with a circle of boulders or tree stumps. Or it can be as elaborate as an artfully crafted stone seating wall surrounding a flagstone patio with a fire pit. If a ring in the woods includes a fire pit, make sure the spot is cleared both overhead and around the edges to prevent the chance of spreading fires.

▲ COUNCIL RINGS of the early 20th century inspired the design of this contemporary outdoor meditation area in the woods. The area has a circular layout, a small water feature, and a stone seating wall that defines the space.

◄ NATURAL MATERIALS such as logs, large tree stumps, and slabs of stone can be converted into garden benches. This bench, crafted from a granite slab held up by two boulders, looks as if it has always been a part of the landscape.

Lighting the Outdoors

IF YOU ARE GOING TO UNWIND, COOK, AND ENTERTAIN OUTDOORS AFTER DARK, you'll need to see what you are doing. Fortunately, there are more practical and aesthetic options than the glare of a floodlight. Downlights placed high on walls, under eaves, or in trees illuminate seating, dining, and recreational areas, while path and step lights allow you to move about safely and with ease. Tabletop and task lights make it possible to see what's cooking in the outdoor kitchen.

Outdoor lighting is also used to create ambience. Uplights accent trees, while spotlights call attention to architectural elements or decorative objects in the landscape; both cast intriguing shadows on nearby walls. Tea lights, torches, and candles all help set a festive or romantic mood. By mixing and matching different types of lighting, you can achieve a dramatic light show or a subtle glow in the yard.

▲ OUTDOOR LIGHTING FIXTURES come in a wide range of styles to match almost any home decor. This Oriental-style lantern hangs from a low copper post. It lights paths and low plantings but stands on its own as a decorative element.

◀ THIS GRANITE LIGHT FIXTURE illuminates a stepping-stone path through a backyard. The sturdy stone post surrounds the bulbs and wiring. The frosted-glass windows produce a soft glow that extends to the ground.

▲ ACCENT LIGHTING calls attention to form and pattern in a landscape. This unusual structure is a recirculating water feature with water flowing from a broad shower head. A single light shines into the streaming water and calls attention to the pattern of the tower's construction.

▼LIGHTS THAT IMPROVE safety are important elements in a backyard. These path lights highlight steps along a woodland path. The light-colored edging on the steps makes it easier to see the grade changes in low light.

▲ LAYERS OF LIGHTING transform this deck into a dramatic space. Uplights mounted on the deck and in the trees highlight playful branching patterns. Downlights mounted on the house wash over the deck to provide overall lighting, and candles add a romantic ambience for dining.

◄ STYLISH LAMPS have been introduced for outdoor use. This floor lamp and companion table lamp feature woven-resin, wicker-style frames, water- and fade-resistant fabric shades, and solid bases that stay stable and upright on windy days.

Understanding Low-Voltage Lighting

LOW-VOLTAGE LIGHTING runs at only 12 volts, making it safe to install yourself. To illuminate a path or small patio, a kit with several fixtures, cable, and a transformer (which plugs into a GFIC-rated outlet to convert household current) may suit your needs. For larger areas or complex lighting schemes, buy fixtures a la carte and choose a transformer that can handle slightly more wattage than your fixtures require (add up the total watts) for potential expansion. Once the cable and fixtures have been laid out, test the lights and make desired adjustments. Finally, bury the cable in a 5-in. trench for protection.

▲ CORDLESS TABLE LAMPS are convenient to use in areas where there are no outlets. This lamp is waterproof, features a dimmer control, and runs for up to eight hours on a single battery charge.

▶ MULTIPLE LIGHTS create exciting outdoor rooms. This space features underwater lights to emphasize the fountain so it can be viewed from both indoors and out. Downlights illuminate the patio and plantings; uplights accent the trees. A wall sconce near the back door was added for safety.

◀ A SPOTLIGHT has a narrower, more precise beam than a floodlight and is an appropriate choice of lighting when accenting sculpture, plants, and architectural elements. To vary the effects a spotlight makes, mount it on the ground (such as the light at the corner of the arbor), to one side, or from above a structure.

▶ ILLUMINATING BOTH A SWIMMING POOL and the surrounding deck improves safety. Underwater spotlights, step lights, and fiber-optic lighting along the rim create a soft glow in this pool. Step lights, ceiling lights, and wall sconces mounted near the deck ensure safe footing around the pool.

Adding Ambience with Accent Lighting

ACCENT LIGHTING ENHANCES THE MOOD OUTDOORS while highlighting special elements in the landscape. Strategically positioned uplights, downlights, and spotlights can highlight the unique branching structure of a tree, cast interesting shadows on nearby walls or paving, emphasize the texture of a stone wall, call attention to the movement of plants in the slightest of breezes, and showcase a garden sculpture or water feature. Candles placed on a table or in a chandelier or torches placed around a pool will create a romantic atmosphere. Strands of tiny lights strung in trees evoke a festive mood. Mix and match several different types of lighting to make the nighttime landscape interesting.

▲ INDOOR LIGHTS can cast a surprising amount of soft light on adjacent outdoor spaces. To enhance the interior lighting that spills out into this backyard, accent lights focused on water features, architectural structures, and plants all work together to bring the landscape to life.

▲ A SPOTLIGHT aimed at this Japanese maple casts a striking shadow on the nearby wall. To achieve a similar effect with a piece of outdoor sculpture, direct a spotlight at the object from one or both sides. Excess light also bounces softly back onto the surrounding patio.

◄ LOW-PROFILE, FLUSH-MOUNTED LIGHTS can be attached to deck railings and fitted with 20-watt bulbs to create a soft glow over the deck's surface. They are also a practical choice for illuminating steps.

12

Backyard Fun and Games

For the ultimate playground, look no farther than your own backyard. Lawns can be used for everything from a game of tag or touch football to badminton or croquet. Patios are the perfect spot for hopscotch, jump rope, and board games. Special areas can also be designated for swimming, play structures, or court games such as basketball or shuffleboard.

Include something for each member of the family in your plan. Start with play spaces for young children that are visible from indoors and out. Older children appreciate gathering places farther away from parental view, with ample room to run, hide, and explore. Teens often prefer group activities such as volleyball or soccer. And don't forget spaces the entire family can enjoy—perhaps a horseshoe pitch, badminton court, or swimming pool.

The backyard can evolve as your family grows, too. Consider the kinds of spaces that may better suit your family five to ten years from now and which ones you may outgrow. A lawn may be the perfect spot for a swimming pool, a playhouse could be converted into a potting shed, or a swing set might be replaced by a tetherball pole. Plan ahead, so changes will have minimal impact on the rest of your yard.

◄ AS CHILDREN GROW OLDER, they tend to prefer more complex play equipment and structures that are located farther from the house. This play structure, nestled on a distant patch of lawn surrounded by trees and shrubbery, is small but includes a lookout, slide, climbing wall, and sandbox.

Kids' Play Spaces

A PLAYHOUSE, TREE HOUSE, OR PLAY STRUCTURE does more than just entertain children. It helps them to develop physically and socially and encourages them to think imaginatively. Design structures that will allow children to swing, climb, balance, slide, dream, and sit quietly in the backyard. Whether play structures are purchased from a store, built from a plan, or designed from scratch, they should be sturdy and free from splinters and rough edges.

Before installing equipment, select a site where young children can be easily observed at all times, and cover the playground with 8 in. to 12 in. of bark, sand, or pea gravel to create a safe, cushioned surface. Older children will appreciate a playhouse or tree house that affords greater privacy. A patch of lawn where young children can learn to walk and older children can play games is an important element of any backyard play space.

▼ A SMALL STONE PATIO was constructed near this play area as a convenient spot to relax while keeping an eye on youngsters. A dense evergreen hedge hugs the patio, creating a cozy seating area and screening the playground equipment from the street.

◄ THIS STURDY CEDAR PLAY STRUCTURE is just the right size for preschoolers. There are opportunities to climb and swing but never very high. The structure includes three swings, a rope and ladder for climbing, and a playhouse with an upper lookout (complete with telescope).

► CREATE SOFT LANDING SURFACES beneath and around play structures with 8 in. to 12 in. of bark mulch, washed pea gravel, or play sand. The sand in this play area offers a beach-like setting perfect for building sandcastles or playing with toy trucks.

Sandbox Options

BUILDING A SANDBOX for young children is an easy afternoon do-it-yourself project. You can construct a 5-ft.-square, bottomless box with rot-resistant lumber (avoid timbers treated with creosote) or interlocking pavers and fill it with play sand. Another option is to design something more naturalistic—such as a sandpit bordered by smooth-surfaced, sitting-sized boulders or timber rounds—that blends into a woodland or garden setting. A sandbox can also be recessed into a brick or flagstone patio. Simply remove a section of pavers, dig out some of the soil, and replace it with sand.

Regardless of style, start with a gravel base for drainage. Add a sheet of landscape fabric to prevent earthworms from making their way up into the sand. Fill the box or area with 10 in. to 12 in. of play sand. (Unlike builders' sand, which will stain clothes, play sand has been filtered and cleaned.) Add a seat around the edge if the walls are not wide enough to sit on comfortably. And finish the project with a hinged, folding cover cut from marine-grade plywood or Plexiglas that will keep falling leaves and small animals out of the play space.

EASY SANDBOX DESIGNS

Wood frame

Interlocking pavers

Timber-round edge

Boulder edge

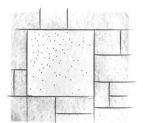
Recessed into patio

▼A SANDBOX AT LEAST 4 FT. SQUARE provides room for more than one child to play. This brightly colored sandbox extends from the garden wall. A broad ledge provides seating, and a hinged cover can be lowered when the sandbox is not in use.

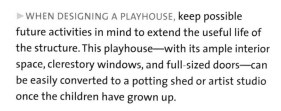

▶ WHEN DESIGNING A PLAYHOUSE, keep possible future activities in mind to extend the useful life of the structure. This playhouse—with its ample interior space, clerestory windows, and full-sized doors—can be easily converted to a potting shed or artist studio once the children have grown up.

▲ THIS PAVED PATH circles the backyard, providing a smooth riding surface for tricycles and scooters. It surrounds a game lawn and leads to a play structure, a pint-sized picnic table, and a children's vegetable garden.

▶ THIS BACKYARD FEATURES a game court and brightly painted raised beds where children can plant and tend easy-to-grow vegetables such as radishes, lettuce, and corn. Both the game court and garden can be easily observed from indoors.

STORE-BOUGHT PLAY STRUCTURES come in modular units with a wide range of add-on features that can be changed as kids grow. This structure includes swings, ladders, monkey bars, a slide, a tree house, and a picnic table.

SWING SEATS come in several styles: molded safety seats for toddlers, soft rubber seats for older children, and tire swings, which can be hung either vertically or horizontally. The seats hang on chains for easy adjustment as children grow.

Playing It Safe

CHILDREN PUSH PLAY STRUCTURES to the limit. They'll swing as high as possible, climb on top of structures, and pack as many friends as they can into a fort or tree house. To keep structures safe, make sure they are built with solid materials, secure them with nuts and bolts, anchor them to the ground, and check them every few months. Kids also tend to run without looking ahead, so place structures away from steps, uneven surfaces, and tripping hazards. Position a swing so there's plenty of room to run around it without getting clunked in the head when the equipment is in use.

▲ BUILDING A PLAY STRUCTURE for older children near a shallow pond provides double the fun by attracting frogs, turtles, and butterflies. Kids access this tree house by climbing over a bridge and exit by sliding over the water.

◀ THIS FREESTANDING TREE HOUSE is built for adventure with a connecting bridge and tower. The hutlike design, combined with the surrounding plantings, makes the climbing structure feel as if it's in the middle of the jungle. The greenery also offers a bit of privacy for tree-house dwellers.

▲ THIS TREE HOUSE is a favorite neighborhood gathering spot for kids, and it's large enough to accommodate several friends at once. It offers open and private spaces and seating areas, plus bridges and ladders for climbing.

◀ A PLAY STRUCTURE MADE FROM WOOD blends into most residential landscapes. This structure has weathered to a natural gray that matches the siding on the house and complements the woodland setting.

▲ TWO SWINGS are almost always better than one. It's more fun to swing with a companion, and a second seat will eliminate any squabbles over whose turn it is to swing. A flowering vine covers this swing frame, helping it blend into the landscape.

Tree-House Innovation

A TREE HOUSE IS FOR CHILDREN and those who are children at heart. Most are built around a tree trunk or between several sturdy trees, but they may also be built out over sturdy branches, on stilts, or as freestanding structures on stilts. Use strong ropes to lash platforms to mature trees, and use screws to secure them to young trees (ropes will constrict a tree's growth over time). Better yet, build a self-supporting structure on posts around a tree to avoid potential tree damage.

Choose sturdy boards for floors and thinner boards for walls and roofs to keep the overall weight down. Build a broad deck or narrow balcony for lounging in the treetops, and add windows, skylights, or a greenhouse-style roof to brighten interior spaces. Both doors and hatches are appropriate in tree houses. Ladders, ropes, firehouse poles, slides, bridges, and climbing walls offer fun ways to come and go from a treetop retreat.

TREE-HOUSE DESIGNS

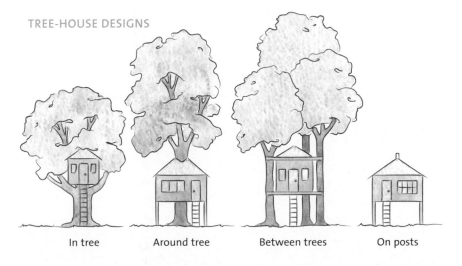

In tree   Around tree   Between trees   On posts

▲ ALTHOUGH MOST TREE HOUSES are built in trees, this one sits atop a sturdy tree trunk that is just the right height for a viewing platform. The tree house is high enough to include a tire swing that hangs from the corner of the structure.

▶ KIDS LOVE PLAYING INSIDE TEEPEES. This one was built with bamboo poles and twine and planted with runner beans that will quickly form a shady, green cover. Hoop tunnels can be formed from willow stems and covered with fast-growing vines to create another fun play structure.

Backyard Bike Paths

Paved bike paths or dirt tracks are an easy addition to many backyards—especially those a quarter acre or more in size. Paths can follow the curve of a lawn, wind through the woods, circle the periphery, and even extend through the side and front yards. A path that is 3½ ft. to 4 ft. wide is ideal for bicycles, tricycles, scooters, and wagons. For safe and easy pedaling, paths should feature a smooth, compact surface such as packed granite fines or concrete, and they should make a complete loop or circle for continuous riding.

▲ LEAVE PLENTY OF SPACE—at least 5 ft. from an extended seat—in front of and behind swings, and avoid placing swings too close to pathways. This will give other children and adults room to safely pass by.

◀ PLAY STRUCTURES constructed from wood, painted natural colors, and surrounded with mulch can be placed unobtrusively in the landscape. This one is only a few feet high for safety purposes. Its low profile also helps it sit discreetly in a clearing among trees.

Recreational Spaces

BACKYARDS OF EVERY SIZE ARE SUITED TO RECREATIONAL ACTIVITIES and offer a convenient place to exercise, improve athletic skills, or simply have fun with friends. Sprawling suburban lawns are superbly suited for impromptu games of touch football, softball, and kick the can. Even in the tiniest of backyards, there's usually room to tuck in a tetherball set, putting green, or plunge pool.

Beyond physical space requirements, consider the characteristics and location of recreational areas. Games should be played on level ground that is free from rocks and roots for safety and enjoyment. They should also be played away from furniture, fireplaces, grills, and fragile plantings. Areas placed closest to the house will get more use, but activities that result in stray balls should be played away from windows. Consider designating areas along your property's periphery for paved, gravel, or grassy courts that may be used for basketball, bocce ball, horseshoes, or shuffleboard.

▲ A REGULATION-PLAY BOCCE COURT measures 13 ft. by 91 ft. but can be easily shortened for smaller spaces like this backyard. This court features a grassy playing surface, but compacted granite fines would work just as well.

◀ TENNIS COURTS, because of their size and tall, surrounding fences, can easily become obtrusive elements in the landscape. Evergreen hedges screen this tennis court, helping it blend in with the environment. A seating area beneath a hemlock tree offers a place to watch the game.

▶ HORSESHOES IS ONE OF THE FEW recreational activities suited to shade—as pools need lots of sun, balls need open space overhead, and running activities need a grassy surface. This horseshoe pitch was tucked into a woodland area defined by boulders and plantings.

◀ THIS OVERSIZED CHESS SET adds an element of surprise to the landscape and provides hours of playing fun. The 8-ft.-square board is a plastic mesh mat that snaps apart for portability, and the chess pieces are made from molded plastic.

The Home-Court Advantage

A HOME GAME COURT **doesn't have to be regulation size. It can be slightly altered to fit available** space in the backyard. General space guidelines for activities are:

Basketball: 30 ft. by 30 ft.

Tennis: 60 ft. by 120 ft.

Badminton: 27 ft. by 54 ft.

Volleyball: 42 ft. by 72 ft.

Croquet: 40 ft. by 50 ft.

Horseshoes: 50 ft. by 6 ft.

Shuffleboard: 52 ft. by 10 ft.

Boule: 40 ft. by 14 ft.

Bocce ball: 13 ft. by 76 ft.

Tetherball: 20 ft. in diameter

TETHERBALL COURT

Turf grass, dirt, or compacted gravel fines for surfaces

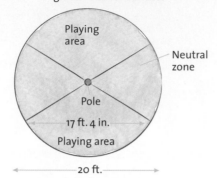

Playing area

Neutral zone

Pole

17 ft. 4 in.

Playing area

20 ft.

CROQUET COURT

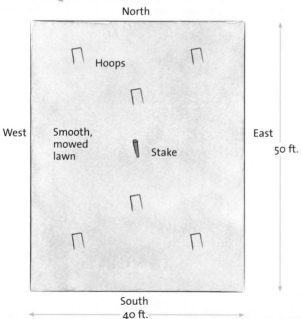

North

Hoops

West

Smooth, mowed lawn

Stake

East

50 ft.

South

40 ft.

BOCCE COURT

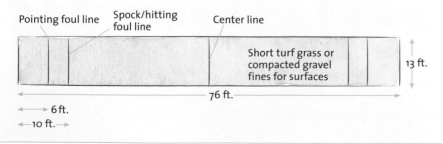

Pointing foul line

Spock/hitting foul line

Center line

Short turf grass or compacted gravel fines for surfaces

13 ft.

76 ft.

6 ft.

10 ft.

▲ CROQUET IS A FUN GAME for players of all ages, and it's an entertaining activity for casual outdoor parties. The game requires a smooth, level lawn, a croquet set, and a few enthusiastic players.

▲ A TENNIS COURT NEEDS a tall fence to contain loose balls. Since it occupies so much space, this tennis court was set along the periphery of the yard. A wildflower garden fills the surrounding yard.

▶ A HOME PUTTING GREEN requires little space and can be adapted to any lot shape. It features an easily maintained, synthetic-turf surface that can be installed by homeowners. The perimeter of this green is put to good use with a stone path, seating area, and garden.

▲ A SMOOTH, LEVEL LAWN cleared of rocks and roots is the most adaptable surface for backyard recreation. For rough-and-tumble activities, choose a tough turf grass such as perennial ryegrass, tall fescue, or St. Augustine grass.

Defining a Play Area

A LAWN LOOKS ITS BEST with crisp, well-defined edges and a distinct shape—either geometric or broadly curving. Edging a lawn with brick or cut-stone cobbles keeps it neat and makes it easy to mow, but for safety reasons, they may not be a good choice for a rough-and-tumble play area. Instead, dig a shallow trench around the play area and fill it with mulch for a safe, attractive, and low-cost alternative. Select a grass that can withstand plenty of wear and tear. Mixtures of perennial ryegrass and tall fescues are the best choices for cool climates, while cultivars of St. Augustine grass are more suitable for warm climates.

▲ FOR HORSESHOES, sink two iron stakes in the ground 40 ft. apart. The stakes should extend approximately 15 in. aboveground, leaning slightly toward the opposite end of the court. Surround the stakes with shallow clay-, dirt-, or sand-filled pits edged with 2-ft. by 6-ft. timbers.

Pools and Spas

SWIMMING IS A FAVORITE AMERICAN PASTIME and a great way to get in shape. Of course, swimming is only half the fun of a backyard pool. A swimming pool is an ideal outdoor gathering space, especially when accompanied by a spacious pool deck, the shelter of an arbor or pool house, the convenience of an outdoor kitchen, and the warmth and ambience of an outdoor hearth.

Pools have changed dramatically in recent years. More shapes, sizes, styles, and special features are available than ever before—from pint-sized plunge pools to long lap pools to naturalistic pools anchored by boulders. Waterfalls, vanishing edges, and fiber-optic lighting add drama to a pool-side setting, while wading areas, underwater benches, and spas make pools a great place to relax. Even without the extra features, there's nothing like a shimmering pool of water in the backyard for cooling off on a blistering hot summer day.

▶ A LAP POOL is a favorite choice for exercise. To establish a comfortable swimming pace and make flip turns, the pool should be at least 40 ft. long, 8 ft. wide, and 4 ft. deep. Wider pools, such as this one, easily accommodate other recreational activities.

▼DESIGNATE BOTH SUNNY AND SHADY sitting areas around the pool. This sunny pool deck is great for drying off after a swim and for soaking up the sun on mild mornings. The shady canopy offers relief from afternoon heat.

▲A POOL CAN BE DESIGNED in any shape, size, or style imaginable. This naturalistic pool was designed to look more like a pond and features a sandy beach at one end. Boulders, streams, and waterfalls are other common additions to naturalistic pools.

▶THIS SMALL, SQUARE POOL is designed to blend into the garden. It is highlighted by a formal wall fountain on one end, is cleverly integrated into a tiered patio, and is surrounded by planters and raised beds.

▲THE STONE SURROUNDING THIS POOL is echoed in the edging around garden beds, establishing a strong sense of unity throughout the landscape. Lawn and plantings come all the way up to the pool's edge, creating a naturalistic setting.

▶STEPS MADE WITH A NONSLIP SURFACE provide safe and easy access to a pool. Well-designed, spacious steps can also provide a place to sit along the water's edge. These steps accentuate the curves of the pool and deck.

Pools for Tight Spaces

EVEN IN A MODEST-SIZED BACKYARD, there's almost always room for a small pool or spa. If exercise is your goal, consider building an 8-ft.-wide by 40-ft.-long lap pool on a narrow lot or installing a small swim spa with adjustable jets that allow you to swim in place. If you simply want to cool off, a plunge pool is a space-saving alternative to the traditional pool; it occupies as little as 36 sq. ft. and requires only a minimal amount of water. For a warm soak, a hot tub or spa can be tucked into a cozy nook near the house. Choose from in-ground, in-deck, and aboveground models.

▲ THIS TEARDROP-SHAPED SWIM SPA takes up a minimal amount of space, yet it has numerous benefits. It is large enough for a refreshing dip on a hot day, and the swim jets can be turned on for an excellent aerobic workout.

▼ A LARGE EXPANSE OF PAVING around a pool can be made more attractive with the addition of planting pockets. Fill pockets with plants that don't drop leaves, flowers, or berries during swimming season, and include some small evergreen plants for year-round interest.

▲ THIS RAISED POOL adds dimension and visual interest to a backyard patio. The wide edge on the pool offers a place to sit. The walls are covered in iridescent tiles, which contribute both color and pattern to the landscape.

◄ IF YOU PLAN TO ENTERTAIN outdoors frequently, include a spacious pool deck that will handle large gatherings and multiple activities, such as sunning, cooking, and dining. This deck is divided by the planting beds and waterfall into multiple gathering spaces.

▲ THE DESIGN OF A POOLSIDE STRUCTURE is as important as the design of the pool. A well-thought out structure can create a feeling of enclosure, establish a sense of style, add a vertical element to a horizontal landscape, and provide necessary shade around the pool.

◀ A DARK INTERIOR POOL FINISH suits a naturalistic pool that is designed to look like a pond. Dark blue (shown here) and dark gray look natural and create excellent reflections yet still allow good visibility to the pool's bottom.

Popular Water Features

NEW SWIMMING POOL DESIGNS often include one or more water features. Falling water is the most popular, and it comes in many forms, from naturalistic streams and waterfalls to spouts, flumes, cascades, and sheet waterfalls. Another dramatic form of falling water is the vanishing edge, in which one or more sides of a pool seem to disappear as the water spills over its edge into a basin below. Fountains are also popular and come in a variety of spray patterns. Powerful underwater jets can transform a shallow seating area or underwater bench in your pool into a relaxing, spa-like gathering space.

▲ TO EXTEND THE SWIMMING SEASON, place a pool in full sun. The sun will warm the water earlier in spring and help keep temperatures comfortable into fall. This pool receives sun all day long, yet swimmers can escape to a nearby porch for relief from summer heat.

▲ THE BRIGHTLY COLORED MOSAIC TILES and contemporary styling of this water feature make it the focal point of a Florida backyard. The soothing sound that emanates from the sheet waterfall helps create a relaxing atmosphere around the pool.

▲ A LARGE, PROTRUDING BOULDER looks at home in this naturalistic pool and provides a gathering area for swimmers. A swim-up bar with seating is another way for swimmers to congregate while keeping cool.

◄ THE LARGE "JUMP ROCK" on the side of this pool replaces a more traditional diving board and helps tie the pool to the surrounding boulder-strewn garden. A small stone patio is positioned on the hillside for enjoying both the pool and garden.

► THE RAISED SPA in this pool includes several water features. It has an infinity edge with water spilling into the pool below, a fountain that can be turned on when the spa is not in use, and four water spouts along the exterior wall of the spa.

▼ TO CREATE A WATERFALL, position a pool near a natural hillside, create a mound from soil excavated during pool construction, or build a raised spa with a dropped edge (like this one) several feet above the pool level.

► NIGHTTIME IS A ROMANTIC TIME around a pool, but good visibility is still essential. This pool features underwater lights and deck lights to illuminate the area for safety. The white pool steps are edged with small blue tiles to improve visibility during night and daytime.

Vanishing-Edge Pools

ONE OF THE MOST DRAMATIC ELEMENTS in modern swimming pool design is the infinity, negative, or vanishing edge in which a rim of the pool is dropped to allow water to flow over it. The water falls into a catch basin and recirculates into the pool. When viewed from above, the water appears to vanish over the pool's edge. The drama of a vanishing edge calls attention to the views beyond the pool—whether rolling hills, woodland groves, or colorful gardens. When the dropped edge overlooks a lake or an ocean, the bodies of water appear to merge.

Viewed from below, that same dropped edge transforms the still surface of the pool into a cascading or tumbling water feature. Both the distance the water falls and the surface over which it falls affect its rhythmic sound. The wall may be straight, sloped, or staggered and can be finished with smooth masonry, colorful tile, or small pebbles to complement the surrounding architecture.

▲ THIS VANISHING-EDGE POOL is positioned so that it can be enjoyed as a formal, cascading water feature from the house and lawn. From the pool deck and garden above, it appears as a quiet reflecting pool.

◀ A PORTABLE SPA can be placed on a patio, deck, or porch. This spa, discreetly tucked into a corner of the patio, is surrounded by greenery and is accessible from both the upper and lower portions of the terrace.

▼ A SPA PLACED CLOSE TO THE HOUSE, like this one near the back door, will be used more frequently throughout the year. The closer the spa is to the house, the shorter the distance to and from the water on chilly days.

◄ THE WATERLINE OF A SPA AND POOL (often referred to as the "scum line") can be difficult to keep clean. Adding ceramic tile around the edge of the pool makes cleaning easier. Here, it also adds a decorative element to the pool.

▼ THIS SPA IS BUILT on the ground, so there was no need to provide added support for the weight of the unit. Its position below the deck railing provides seclusion and integrates it into the deck.

▲ THE BROAD LEDGE around this raised spa provides a place to set down towels and drinks while relaxing in the water. Since the spa is about 15 in. above the ground, the ledge is just the right height for additional poolside seating.

POOL HOUSES

▶THIS COLORFUL YURT creates a festive poolside atmosphere. Yurts, which range in size from 12 ft. to 30 ft. in diameter, are constructed from stronger materials than those used for tents but utilize fewer materials than would a pool house. They can house a spa or be furnished like a pool house.

▼THIS BACKYARD AREA is set up to extend the time spent outdoors. For sun-lovers, the area by the pool is unobstructed. As the hot afternoon sun beats down, though, the shaded area offers relief. An outdoor heater takes the chill off once the sun goes down.

◄ THE FOUR DOORS on this pool house fold back on hinges to allow sun and breezes into the structure. When a sudden shower rolls in, homeowners can seek shelter in the pool house, leaving the doors partially open for fresh air.

▼ WHEN A POOL IS LOCATED a distance away from the main house, a pool house is a convenient place for swimmers to dry off or change clothes before heading back to the house. A pool house can include a bathroom, kitchen, comfortable gathering spaces, and storage for pool equipment and towels.

Pool Storage Ideas

A SWIMMING POOL COMES WITH ASSORTED GEAR that needs to be stored nearby. The pool pump and filter should be placed within 100 ft. of the pool for operating efficiency—but away from your house and outdoor gathering areas to minimize noise. They may be enclosed in a ventilated shed or closet, placed behind an outbuilding, or screened from view with fences and plantings.

Store recreational gear in a nearby closet or shed. If you have a pool house, stash supplies in chests, drawers, or beneath skirted tables. Stack colorful dinnerware on open wall shelves, and fill decorative baskets, crates, and hampers with fresh towels.

OUTDOOR SHOWERS

▼ AN OUTDOOR SHOWER is a refreshing way to rinse off after a swim. Teak weathers well outdoors, making it a handsome and natural choice for an outdoor shower floor and surrounds. Space floor planks so that water can flow into a drainage system beneath the deck.

▶ AN OUTDOOR SHOWER can be located against the wall of a pool house, tool shed, or other outdoor structure. This one features a partial wall for bathing privacy, while a dense thicket of shrubs screens the entire building from neighboring properties.

▼ PLACE A SMALL BENCH, or shelves and hooks, near an outdoor shower to hold wet and dry towels, a change of clothes, and other bathing amenities. A bath mat is also essential for drying wet feet.

▲ THE OUTDOOR SHOWER and steel tub on this porch were designed for the pleasure of bathing and relaxing outdoors. They were built adjacent to the master bathroom for easy access to the home's plumbing.

▶ THIS OUTDOOR SHOWER was designed and painted to match the home's contemporary architecture. An angled wall provides screening while allowing the bather to enjoy the scenic view. The nearby railing is a handy place to toss towels.

Specialty Gardens

OR SOME HOMEOWNERS, GARDENING IS A PASSION as important as entertaining or playing games. In fact, gardens are often the focal point of a backyard—as distinctive and dominant as any deck, patio, or swimming pool.

Gardens may be integrated in the landscape in any number of ways— as foundation plantings around the house and outbuildings, as mixed borders against fences or along paths, as island beds floating in a sea of lawn, as edible gardens just beyond the kitchen door, in containers on patios and decks, or as dense plantings that offer screening and privacy. These may be small, enclosed gardens or more expansive gardens that wrap around the periphery of a backyard, and they may be placed in sun or shade.

Landscaping elements such as fences, arbors, and paths give a garden structure, while decorative accents—from birdhouses and benches to outdoor sculpture and water features—help give it character.

▼ A VINE-DRAPED ARBOR frames the entry into a backyard garden of raised beds filled with a variety of vegetables, herbs, and edible flowers. Beyond the garden are several small henhouses where the homeowner gathers eggs each day.

◄ THIS SMALL AND ORDERLY GARDEN is the focal point of the backyard. The white fence with its unique birdhouse posts defines the garden, which is filled with cosmos, artemisia, thyme, basil, and nasturtiums and traversed on a stepping-stone path.

NATURALLY ROT-RESISTANT locust branches make sturdy garden structures and furniture. This rustic arbor features a hanging swing, the perfect spot for a gardener to take a break from the day's gardening chores.

THIS HEDGED CORRIDOR features a clipped boxwood parterre and a rustic pergola draped with climbing roses and other flowering vines. It serves as a formal, ornamental passageway amid a series of backyard garden rooms.

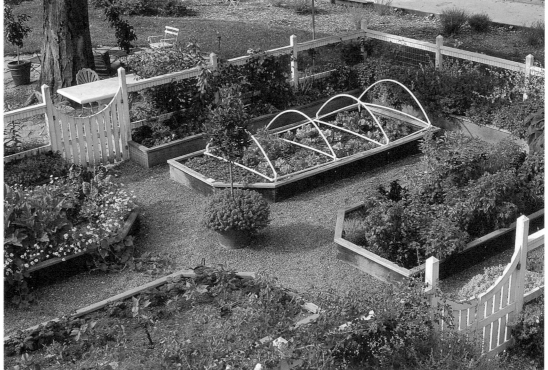

▲ A KITCHEN GARDEN suits even the most formal landscape. This one is designed like a traditional French potager, with separate beds devoted to different herbs and salad greens. The beds with trellises support climbing and rambling vegetables such as squash, beans, peppers, and tomatoes.

► RAISED BEDS provide better drainage and are easier to access than in-ground gardens. The ledges of a bed can offer seating as well. Though beds are used most often to grow vegetables and herbs, they can also accommodate cutting gardens for flowers.

Edible Gardens

NOTHING BEATS THE FLAVOR of home-grown vegetables or freshly picked herbs. A compact kitchen garden filled with colorful herbs, vegetables, and edible flowers can be conveniently located near the back door—where it can be quickly and easily reached while planning and cooking meals. Raised planting beds—which are built from stone, brick, boards, or timbers and filled with improved soil to increase plant production—are attractive and can be more easily tended than in-ground beds. Sprawling vegetables, such as squash, tomatoes, and beans, can be grown in cages or trained up trellises and garden teepees to maximize space. The growing season can be extended by using protective plant covers such as glass cloches (bell jars), plastic and synthetic-cloth row covers, or portable cold frames.

▲ ALTHOUGH IT'S A SMALL PLOT, this charming country garden is framed by a handcrafted stick fence and filled with old-fashioned flowers, vegetables, and herbs. A rustic garden shed was built nearby as a convenient place for tools.

▲ A KITCHEN GARDEN can be much more than a functional space. With decorative features, such as these homemade concrete pavers imbedded with bits of ceramic tile, it can add style and personality to a backyard.

13

Backyard Buildings

A backyard building can expand your living space outdoors, get the office out of the house, or store your overflow of tools, toys, and pool supplies. Small buildings—from potting sheds and firewood shelters to artists' studios and woodworking shops—come in all shapes, sizes, and styles. Some are strictly utilitarian; others are comfortably furnished, with access to utilities, making them destinations for everyday activities. Buildings can be purchased as ready-to-assemble kits, created from a set of plans, or designed and built from scratch.

An outbuilding can be the focal point of the backyard, thoughtfully designed to complement a home's architecture and positioned to catch the eye. Likewise, a backyard structure can be painted a dark color or screened with plantings so that it recedes into the landscape.

When selecting a location for a backyard structure, consider its accessibility, exposure to the sun, and proximity to utilities. A firewood shelter should be built close to the house, a potting shed should be near the garden, and a retreat can be placed along the property's periphery. Adding a path from the house makes a backyard building easier to reach, especially during inclement weather. To accommodate wheelbarrows, carts, and mowers, make paths at least 4 ft. wide.

◄ BACKYARD RETREATS are often designed around a specific theme. This gardener's retreat is a casual, light-filled space decorated with rustic finds from antique stores and flea markets. The sunny window provides an ideal spot for growing herbs and getting seedlings off to a good start.

Studios and Retreats

KIDS LOVE FORTS, PLAYHOUSES, AND TREE HOUSES. Adults are similarly drawn to backyard retreats—cozy outbuildings for painting, writing, reading a good book, or relaxing with a cup of coffee. These are personal spaces designed for escaping the stresses of day-to-day living.

Some homeowners transform existing garages, playhouses, or sheds into inviting and functional spaces. For others, designing and building a retreat from scratch can be just as much fun as spending time in it later. Even the most rustic backyard retreat can be enjoyed during warmer seasons when there's good weather and natural light. Equipped with some of the luxuries of home—such as comfortable furnishings, a half-bath, and utilities—it can serve as a guesthouse, home office, or relaxing year-round refuge.

▼THIS WOOD-AND-STONE DINING PAVILION is the hub of the backyard and a destination for many gatherings. The canvas canopy provides shade and cover from light rain, while the fireplace adds warmth on cool evenings. Storage for firewood is built conveniently into adjacent walls.

▼ WHEN AN OUTBUILDING PLAYS a dominant role in the backyard, details provide personality. This colonial-style building features a cantilevered roof with cedar-shake shingles, board shutters with wrought-iron shutter dogs, and a brick foundation. It doubles as a potting shed and children's playhouse.

▲ A LANDSCAPE ARCHITECT converted his one-car garage into a home office and studio that anchors one end of the small backyard courtyard. A pergola runs along the front of the studio, providing a shady outdoor seating area next to a water feature.

WHAT THIS WRITER'S STUDIO lacks in size and amenities it more than makes up for in style with natural timbers, weathered siding, and a stone stoop. Quiet places without distractions such as telephones and radios are exactly what many writers desire in a backyard studio.

THIS BUILT-IN DESK FEATURES a long work surface and handy shelving for supplies. The old-fashioned typewriter can be put aside to make room for a laptop computer when it's time for serious writing. A view to the water and personal mementos provide inspiration.

WINDOWS ARE ESSENTIAL in backyard retreats that lack electricity. These windows provide ample natural light and fresh, salt-air breezes for the writer. The small stained-glass window tucked into one corner of the far wall adds personality to the space.

Before You Build

BEFORE YOU BREAK GROUND FOR A BACKYARD OUTBUILDING, **make sure your plans comply with local building codes, ordinances, and deed restrictions. If your project requires grading or running power, gas, telephone, or water lines to the outbuilding, you will probably need building permits and inspections. Find out if there are issues regarding public rights-of-way, property setbacks, structure height standards, or environmental sensitivities (such as wetland areas). Local officials, architects, landscape architects, builders, and engineering professionals familiar with local building codes can help you obtain appropriate permits and approvals.**

▼ OUTDOOR RETREATS are great places to use materials creatively. This rustic, Finnish-style sauna is housed in a log-cabin structure with a roof shingled with thin flagstone. The carved door and door frame have been brightly painted to contrast with the natural building materials.

▲ THIS GARDEN HOUSE FEATURES a distinctive Japanese-style design. Paneled-glass sliding doors and skylights along the roof's ridge fill the structure with natural light. The doors also allow the space to be opened up to the outdoors.

▶ INSIDE THE GARDEN HOUSE, storage and work spaces have been cleverly screened behind folding doors, allowing the homeowners to close off supplies, a large-basin sink, and flower-arranging works-in-progress when hosting other activities.

▲THIS ARTIST'S STUDIO in Maine is located in a historic neighborhood, so it was carefully designed to match the local architecture. Although it looks like a structure original to the site, it was recently constructed.

▲SLATE FROM RECYCLED SCHOOL BLACKBOARDS was purchased at a salvage yard and used to cover this sauna. A bridge with hand-cut and bark-stripped timber railings provides easy passage over rough terrain to this woodland retreat.

◄TUCKED INTO A SWEEPING BORDER that surrounds the lawn, this brightly painted shed serves as the primary focus of the garden. It has been landscaped much like a house, surrounded by foundation plantings and accented with a window box.

►A PORTABLE SPA is transformed into a secluded, relaxing retreat when wood posts, bamboo fencing, and lush container plantings surround it. Architectural accents and pots with an Asian flair give the setting a distinct character.

▲ GET CREATIVE with storage in a backyard retreat. Unusual pieces of furniture, bins, crates, baskets, and buckets can be filled with tools, supplies, and collectible items. The space above the rafters can be converted into storage for less-frequently-used or hard-to-store items.

▲ A FLAGSTONE PATH leads to this garden cottage, making it the highlight of the backyard. In addition to serving as a garden feature, this small building includes an outdoor seating area. An abundance of windows allows natural light to flood the interior.

Designing a Studio

FOR SOME ARTISTS, WRITERS, AND CRAFTSPEOPLE, the backyard studio is their primary place of work. For others, it's a seasonal working space that offers a welcome change of pace.

While some people want their surroundings filled with personal effects, others prefer a spare, uncluttered space without distractions. To create a bright studio filled with natural light, install large windows and skylights. Add built-in or freestanding tables, desks, easels, or workbenches to create generous work surfaces. Use baskets, crates, and wall ledges to store small tools and materials, while reserving furniture and cabinetry for larger objects. Most important, include a comfortable seating area where you can indulge in a little dreaming.

◀ THIS RETREAT, built above a stone patio, blends a Japanese teahouse concept with Craftsman–style architecture. The structure features two large, sliding barn doors, a small sitting room with a fireplace, and an upstairs loft with a mattress.

Greenhouses and Potting Sheds

ANYONE WHO SPENDS TIME GARDENING OR TENDING A LAWN appreciates a dedicated work space—whether it's used for sharpening tools, starting seedlings, or hanging the water hose. Although greenhouses traditionally are for growing plants and potting sheds are for potting up seedlings and storing tools, the lines between the two are often blurred. It's not unusual to find a potting bench in a greenhouse or a sunny, plant-filled windowsill in a potting shed.

Just as often, these two spaces are connected or built close together—and never far from the garden. Greenhouses are bright, humid spaces used for protecting tender plants over winter, propagating new plants, and growing a wider range of plants than possible in a garden. They should be positioned for maximum sun exposure and away from trees to avoid falling branches. Both greenhouses and potting sheds benefit from access to water, whether provided by a spigot or a sink.

◄ BY USING SMALL WINDOWS in this shed, interior wall space is freed up for shelving, potting benches, and hanging tools, while supplemental lighting improves visibility on overcast days and during evenings. For buildings without electricity, rechargeable, battery-powered lamps or lanterns are affordable lighting options.

▼ ALTHOUGH THE HERBS AND FLOWERS in this garden are at their peak of perfection, the extensive use of structures—such as the potting shed, fence, raised beds, and arbor—will make the garden attractive even in the off-season.

▲ TOOLS, PLANT STAKES, TWINE, and fertilizers are just steps away when a potting shed is conveniently located in the middle of a garden. A nearby location means that containers can be easily potted up and set in place, and flowers can be carried into the shed to be immediately hung in the rafters to dry.

Choosing a Greenhouse

SIZE IS THE MOST IMPORTANT FACTOR to consider when choosing a greenhouse. Freestanding greenhouses are available as small as 6 ft. by 8 ft., but most gardeners find that a structure measuring at least 8 ft. by 10 ft. better accommodates plants and people. It's easier to grow into a larger greenhouse than it is to expand a greenhouse when you outgrow your space.

There are numerous styles of greenhouses. Freestanding rectangular or hexagonal greenhouses, lean-to–style greenhouses that attach to a house or garage, and portable greenhouses with just enough room for a few small plants are several choices. Roofs may be peaked, rounded, or domed. Doors may swing or slide open. And windows or roofs may open to improve ventilation.

Greenhouse frames come in a variety of materials. Painted wood is beautiful, but rot-resistant cedar and anodized or enamel-coated aluminum is much easier to maintain. Although most greenhouses still have glass panels, new UV-treated polycarbonate panels are more energy efficient and less susceptible to breakage. Pea gravel is a practical choice for greenhouse flooring. It won't become slick when wet and allows excess water to soak into the soil.

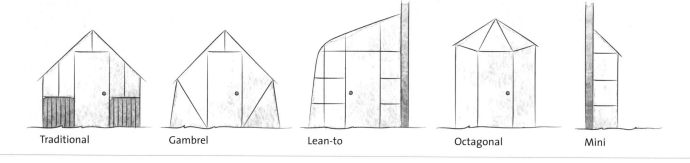

Traditional   Gambrel   Lean-to   Octagonal   Mini

►THIS GARDEN HOUSE FEATURES a shingled roof, but the many windows on each wall make it a bright place for over-wintering tender plants and growing houseplants during the summer. Inside, there's room to sit and enjoy the view and make notes in a garden journal.

A GREENHOUSE CAN BE BOTH decorative and functional. This Victorian-style greenhouse is the highlight of the garden, positioned at a bend in the path where you can't help but notice it as you move into the yard.

▼ INSIDE THE GREENHOUSE, dry-laid brick floors allow excess water to soak into the ground, while a long counter affords plenty of space for starting seeds and potting up containers. Window shelves are lined with plants, while potting soil and supplies are stashed under the counter.

Warming a Greenhouse

GREENHOUSE HEATING REQUIREMENTS depend on what you are growing and where the structure is located. Cooler greenhouses are ideal for protecting frost-tender plants and growing cool-season vegetables. Warmer greenhouses are required for starting seedlings or growing tropical plants. Greenhouses in northern regions need a more reliable heat source than those in southern climates. Start by placing a greenhouse in an open, sunny area, with the longest side running east to west to maximize sun exposure. Several large barrels, filled with water and painted black, will absorb heat during the day and radiate that heat at night. Electric, oil, and gas heaters will provide additional warmth and more precise control over temperatures.

◂ A LATH HOUSE is a shaded structure used for hardening off tender seedlings or growing shade-loving plants like orchids and ferns. A lath house also provides a shaded holding area for nursery plants awaiting a permanent home in the garden.

▴ A GREENHOUSE is an ideal location for growing plants from seed. The benches, or tables, that hold flats and pots should drain easily after the plants are watered. They should also be sturdy enough to support pots filled with wet soil.

◂ A TRANSLUCENT ROOF allows enough light into this potting shed so that it doubles as an unheated greenhouse, sheltering tender plants from winter's cool weather. The top half of the barn-style door can be opened to improve ventilation.

A GREENHOUSE can be built against the south-facing wall of a house for convenient access, as well as for added protection against extreme temperature swings. The house wall shields the greenhouse from harsh northern winds and adds an insulating layer along one side.

Making Compost Convenient

COMPOST BINS AREN'T USUALLY THE MOST ATTRACTIVE GARDEN STRUCTURES, but to encourage their use, they must be conveniently located near the kitchen. So instead of looking at a pile of decaying leaves and vegetable peels, build an attractive wood or brick bin with a hinged lid that keeps the mess at bay and blends in with your home's architecture. As an alternative, screen less attractive but functional compost bins with an evergreen hedge, fence, or vine-draped trellis. A bin that holds approximately 1 cu. yd. (3 ft. wide by 3 ft. long by 3 ft. high) of materials is the most efficient at converting waste into rich compost.

WELL-WATERED PLANTS DRIP, so it's best to have a permeable greenhouse floor. A 2-in. to 4-in. layer of mulch (shown here), pea gravel, or crushed gravel will allow the water to drain and keep the floor from becoming slippery or muddy.

▶LANDSCAPING HELPS PLAY DOWN the prominence of this large working greenhouse by providing a buffer of dense foliage with trees and shrubs. Including a few evergreens—such as junipers, cypress, laurels, or rhododendrons— increases year-round screening.

▼ALTHOUGH POTTING AND GROWING ACTIVITIES can take place under the same roof, moving the potting bench to a separate location frees up additional space for plants in a greenhouse. This nearby potting shed also provides ample storage for tools, potting soils, and other gardening gear.

▲THIS BACKYARD SHED IS DIVIDED into two sections. The front section, with a single door and windows, offers ample space for a workbench, as well as for storing tools and gear. The rear section, accessed through double doors, is for storing large power equipment.

Potting Shed Alternatives

I F YOU DON'T HAVE SPACE FOR A FREESTANDING SHED for potting up seedlings, stashing gardening tools, or storing pots in winter, simply improvise with what you do have. A garage or basement may have enough space for a table and shelves. A potting bench and hanging wall rack for tools can be tucked under the eaves of a house, garage, or other outbuilding. In a pinch, use an oversized wheelbarrow as a basin for mixing and storing custom potting soils. It can also serve as a portable workstation filled with gardening gear and rolled from one area to the next.

▼ THIS POTTING SHED FEATURES enclosed storage for tools, wheelbarrows, and power equipment. A potting bench and staging area are located beneath an attached shelter, part of which is covered in lattice. The lattice offers partial shade for acclimating plants started indoors or in a greenhouse.

▶ WITH ITS FRESH COAT of white paint, green roof shingles, and black shutters, this strategically placed potting shed is alluring. It's tucked into the woodland edge, just beyond a border, where it's a retreat as well as a place to take a break from gardening.

Storage Buildings

At the end of the day, there's rarely a shortage of toys, tools, bikes, hoses, ladders, or pool supplies to put away. Storage buildings can help keep things under control. A freestanding shed can be built from scratch or delivered to your property already assembled. Some are made from wood or metal; others are built from brick or stone. Choose materials that suit your budget and complement your home's architectural style.

An unused playhouse can often be adapted for reuse. If there's no room in your backyard for a freestanding storage shed, consider attaching a lean-to–style closet to your house or garage. There are other inexpensive options, too—mount a hanging rack for essential garden tools on an exterior wall near the back door, encase deck benches with lift-top seats, or enclose the space beneath your deck or porch with lattice to create convenient walk-in storage.

▲ INSTEAD OF A SHED, these homeowners built a row of waist-high, painted-wood storage cabinets along an exterior wall of their garage. The tops of the cabinets, which are protected by roof shingles, double as a holding area for recently purchased plants.

◄ A SMALL SECONDARY SHED is a good idea on larger properties with multiple or outlying gardens. This homeowner keeps an extra set of essential gardening tools in a refurbished outhouse to reduce the number of trips made to the main storage shed.

▲FIREWOOD STORAGE should be conveniently located near the door with the easiest access to the fireplace. Well-seasoned firewood is rarely infested with bugs, but to be safe, don't store wood against your house for longer than a few weeks.

◄WHEN SHEDS ARE DESIGNED to complement your house, they can be placed prominently in the landscape. This one features a hipped roofline and paneled double doors. The wide path both calls attention to the shed and improves access for mowers and wheelbarrows.

▼ SPACE IS AT A PREMIUM in this small, in-town backyard. The owner designed an attractive peg rack for an exterior wall where garden tools can be hung and has arranged the tools so they add a sculptural accent to the garden.

◄ IN THIS CLEVER DECK DESIGN, colorful box planters of varying heights filled with foliage plants help camouflage a cubbyhole used for storing a bicycle and toys. A shallow planting bed with a built-in drainage system sits atop the storage unit.

► THE OVERSIZED BARN-STYLE DOORS on this shed open wide, making it easy to move riding mowers, tractors, boats, trailers, and even outdoor furniture in and out of storage. An adjacent area, accessed through a standard doorway, provides space for a workbench and storage shelves.

Stretching Your Storage Space

NEARLY EVERY STORAGE SHED, GARAGE, POOL HOUSE, POTTING SHED, AND BACKYARD STUDIO can benefit from increased storage capacity. Here are some ideas for organizing your storage areas to better accommodate toys, recreational gear, garden tools, power equipment, and pool-cleaning supplies.

- Place items in stackable bins, and then label the bins.
- Group items by size, and adjust shelf height to eliminate wasted space.
- Hang under-shelf baskets on fixed shelves to make the most of in-between spaces.
- Divide drawer space with adjustable inserts so that contents can be organized.
- Build cabinets or shelves from the floor all the way to the ceiling.
- Lay boards across rafters to create out-of-the-way shelving.
- Install a grid system on walls to support hanging items.
- Build a fold-down worktable into wall shelving, and line the back with pegboard for hanging small tools.
- Install a pocket door that slides into the wall rather than taking up floor and wall space.
- Mount bicycles on wall racks, and hang canoes from the ceiling using ropes and pulleys.
- Store large power equipment in the center of a room so the walls are still accessible.

▲ STORAGE SHEDS such as this one are often built on a concrete slab or piers raised slightly above ground level, so a ramp is necessary for rolling large equipment and wheelbarrows in and out of storage.

MODULAR SHELVING

Peg rack with hooks for scissors, pliers, pruning shears, string, and wire

Built-in work counter

Small, upright boxes for hand tools, plant labels, pens, gadgets, and screws

Broad shelf for lightweight but bulky buckets and watering cans

Under-counter storage for trash can or recyling bins

Shelf for fertilizers, books, pots, tool boxes, or pool supplies

Bins for bulbs, balls, or toys

Cubed drawers for gloves, seed packs, small tools, and gadgets

Upright storage or hooks for rakes, shovels, axes, and hoes

▶ 'AMERICAN PILLAR' ROSES CLAMBER over a historic Nantucket shed and picket fence. Since roses aren't true climbers, they need the additional support of a trellis when grown against a building. The trellis also improves plant health by increasing air circulation around foliage.

▶ STORAGE SHEDS can be dressed up by training espaliered trees, climbing roses, or other vines along wire supports or trellises. On wooden structures, avoid vines that cling with aerial rootlets, such as ivy or climbing hydrangea, because they can damage the surface or work their way under shingles.

▼ A NARROW CEDAR SHED HOUSES the swimming-pool pump, filter, and cleaning supplies. It features two large doors that slide easily out of the way—a smart, space-saving feature. The shed screens the equipment from view and helps buffer noise generated by the pump.

◀ THIS EXTERIOR CLOSET provides an easily accessible place to stash heavy clay pots for the winter. Exterior closets may be part of the original design of a storage shed, potting shed, garage, or studio or later added as a lean-to structure.

▼ TRASH CANS CAN BE discreetly enclosed in a simple but attractive storage bin. This one is painted green so that it blends in with the landscape. Front-opening doors provide easy access when it's time to take the cans to the curb.

◀ FIREWOOD SHOULD BE STACKED under dry cover and seasoned for a year before use. This cedar-shingled firewood shelter features a large covered storage area, along with an uncovered, screened work area where firewood can be split.

Acknowledgments

FRONT YARD IDEA BOOK

First and foremost, I want to thank and acknowledge my editor, photographer, and friend, Lee Anne White. Without her continuous inspiration and dedication, this book would have simply remained a concept. Her way with a camera amazes me; I am always impressed by her ability to capture the essence of a garden. I can't thank Lee Anne enough for her friendship, craftsmanship, and generous assistance through all aspects of the project.

My longtime friend Anna Kondolf generously shared her expertise on lighting design. Anna contributed essential information and

landscapes to shoot for the chapter on lighting. Her artful lighting illuminates many fine homes and businesses in the San Francisco Bay area.

While working on this book, I have met so many kind and inspiring people. I want to thank all the homeowners who shared their homes and their stories and allowed us to photograph their gardens. I am very grateful to the many designers who helped us find front yards for inclusion in the book.

My aunt Sydney Eddison is a woman who always either has dirt on her hands or her hands on a keyboard. A dedicated and talented gardener and writer who has shown me what one can create and accomplish in a lifetime, she has both inspired and encouraged me along the way.

I would also like to thank the many wonderful individuals who have supported me through the years, inspired me in the ways of creativity, and encouraged me to follow my dreams: my high school art teacher Jack Bledsoe; my dear friends Susan Corfman, Barbara Guarino, and Jayme Martinez; my brother Russ Webber; my family in Yorkshire, England; Bev Thorne, his sons, and my colleagues at the design studio; and many other friends too numerous to mention by name. I'd like to acknowledge the many designers, past and present, whose work has become my library. And last, but not least, I want to thank my clients for their warm encouragement while I was working on this book and for allowing me to use their land as a canvas for learning.

—Jeni Webber

BACKYARD IDEA BOOK

Writing a book is often a solitary task. And often, it does begin to feel that way. But pulling together an idea book is a wonderfully collaborative experience, and I have many to thank for their creativity, advice, support, and encouragement.

Most importantly, I'd like to acknowledge the many photographers who contributed images; the landscape architects, architects, landscape designers, interior designers, and garden designers who created these spaces; and the homeowners who have so graciously shared their backyards with us. They are listed individually in the credits for this book.

On a more personal note, there are those who consented to interviews, answered questions, helped arrange photo shoots, shared plans of their projects, or contributed to my education as a designer. Their thoughts, ideas, and advice are woven throughout this book. To Barbara Allen, Betty Ajay, Barbara Blossom Ashmun, Jeff Bale, Margaret de Haas van Dorsser, Michelle Derviss, Tracy DiSabato-Aust, Kevin Doyle, Sydney Eddison, David Ellis, Brooks Garcia, Keith Geller, Erica Glasener, Nancy Goodwin, John Harper, Gary Keim, Ann Lovejoy, Anna Kondolf, Brad McGill, David Bennett McMullin, Richard McPherson, Keeyla Meadows, Carrie Nimmer, Carole Ottesen, Paula Refi, Doug Ruhren, Warren Simmonds, Andrew Schulman, David Schwartz, Isis Spinola-Schwartz, Michael Thilgen, and David Thorne, I offer my deepest gratitude. To landscape architect Jeni Webber, who has been so generous with her knowledge and experience and is never more than a phone call away, I am especially grateful.

Several organizations were particularly helpful in providing information regarding trends, safety issues, construction, and new products. Many thanks to the Hearth, Patio & Barbecue Association, the National Spa & Pool Institute, Master Pool Builders Association, Laneventure, Frontgate, *Fine Gardening,* and *Fine Homebuilding.*

A special note of appreciation goes to the editors, art directors, production staff, and marketing group at The Taunton Press who helped make this book possible—especially managing editor Carolyn Mandarano, editor Marilyn Zelinsky-Syarto, and editorial assistants Robyn Doyon-Aitken and Jenny Peters. You have all been a pleasure to work with.

—Lee Anne White

Resources

Associations

The American Institute of
Architects
1735 New York Avenue, NW
Washington, DC 20006
202-626-7300
www.aia.org

American Society of Landscape
Architects
636 Eye Street, NW
Washington, DC 20001
202-898-2444
www.asla.org

Association of Professional
Landscape Designers
1924 North Second Street
Harrisburg, PA 17102
717-238-9780
www.apld.org

International Play Equipment
Manufacturers Association
1924 North Second Street
Harrisburg, PA 17102
888-944-7362
www.ipema.org

Master Pools Guild
9601 Gayton Road, Suite 101
Richmond, VA 23233
800-392-3044
www.masterpoolsguild.com

National Association of
Home Builders
1201 15th Street, NW
Washington, DC 20005
800-368-5242
www.nahb.org

National Spa & Pool Institute
2111 Eisenhower Avenue
Alexandria, VA 22314
703-838-0083
www.nspi.org

Manufacturers & Suppliers

Charley's Greenhouse & Garden
17979 State Route 536
Mount Vernon, WA 98273
800-322-4707
www.charleysgreenhouse.com
(greenhouses and gardening
supplies)

Childlife
55 Whitney Street
Holliston, MA 01746
508-429-4639
www.childlife.com
(backyard play structures)

Frontgate
800-626-6488
www.frontgate.com
(outdoor living and home
furnishings)

Laneventure
P. O. Box 849
Conover, NC 28613
800-235-3558
www.laneventure.com
(outdoor furniture, kitchens,
and fireplaces)

Pacific Yurts Inc.
77456 Highway 99 South
Cottage Grove, OR 97424
541-942-9435
www.yurts.com
(yurts)

Putting Greens Direct
866-743-4653
www.puttinggreensdirect.com
(residential putting greens)

Smith & Hawken
800-940-1170
www.smithandhawken.com
(patio and garden furnishings)

Warmly Yours
1400 E. Lake Cook Road Ste. 140
Buffalo Grove, IL 60089
800-875-5285
www.warmlyyours.com
(radiant floor heating)

WaterSports Products
619-271-2750
www.watersportsproducts.com
(outdoor games including oversized chess sets)

Additional Reading

Architecture in the Garden by
James Van Sweden. Random
House, 2002.

*Fine Gardening Design Guides:
Landscaping Your Home.* The
Taunton Press, Inc., 2001.

John Brookes Garden Masterclass
by John Brookes. Dorling
Kindersley, 2002.

*Taylor's Master Guide to Land-
scaping* by Rita Buchanan.
Houghton Mifflin, 2000.

The Essential Garden Book
by Terence Conran and Dan
Pearson. Crown Publishers,
Inc., 1998.

The Landscape Makeover Book
by Sara Jane von Trapp. The
Taunton Press, Inc., 2000.

The Pool Idea Book by Lee Anne
White. The Taunton Press, Inc.,
2004.

Credits

p. 109 (bottom): Wayland, MA, residence; photo © Lee Anne White.

pp. 110, 132 (top): Selina & Bill Dwight residence, Palo Alto, CA; designed by Selina Dwight and Jeni Webber; photos © Lee Anne White.

pp. 112 (bottom), 146, 180: Karen King residence, Atlanta; designed by Jeremey Smearman, Planters Nursery; photos © Lee Anne White.

p. 114: Gary & Sue Homsey residence, Nichols Hills, OK; designed by Bill Renner; photo © Lee Anne White.

pp. 116–117: Dave & Anne Hall residence, Seattle; photos pp. 116 and 117 (top) designed by Lisa Ravenholt; photos © Lee Anne White.

p. 118: Boston residence; designed by Kevin Doyle; photo © Lee Anne White.

pp. 119, 138: Oklahoma City residence; designed by Bill Renner; photos © Lee Anne White.

pp. 123 (top), 147: Rosemary Kent residence, Palo Alto, CA; designed by Lawrence Booth; photos © Lee Anne White.

p. 127: Alan & Lee Anne White residence, Cumming, GA; photo © Lee Anne White.

pp. 130, 142: Ronald Cobb residence, Atlanta; photos © Lee Anne White.

pp. 131, 154–55: David & Patricia Ketchum residence, Palo Alto, CA; designed by Jeni Webber; photos © Lee Anne White.

p. 132 (bottom): Philip & Kate Zoercher residence, Gainesville, GA; photo © Lee Anne White.

pp. 134-135: Betty Ajay residence, Bethel, CT; photos © Lee Anne White.

p. 140: Sudbury, MA, residence; designed by Maria von Brincken; photo © Lee Anne White.

p. 149: Michael & Susanne Snyder residence, Atlanta; photos © Lee Anne White.

p. 151 (right): Marc & Rowena Singer residence, Oakland, CA; designed by Jeni Webber; photo © Lee Anne White.

p. 160 (top): Perry & Brooke Thacker residence, Issaquah, WA; photo © Lee Anne White.

p. 164: Andrew Schulman residence, Seattle; photo © Lee Anne White.

p. 165: Brooks Garcia residence, Atlanta; photo © Lee Anne White.

p. 170: Atlanta Botanical Garden; photo © Lee Anne White.

pp. 173, 185 (bottom left): San Francisco residence; landscape design by Betsy Everdell; lighting design by Anna Kondolf; photos © Lee Anne White.

p. 174: Gail Giffen residence, Lafayette, CA; designed by Michael Thilgen, Four Dimensions; photos © Lee Anne White.

p. 175: Elizabeth Greenberg residence, San Rafael, CA; designed by Warren Simmonds; photo © Lee Anne White.

pp. 176, 178, 182, 183: San Francisco residence; designed by Sonny Garcia; photos © Saxon Holt.

p. 179: Clari & Bob Davis residence, Denver; photo © Lee Anne White.

p. 181: Pete & Mavin Howley, Mill Valley, CA; landscape design by Suzman Design Associates; lighting design by Anna Kondolf; photo © Lee Anne White.

p. 188: Photo: © Brian Vanden Brink, Photographer 2004.

p. 189: Photo: © Lee Anne White, Design: Hermann Weiss, landscape architect.

p. 190-91: (top) Photo: © www.david-duncanlivingston.com; (bottom) Photo: © Lee Anne White, Design: Louise Poer.

p. 192: (top) Photo: © Allan Mandell, Design: Jeff Glander; (bottom) Photo: © Tim Street-Porter, Design: Arthur Erickson, architect, and Barbara Barry, interior designer.

p. 193: (top) Photo: © www.daviddun-canlivingston.com; (bottom) Photo: © Allan Mandell, Design: Linda Ernst.

p. 194: (top) Photo: © www.daviddun-canlivingston.com; (bottom) Photo: © 2004 Samu Studios, Inc.

p. 195: Photo: © Alan & Linda Detrick, Design: Cording Landscape Design.

p. 196: (top) Photo: © Saxon Holt/Photo Botanic, Design: Diana Stratton; (bottom) Photo: © Lee Anne White, Design: Sonny Garcia.

p. 197: Photo: Steve Silk © The Taunton Press, Inc., Design: Betty Ravenholt.

p. 198: (top) Photo: Charles Bickford © The Taunton Press, Inc., Design: David Sellers, Sellers and Company Architects; (bottom) Photo: © Tria Giovan.

p. 199: (top) Photo: Roe Osborn © The Taunton Press, Inc., Design: David D. Quillin, architect; (bottom) Photo: © Lee Anne White, Design: John Harper, Urban Earth.

p. 200: Photo: © www.daviddun-livingston.com.

p. 201: Photo: © Lee Anne White.

p. 202: (bottom) Photo: © Brian Vanden Brink, Photographer 2004, Design: Stephen Blatt, architect.

p. 203 (top) Photo: © Brian Vanden Brink, Photographer 2004, Design: Bullock & Company; (right) Photo: Charles Bickford © The Taunton Press, Inc., Design: Paul MacNeely, architect; (bottom) Photo: © Brian Vanden Brink, Photographer 2004, Design: Rob Whitten, architect.

p. 204: (top) Photo: © 2004 Samu Studios, Inc., Design: Bruce Nagle, AIA; (bottom) Photo: © Brian Vanden Brink, Photographer 2004, Design: Rob Whitten, architect.

p. 205: (left) Photo: © Tim Street-Porter; (top right) Photo: © 2004 Samu Studios, Inc., Design: Luciana Samu; (bottom right) Photo: © Brian Vanden Brink, Photographer 2004, Design: Roc Caivano, architect.

p. 206: (top) Kevin Ireton © The Taunton Press, Inc., Design: Cass Calder Smith, architect; (bottom) Photo: © 2004 Samu Studios, Inc., Design: Boccard/ Suddell.

p. 207: Photos: © Brian Vanden Brink, Photographer 2004, Design: (left) Weather End Estate Furniture, (right bottom) Scholz & Barclay, architects.

p. 208: (left) Photo: © Lee Anne White, Design: Paula Refi, landscape designer; (top right) Photo: © 2004 Samu Studios, Inc., Design: Brian Shore, AIA; (bottom right) Photo: © Brian Vanden Brink, Photographer 2004, Design: John Gillespie, architect.

p. 209: (top) Photo: © Brian Vanden Brink, Photographer 2004; (bottom) Photo: © www.davidduncanlivingston.com.

p. 210: (top) Photo: Roe Osborn © The Taunton Press, Inc., Design: Laura Craft; (bottom) Photo: © www.david-duncanlivingston.com.

p. 211: (left) Photo: © www.daviddun-canlivingston.com; (right) Photo: © Tim Street-Porter.

p. 212: (top) Photo and Design: courtesy of Richard McPherson, Landscape Architect, San Francisco; (bottom) Photo: Charles Bickford © The Taunton Press, Inc., Design: Adam Turner, Dovetail, Inc.

p. 213: Photo: Steve Silk © The Taunton Press, Inc.

p. 214: (left) Photo: © Brian Vanden Brink, Photographer 2004, Design: John Silverio; (right) Photo: © Brian Vanden Brink, Photographer 2004, Design: Weather End Estate Furniture.

p.215: Photos: © Brian Vanden Brink, Photographer 2004, Design: Rob Whitten, architect.

p.216 (top) Photo: © Brian Vanden Brink, Photographer 2004, Design: John Silverio; (bottom) Photo: © SaxonHolt/ Photo Botanic.

p. 217: (top) Photo: © 2004 Samu Studios, Inc.; (bottom) Photo: © Lee Anne White, Design: Warren Simmonds, landscape architect.

p. 218: (top) Photo: © judywhite/ GardenPhotos.com, Design: Nigel Boardman, Stephen Gelly & Jennifer Harkins; (bottom) Photo: © www.david-duncan livingston. com.

p. 219: Photo: © 2004 Samu Studios, Inc., Design: Sherill Canet Design.

p. 220: (top) Photo: © www.daviddun-canlivingston.com; (bottom) Photo: © Eric Roth.

p. 221: (top) Photo: © www.carolynbates.com, Design: Milford Cushman, Cushman & Beckstrom, Inc.; (bottom left) Photo: © Tria Giovan; (bottom right) Photo: © www.davidduncanliv-ing-ston.com.

p. 222: (left) Photo: © Brian Vanden Brink, Photographer 2004, Design: Elliott, Elliott, Norelius, architects; (right) Photo: © Brian Vanden Brink, Photographer 2004, Design: Sam Van Dam, architect.

p.223: Photo: © Brian Vanden Brink, Photographer 2004, Design: John Morris, architect.

p. 225: (top left) Photo: © Brian Vanden Brink, Photographer 2004, Design: Mark Hutker & Associates; (top right) Photo: © Tim Street-Porter, Design: Speigelman Interior Design; (bottom) Photo: © Lee Anne White.

p. 226: (top) Photo: © www.daviddun-can-livingston.com; (bottom) Photo: © Brian Vanden Brink, Photographer 2004, Design: Lo Yi Chan.

p. 227: (top left) Photo: © Brian Vanden Brink, Photographer 2004, Design: Centerbrook Architects; (top right) Photo: © Anne Gummerson Photography; (bottom left) Photo: © Brian Vanden Brink, Photographer 2004, Design: Weather End Estate Furniture; (bottom right) Photo: © Allan Mandell, Design: Lucy Hardiman.

p. 228: (left) Photo: © Allan Mandell, Design: Jeffrey Bale, landscape architect; (top right) Photo: © www.david-duncanlivingston. com; (bottom right) Photo: © Lee Anne White, Design: Hermann Weiss, landscape architect.

p. 229: Photo: © Tria Giovan.

p. 230: (top) Photo: © Lee Anne White; (bottom) Photo: © www.davidduncan-livingston.com.

p. 231: (top) Photo: © Lee Anne White, Design: Warren Simmonds, landscape architect; (bottom) Photo: © Lee Anne White, Design: Richard McPherson, Landscape Architect, San Francisco.

p.232: (top) Photo: © Lee Anne White; (bottom) Photo: © www.davidduncan-livingston.com.

p.233: (top) www.davidduncanliv-ingston.com, Design: David Yakish, landscape architect; (bottom) Photo: © Lee Anne White.

p. 234: (top left) www.davidduncanliv-ing-ston.com; (top right) Photo: © Alan & Linda Detrick, Design: Cording Land-scape Design; (bottom left) Photo: © Alan & Linda Detrick; (bottom right) Photo: © Lee Anne White.

p. 235: Photo: © Alan & Linda Detrick, Design: Dean Riddle.

p. 236: (top) Photo and Design courtesy of Jeni Webber, landscape architect; (bottom) Photo: © Alan & Linda Detrick.

p. 237: (top) Photo: © www.carolyn-bates. com, Design: Birgit Deeds; (right top) Photo: © www.carolynbates. com, Design:Chris Dunn; (right bottom) Photo: © Saxon Holt/ Photo Botanic, Design: Cynthia Woodward.

p. 238: (left) Photo: © Lee Anne White; (right) Photo: © judywhite/Garden-Photos.com, Design: Guy Farthing.

p. 239: (top) Photo courtesy of Sals-bury-Schweyer, Inc.; (bottom) Photo: © Lee Anne White.

p. 240: (top) Photo: © Lee Anne White, Design: Warren Simmonds, landscape architect; (bottom) Photo: © Lee Anne White, Design: Hermann Weiss, land-scape architect.

p. 241: (top left) Photo: © Lee Anne White,Design: Dan Cleveland; (top right) Photo: © Lee Anne White, Design: Warren Simmonds, landscape architect; (bottom) Photo: © www.carolynbates. com, Design: Catherine Clemens, Clemens and Associates.

p. 242: (top left) Photo: © Brian Vanden Brink, Photographer 2004, Design: Horiuchi & Solien, landscape architects; (bottom left) Photo: ©www.david-duncanlivingston.com; (right) Photo courtesy of Laneventure 2003.

p. 243 (top) Photo: © www.daviddun-canlivingston.com; (bottom) Photo: © Allan Mandell, Design: Pamela Burton.

p. 244: (top) Photo: © Lee Anne White, Design: Jeni Webber, landscape archi-tect; (bottom) Photo: © Tria Giovan.

p. 245: Photo: © Dency Kane.

p. 246: Photo: © Lee Anne White.

p. 247: Photo: © Saxon Holt/Photo Botanic.

p.248: (left) Photo: © Tim Street-Porter, Design: Speigelman Interior Design; (right) Photo: Charles Miller

© The Taunton Press, Inc., Design: Jon Stoumen, architect.

p.249: (left) Photo: © Allan Mandell, Design: Sonny Garcia; (right) Photo: © Tim Street-Porter, Design Tichenor and Thorp, landscape architects.

p. 250: (top left) Photo: © Tria Giovan; (top right) Photo: © Lee Anne White; (bottom) Photo: © Anne Gummerson Photography.

p. 251: Photo: © Lee Anne White, Design: Sonny Garcia.

p. 252: Photo: © 2004 Samu Studios, Inc., Design: Andy Levtovsky.

p. 253: (top) Photo: © www.daviddun-canlivingston.com; (bottom) Photo courtesy Richard McPherson, Land-scape Architect, San Francisco.

p. 254: Photo courtesy Frontgate catalog.

p. 255: (top left) Photo: © Tim Street-Porter; (bottom left) Photo: © Eric Roth, Design: Bill Harris Architecture; (right) Photo: © www.carolynbates.com, Design: Catherine Clemens and Elizabeth Robechek, landscape archi-tects, Clemens & Associates, Inc.

p. 256: (top left) Photo: © Jerry Pavia Photography, Inc.;(bottom left) Photo: © Lee Anne White, Landscape design: Beverley Ross/Live in Color, Pool design: Leisure Living Pools; (right) Photo: © Robert Stein, Design: Barry Sugerman, architect.

p. 257: (top) Photo: © Robert Stein, Design: Barry Sugerman, architect; (bottom) Photo: © Lee Anne White.

p. 258: (left) Photo: © Deidra Walpole Photography, Design: Ruby Begonia Fine Gardens; (top right) Photo: © Deidra Walpole Photography, Design: Mark David Levine Design; (bottom right) Photo: © Deidra Wal-pole Photography, Design: Mayita Dinos Garden Design.

p. 259: Photo courtesy of Laneventure 2003.

p. 260: (top) Photo: © 2004 Samu Studios, Inc.; (bottom) Photo: © Tim Street-Porter, Design: Tichenor and Thorp, landscape architects.

p. 261: (top) Photo: © Tim Street-Porter; (bottom) Photo: © Tim Street-Porter.

p. 262: (top left) Photo: © Tim Street-Porter, Design: Dunas Landscape Architecture; (bottom left) Photo: © www.davidduncanlivingston.com; (right) Photo: © www.davidduncanliv-ingston.com.

p. 263: (top) Photo: © www.carolyn-bates.com, Design: Catherine Clemens,

Clemens and Clemens Associates, Inc., Construction: Jess Clemens, Clemens and Associates, Inc.; (bottom) Photo: © www.davidduncanlivingston.com.

p. 264: (top) Photo: © www.carolyn-bates. com, Design and construction: Matt Furney, Firestone Landscaping; (bottom) Photo: © Dency Kane.

p. 265: (top left) Photo: © Deidra Wal-pole Photography, Design: New Leaf Garden Design; (bottom left) Photo: © Deidra Walpole Photography, Design: Green Scene; (top right) Photo courtesy of Laneventure 2003; (bottom right) Photo: © Deidra Walpole Photography, Design: Tony Miller/Scott Smith.

p. 266: (left) Photo: © Allan Mandell, Design: Lucy Hardiman; (right) Photo: © Allan Mandell, Design: Eryl Morton.

p. 267: Photo: © Lee Anne White, Design: David Bennet McMullin, garden designer.

p. 268: (left) Photo: © Allan Mandell, Design: Portland International Gar-dens; (right) Photo: © Allan Mandell, Design: Les Bugajski.

p. 269: (top left) Photo: © www.david-duncanlivingston.com; (bottom left) Photo: © 2004 Samu Studios, Inc., Design: Keller Sandren, AIA; (right) Photo: © Lee Anne White, Design: Ellis LanDesign.

p. 270: (top left) Photo: © Lee Anne White, Design: Michelle Derviss Land-scapes Designed; (top right) Photo: Lee Anne White

© The Taunton Press, Inc.; (bottom) Photo: © Tria Giovan.

p. 271: Photo: © Brian Vanden Brink, Photographer 2004, Design: Horiuchi & Solien, landscape architects.

p. 272: (top) Photo: © Robert Stein; (bot-tom) Photo: © 2004 Samu Studios, Inc.

p. 273: (top) Photo: © Alan & Linda Detrick; (bottom) Photo: © Tim Street-Porter, Design: Tichenor and Thorp, landscape architects.

p. 274: (left) Photo: © Jerry Pavia Photography, Inc.; (right) Photo: © Saxon Holt/PhotoBotanic, Design: Sally Robertson.

p. 275: (top) Photo: © Saxon Holt/PhotoBotanic; (bottom) Photo courtesy of Salsbury-Schweyer, Inc.

p. 276: Photo: © Allan Mandell.

p. 277: (top) Photo: © www.daviddun-canlivingston.com; (bottom) Photo: © Lee Anne White.

p. 278: (top left) Photo: © Lee Anne White; (top right) Photo: © Eric Roth; (bottom) Photo: © Allan Mandell.

p. 279: (top) Photo: © Lee Anne White, Design: Jeni Webber, landscape archi-tect; (bottom) Photo: © Eric Roth.

p. 280: (left) Photo: © Jerry Pavia Photography, Inc.; (right) Photo: © Saxon Holt/PhotoBotanic.

p. 281: (top) Photo: © Brian Vanden Brink, Photographer 2004, Design: Horiuchi & Solien, landscape archi-tects; (bottom) Photo: © Alan & Linda Detrick.

p. 282: (left) Photo: © Brian Vanden Brink, Photographer 2004, Design: Horiuchi & Solien, landscape archi-tects; (center) Photo: Positive Images/ Karen Bussolini, Design: John McKay; (right) Photo: © Alan & Linda Detrick.

p. 283: Photo: © Brian Vanden Brink, Photographer 2004.

p. 284: (top) Photo: © Kenneth Rice Photography/www.kenricephoto.com; Lighting Design: Randall Whitehead; (bottom) Photo courtesy Frontgage catalog.

p. 285: (top) Photo courtesy Frontgate catalog; (bottom) Photo: © Kenneth Rice Photography/www.kenricephoto. com, Builder: Renown Enterprises.

p. 286: (top) Photo: © Eric Roth; (bottom) Photo: © Kenneth Rice Photography/ www.kenricephoto.com, Lighting design: Ruud Lighting.

p. 287: (top left) Photo: © Kenneth Rice Photography/www.kenricephoto.com, Lighting design: Janet Lennox Moyer, MSH Visual Planners; (top right) Photo: © Kenneth Rice Photography/ www.kenricephoto. com, Lighting design: Janet Lennox Moyer, MSH Visual Planners; (bottom left) Photo: © Kenneth Rice Photography/ www.kenricephoto.com, Lighting design: Kichler Lighting.

p. 288: Photo: © Dency Kane.

p. 289: Photo courtesy of Laneventure 2003.

p. 290: Photo: © Lee Anne White, Design: Betty Ajay.

p. 291: (top) Photo: © Kenneth Rice Photography/www.kenricephoto.com; (bottom) Photo: © Kenneth Rice Photography/www.kenricephoto.com.

p. 292: (left) Photo: © judywhite/ GardenPhotos.com, Design: Jane Mooney, Installation: Hillier Landscapes; (right) Photo: © Saxon Holt/ PhotoBotanic.

p. 293: (top) Photo: © Lee Anne White, Design: Michelle Derviss Landscapes Designed; (bottom) Photo: © judy-white/GardenPhotos.com.

p. 294: (top) Photo: © Lee Anne White, Landscape design: Don Dickerson, Inc.; (bottom) Photo: Liz Ball/Positive Images.

p. 295: (top) Photo: © judywhite/GardenPhotos.com, Design: David Stephens, Installation: Peter Dowle Plants & Gardens; (bottom) Photo: © Jerry Pavia Photography, Inc.

p. 296: Liz Ball/Positive Images.

p. 297: (left) Photo: © Saxon Holt/PhotoBotanic; (right) Photo: © Jerry Pavia Photography, Inc.

p. 298: (top) Photo: © www.carolynbates.com, Design: Pleasant Valley Landscaping; (bottom) Photo: © Saxon Holt/ PhotoBotanic.

p. 299: (left) Photo: © Brian Vanden Brink, Photographer 2004, Design: Elliott Elliott, Norelius Architecture; (right) Photo: © Brian Vanden Brink, Photographer 2004, Design: Horiuchi & Solien, landscape architects.

p. 300: (left) Photo: © Lee Anne White, Design: Betty Ajay; (right) Photo: © Allan Mandell, Design: Ron Wagner & Nani Waddoups.

p. 301: (top) Photo: © Lee Anne White; (bottom) Photo: © judywhite/GardenPhotos.com, Design: Geoffrey Whiten.

p. 303: Photo: © www.carolynbates.com, Design: Barbara Van Raalte, Construction: Luanne Rotax.

p. 304: (top) Photo: © www.carolynbates.com, Design: Vincent and Allyson Bolduc; (bottom) Photo: © Deidra Walpole Photography, Design: Kennedy Landscape Design Associates.

p. 305: (top) Photo: © www.carolynbates.com, Design: Barbara Weedon Landscape Design; (bottom) Photo: © www.carolynbates.com, Styling: Caitrin Roesler.

p. 306: (top) Photo: © E. Andrew McKinney, Design: Jack Chandler & Associates, landscape architects; (bottom) Photo: © Robert Perron, Photographer.

p. 307: (top) Photo: © 2004 Samu Studios, Inc., Design: Bruce Nagel, AIA; (bottom) Photo: © Tim Street-Porter.

p. 308: (top) Photo: © Tim Street-Porter; (bottom) Photo: © Lee Anne White.

p. 309: Photo: © Lee Anne White, Design: Ellis LanDesign.

p. 310: (top left) Photo: © Alan & Linda Detrick, Design: Cording Landscape Design; (top right) Photo: © Eric Roth, Design: Nancy Smith; (bottom) Photo:

© Alan & Linda Detrick, Design: Cording Landscape Design.

p. 311: (top) Photo: © www.carolynbates. com, Design: Keight Wagner, landscape architect; (bottom) Photo: © Eric Roth, Design: Bill Harris Architecture.

p. 312: (left) Photo: © Robert Stein, Design: Barry Sugerman, architect; (right) Photo: © www.carolynbates. com, Design and construction: Pleasant Valley Landscaping.

p. 313: (top) Photo: © Eric Roth; (bottom) Photo: © Alan & Linda Detrick, Design: Cording Landscape Design.

p. 314: (left) Photo: © Robert Stein, Design: Raymond Jungles, landscape architect; (top right) Photo: © Robert Stein, Design: Barry Sugerman, architect; (bottom right) Photo: © Barbara Bourne Photography, Design: London Pool & Spa, Inc.

p. 315: Photo: © Saxon Holt/PhotoBotanic.

p. 316: (top) Photo: © judywhite/GardenPhotos.com, Design: Geoffrey White; (bottom) Photo courtesy of Tony Benner Photography/Artistic Pools.

p. 317: (top) Photo: © Robert Stein, Design: Barry Sugerman, architect; (bottom left) Photo: © Robert Stein, Design: Barry Sugerman, architect; (bottom right) Photo; © www.carolynbates.com, Design: Michael Dugan, AIA, Construction: Tom Sheppard, Sheppard Custom Homes.

p. 318: (top) Photo: © Barbara Bourne Photography, Pool design: London Pool & Spa, Inc.; (bottom) Photo: © Alan Geller, San Francisco, Design: Michael McKay.

p. 319: (top) Photo: © www.carolynbates.com, Design: Keith Wagner, landscape architect; (bottom) Photo: © Eric Roth, Design: Bill Harris Architecture.

p. 320: (top) Photo: © Brian Vanden Brink, Photographer 2004, Design: Horiuchi & Solien, landscape architects; (bottom) Photo: © Eric Roth.

p. 321: (left) Photo: Kevin Ireton © The Taunton Press, Inc., Design: Cass Calder Smith, architect; (top right) Photo: © Eric Roth; (bottom right) Photo: Roe Osborn © The Taunton Press, Inc., Design: David R. Quillen, AIA.

p. 322: (left) Photo: © Brian Vanden Brink, Photographer 2004, Design: Ron Forest Fences; (right) Photo: © Lee Anne White.

p. 323: (top) Photo: © Lee Anne White,

Design: Ellis LanDesign; (bottom) Photo: © Lee Anne White.

p. 324: (top left) Photo: © Tim Street-Porter; (top right) Photo: © Alan & Linda Detrick, Design: Dean Riddle; (bottom) Photo: © Saxon Holt/PhotoBotanic, Design: Diana Stratton.

p. 325: Photo: Lee Anne White © The Taunton Press, Inc.

p. 326: Photo: © Eric Roth, Design: Polly Peters.

p. 327: Photo: © Jerry Pavia Photography, Inc.

p. 328: (bottom) Photo: © Brian Vanden Brink, Photographer 2004, Design: Sam Williamson, landscape architect; (top) Photo: © Allan Mandell, Design: Ron Wagner & Nani Waddoups.

p. 329: (left) Photo: © Allan Mandell, Design: Michael Schultz & Will Goodman; (right) Photo: © Lee Anne White.

p. 330: (top left) Photo: © Brian Vanden Brink, Photographer 2004, Design: South Mountain Builders; (top right) Photo: © Brian Vanden Brink, Photographer 2004, Design: South Mountain Builders; (bottom) Photo: © Brian Vanden Brink, Photographer 2004, Design: South Mountain Builders.

p. 331: Photo: © Brian Vanden Brink, Photographer 2004.

p. 332: (top) Photo: © Brian Vanden Brink, Photographer 2004, Design: Carol Wilson, architect; (bottom) Photo: © Brian Vanden Brink, Photographer 2004, Design: Carol Wilson, architect.

p. 333: (left) Photo: Charles Bickford © The Taunton Press, Inc., Design: David Sellers, Sellers and Company Architects; (right) Photo: © Lee Anne White.

p. 334: (top) Photo: © 2004 Samu Studios, Inc., Design: Jim De Luca, AIA; (bottom) Photo: © Allan Mandell, Design: Jeffrey Bale.

p. 335: Photo: © Eric Roth, Design: Polly Peters.

p. 336: Photo: courtesy of John L. Harper.

p. 337: Photo: © Lee Anne White, Design:F. Malcom George, architect.

p. 338: (left) Photo: © Brian Vanden Brink, Photographer 2004, Design: Horiuchi & Solien, landscape architects; (right) Photo: © Brian Vanden Brink, Photographer 2004, Design: Horiuchi & Solien, landscape architects.

p. 339: Photo: © Brian Vanden Brink, Photographer 2004, Design: Horiuchi & Solien, landscape architects.

p. 340: Photo: © Brian Vanden Brink, Photographer 2004.

p. 341: (left) Photo: © Allan Mandell; (right) Photo: © Allan Mandell.

p. 342: (top left) Photo: © Tim Street-Porter; (top right) Photo: © Eric Roth; (bottom) Photo: © Tim Street-Porter, Design: Kathy Spitz, landscape architect.

p. 343: (top) Photo: © Tria Giovan; (bottom) Photo: © www.davidduncanlivingston.com.

p. 344: (top) Photo: © Eric Roth; (bottom left) Photo: © Alan & Linda Detrick; (bottom right) Photo: © Alan & Linda Detrick.

p. 345: (top) Photo: © Saxon Holt/PhotoBotanic; (bottom) Photo: © Alan & Linda Detrick.

p. 346: (left) Photo: Lee Anne White © The Taunton Press, Inc.; (left) Photo: © Allan Mandell, Design: Scott Kasterson.

p. 347: (top) Photo: © Brian Vanden Brink, Photographer 2004, Design: Scholz & Barclay, architects; (bottom) Photo: © Lee Anne White, Design: Mahan Rykiel Associates.

p. 348: (left) Photo: © Lee Anne White, Design: Hermann Weiss, landscape architect; (top right) Photo: © judywhite/GardenPhotos.com, Design: Natialie Charles; (bottom right) Photo: © Brian Vanden Brink, Photographer 2004, Design: Horiuchi & Solien, landscape architects.

p. 349: Photo: © Brian Vanden Brink, Photographer 2004, Design: Elliott, Elliott, Norelius Architecture.

p. 350: (top) Photo: © www.carolynbates. com; (bottom left) Photo: Karen Bussolini/Positive Images; (bottom right) Photo: © www.carolynbates.com.

p. 351: (top left) Photo: © Eric Roth; (top right) Photo: © Paula Refi; (bottom) photo: © Brian Vanden Brink, Photographer 2004, Design: John Silverio, architect.